The Things We've Handed Down

The Things We've Handed Down

By

Colman Rushe

DEDICATION

To Bridget.

Preface

My parents did me no favours as a writer.

It seems to me that most writers, especially Irish ones, were blessed with parents who imparted sufficient neuroses to sustain them through a lifetime of writing. In some cases, the Irish writer's mother died early, leaving behind a child racked with guilt or burdened with a sense of abandonment. Otherwise, the mother lived on to smother her offspring with stifling affection so that escape and retribution seemed to be the only valid responses. The fathers of writers were either drunken philanderers or cold, emotionless figures who withheld from their children any display of affection or validation and, as a result, the writer was obliged to spend a lifetime vainly seeking the approval of the parent. All the better if the childhood was played out against a background of grinding poverty and bleak hopelessness. Then, in the vernacular of rural Ireland, the writer was sucking diesel.

The portrayal in memoirs of the stereotypical Irish family is vividly described by Frank McCourt. "The poverty; the shiftless loquacious alcoholic father; the pious defeated mother moaning by the fire." McCourt cautions that "the happy childhood is hardly worth your while". Colm Toibin goes further: "A happy childhood may make good citizens, but it is not a help for those of us facing a blank page". Alan Bennett treads a similar path. He references the Philip Larkin poem "This Be The Verse" which begins: "They fuck you up, your mum and dad". Bennett elaborates: "If your parents do fuck you up, and you're going to write, that's fine because then you've got something to write about. But if they don't fuck you up, then you've got nothing to write about. So then they've fucked you up good and proper".

Tolstoy doesn't offer much encouragement either : "Happy families are all alike; every unhappy family is unhappy in its own way" .

Are all happy families alike? Was Tolstoy correct? Or was finding an arresting opening line of more importance to him than stating a universal truth? Would it not be equally true to claim that each happy family is happy in its own way? It is true that happy families share many common characteristics. Those in the parental role do their utmost to protect and shield the children from everything that might cause unhappiness. They offer encouragement and support. They elevate the expectations and self esteem of the children to a sustainable level but are careful not to impart a sense of entitlement or an unrealistic level of aspiration. But how do they achieve this? Not in an identical manner, surely?

As I grew up, I compared my family to others around me. There were wide variations in the manner in which children were raised. In our home, there was much emphasis on education; it was regarded as the means by which we could improve our prospects in life. Yet some other parents had little regard for education so that farm work or household chores often took precedence over school attendance or homework. Such parents limited the expectations and ambitions of their children. In the harsh economic climate of the 1950s, when most Irish children were destined for emigration, it could be argued that such a pragmatic approach was fair and reasonable. If the children nurtured a belief that they deserved and were entitled to the best, this could lead to disillusionment and resentment. Better to tell them that they have to fight for everything in life. And even then, it's likely that others of "better" birth or with more potent family or political influence will snatch the prize from them. Many Irish parents accepted that no real progress was possible for their children unless they emigrated. They prepared their sons and daughters for the mail boat to England where the prospect of a better life beckoned. These families were quite unlike mine. But weren't many of them happy in their own way?

Is chronicling the lives of happy families "worth your while"? Tolstoy, McCourt, and Toibin don't think so. It seems that, unless you were neglected and abused by your parents, you have nothing to say - nothing worth hearing or writing about. If your parents were the kind of people who, nowadays, would have their children taken away by social services, then write about them. Celebrate them. Or at a minimum, demonstrate that, despite their inadequacies as parents, you emerged as a rounded human being who is magnanimous enough to pat them on the head and forgive them.

In my case, there were none of these "advantages". My father was never out of work for more than a week or two, did not drink alcohol, and routinely displayed affection towards his wife and children. My mother, in the more demanding role, kept the home and family together. Both of them were loved and revered by their children and later by their grandchildren.

We were among the lucky ones. That's what I would say as an adult when questioned about growing up in the 50s and 60s. But, when I began to research my family history, I was confronted with the realisation that, rather than having a relatively privileged and care-free existence, my parents were faced with a potentially disastrous sequence of set-backs and tragedies during the first fifteen years of their marriage. Any one of these dramatic occurrences had the potential to destroy the marriage and the family. This dreadful accumulation of events would be expected, at the very least, to have had a traumatic impact on the parents or children who would emerge damaged from the wreckage.

But my parents didn't burden us with their problems as they struggled to cope. They ensured that we, the children, sailed through unscathed. At least I did. Or I think I did. Which is probably the same thing.

Was the Red Lemonade Syndrome at work here?

For Irish children of my generation, mention of lemonade conjures up the image of a red, fizzy, lemon-flavoured beverage. It was the drink that was routinely given to a child while adults were drinking alcohol. We loved our occasional treat of a reliable, comforting, glass of lemonade. In Ireland, lemonade was red just as milk was white, porter was black, whiskey was amber, and water was no colour at all. But over the years, a strange, mysterious hybrid named white lemonade began to appear in Irish pubs. If you asked the barman for lemonade, you were given proper red lemonade - if you wanted the new-fangled, unnatural stuff, you had to specify the colour.

"A white lemonade, please".

Simple. Natural.

As children, it didn't occur to us that, if you squeeze a lemon, you get clear juice without a trace of red. We didn't pause to think about it. As a child, you don't spend your time pondering why blood is red, grass is green, or the Irish sky is usually grey. You accept that this is the natural order of things. This acquiescence, which I call the Red Lemonade Syndrome, leads to an unquestioning acceptance of things as we experience them despite clear evidence to the contrary. Did the Red Lemonade Syndrome cloud my memory? Was my childhood as care-free as I remember?

The biographer Peter Manso states, "Memory is fragile. Recollection is everyone's second chance." The same event can be recalled differently or can have a disparate impact on each child depending on age or sensibility. My brothers and sisters each have their own story. But I am writing about my parents, not theirs. As William Zinsser writes, "The same past has many different owners". My father and mother brought us up and cared for us without showing any favouritism. Nevertheless, as I will explain later, each of us had a unique relationship with them. They recognised that we had varying aptitudes and skills and we were encouraged to pursue our own interests and to develop our individual talents. We all eventually left home and have maintained good, supportive relationships with one another. All of us remained close to our parents throughout their lives. Nevertheless, I realise that each of us has a different story.

What I consider remarkable, and what I am trying to understand, is how my own parents managed to steer the family ship through turbulent waters while their children lounged on the deck, blissfully unaware that anything unusual was happening. It was only when I became a parent that I was able to fully appreciate the complexity of the task which they had completed without drama or fuss. They deserve to be written about. As Walter Junior says in the TV series Breaking Bad: "The good guys never get ink like the bad guys do."

When Alan Bennett mused on whether your parents really do "fuck you up" as a writer, he came to the conclusion that you don't write in order to write about your youth; you write to find out about your youth. I want to find out about my youth and specifically about my parents.

What motivated these people who steered their happy children through these turbulent years? That's what I want to know. That's what I want to find out about by writing.

I'll try.

But, my parents did me no favours as a writer…

CHAPTER ONE

A Fine Romance

CRACKED
Adjective
Damaged but not unusable, reduced in value, reparable but never to original state, mad, demented, opened (as in safe or deck of cards), solved (as in code), broken in tone (as in voice).

Their first meeting didn't augur well. Coleman Rushe had seen and admired the new girl in town and had found out that she was Kitty Ryan from down south in Limerick. He knew that she worked in the saloon at the railway station and that she spent her spare time with May Tighe and Julia Connolly, two friends of his, but he hadn't had the opportunity to meet her. If he had a choice, he would have preferred to be introduced to her when he was scrubbed and spruced up at the weekend, not when he was in his work clothes in the brush factory. Yet, here she was, standing beside his work bench, wearing an expression of faint amusement as she watched him chatting to Julia Connolly. Julia had called to the Ronayne's brush factory on an errand and Kitty had tagged along. As the girls were passing Coleman's work-bench, Julia stopped to greet him. They had known each other since childhood and now, as teenagers, hung around with the same group of friends, going to dances and the cinema.

As they chatted, Julia playfully introduced Coleman to her friend. Kitty was a pretty, buxom, healthy-looking, eighteen year old of average height with shoulder length black hair which was fashionably waved and pinned back to reveal her slightly shy smile and sparkling, penetrating eyes. Coleman was a year older and a few inches taller, lean and rangy, with chiseled features and a full head of black hair with a carefully prepared, off-centre parting.

"Kitty. This is Coleman Rushe. Don't be taken in by his *plamás*; he'll try to sweet-talk you because you're new in town. He plays music with a dance band and all of them musicians think they're God's gift."

Kitty laughingly agreed that she would heed the warning. As the two girls turned to leave, Coleman protested to Kitty that he had been unfairly maligned.

"Pay no heed to Julia. Maybe, I'll call for you for the pictures."

"Fine!" Kitty answered over her shoulder with a laugh as they left.

Was she serious, he wondered, as he resumed his work. The tone of their exchange had been light-hearted. Was Kitty merely bantering or was she willing to go to the cinema with him?

Kitty was similarly perplexed. As they strolled up the pathway towards Mount Street, she broached the subject with Julia. Was he serious about taking her to the cinema? Did he even know where to pick her up? And at what time? Was it tonight even?

Julia was adamant. Coleman Rushe didn't mess about. Of course it was tonight - if not, he would have said so. And didn't everyone in town know what time the pictures started? And he must know that she always went to May Tighe's lodgings to get ready before going out. Otherwise, he would have asked. Wouldn't he?

As they walked, Julia passed on some facts to Kitty about her friend. He was a non-drinker, which was a bonus in Julia's opinion. He lived with his parents and, as an only son, was particularly idolised by his mother and three younger sisters. Despite this, he was never a spoilt child, reassured Julia.

Kitty wasn't convinced that he was going to show up but she was waiting with May Tighe later that evening when Coleman apprehensively knocked on the door.

"Your mother and father were cracked about one another right from the start", a contemporary of theirs told me many years later.

People in the west of Ireland didn't "fall in love". Falling in love was the preserve of Doris Day or Rock Hudson on the cinema screen or in the movie magazines. In Claremorris, you were cracked about somebody. If you were lucky, he or she was equally cracked about you. The term was much more descriptive than the cliched "in love" and covered all conditions from short-lived infatuation to lifelong devotion and commitment. The expression implied that, like a cracked container, you were permanently changed but the damage was not irreparable. You could be mended and might continue to have a lifetime of use. Nevertheless, you would never be quite the same again.

When they met in 1943, he was nineteen years old and she was eighteen.

Coleman Rushe, my father, was born in 1924 on a farm in Meelickroe in County Roscommon. His father, Tom Rushe, was a Galway-born carpenter who married Mary Reynolds, the only daughter in a local farming family.

I should point out here that, when I first began to take a tentative interest in family history, my parents answered all my questions openly and honestly. I have since been able to verify much of their information from other sources. They were unable, however, to tell me much about their own parents. There were many vague areas and, as I was to discover, some important topics that were "not talked about".

For example, during my youth, the childhood of my paternal grandfather, Tom Rushe, was not talked about. I knew that he was born at the dawn of the new century in Claddagh, a fishing village adjacent to Galway city and that his family broke up when he was very young. The reasons for the dispersal of the family were unclear but a house-fire was sometimes mentioned as a possible cause. I knew that Tom and the younger Rushe siblings were taken into care and he spent some time in Glenamaddy Workhouse. Any historical family connection with the workhouse was a source of embarrassment to an Irish family and, as such, was not talked about. Tom was fostered in his teens by Maurice and Sarah Mitchell who brought him to live on their farm near Ballinlough, County Roscommon. He served his apprenticeship as a carpenter and the Mitchells built a workshop for him near their home. He was working locally, repairing horse-drawn carts and carriages, when he married Mary Reynolds, who lived nearby on her parents' farm.

Mary's father had died in July 1922, a year before she married. When my brother Sean visited Meelickroe in the company of my father many years later, they met an elderly neighbour who remembered my grandmother's parents. He described her father, William Reynolds, as the kind of man to whom people turned when they needed help. We do not know what hopes the Reynolds had for their only daughter or how the widow, Mrs Reynolds, felt about her decision to marry Tom Rushe, a man who had been rescued from the local workhouse.

In April 1924, Tom and Mary Rushe had their first child, my father, and they named him Coleman. After the birth of my father in the

Reynolds' farmhouse, the young family moved to a rented house in Ballinlough, a few miles away, but they later moved back into Mary's family home which they shared with Mary's mother and her two brothers, Jack and Martin Reynolds. Mary's mother died in 1929 but, by then, Tom and Mary had moved away and were living in County Mayo.

A second child, Mary, arrived in 1926 while the Rushe family were living with the Reynolds. As time went on, the young family were anxious to set up home on their own. Tom Rushe heard about an opportunity in Claremorris, County Mayo, which is about 22 miles west of Ballinlough. Martin Gilligan, who had a woodwork and undertaking business, was seeking a carpenter who would be responsible for coach building and coffin making. Tom got in touch with Martin Gilligan and was offered the job. The outcome was the relocation of the Rushes to Claremorris. The family rented a house from Tom's new employer at Gilligan's Arch at the rear of the town square. While the family lived there, another daughter, Patricia (known as "Patsy") was born in 1929.

The Rushes later moved to a better house in Mount Street where a third daughter, Chris, was born in 1931. The children were soon attending the local national school. During the summer, the family had a few days holiday in Ballinlough with the Mitchells, Tom Rushe's foster parents, or with his relatives in Galway.

In 1936, my father was presented with a baby brother, Michael, who was known as Mikey. At the age of two, Mikey was struck down by meningitis. There was no effective treatment for the lethal viral infection and Mikey died within twenty-four hours. The child was buried with his Reynolds grandparents at Granlahan cemetery in Roscommon.

I did not know about Mikey's existence until many years later - another example of things that were not talked about. When I questioned my father about the event, he spoke freely. He was eleven years old when Mikey died. His predominant memory was not of the impact on himself of the death of his only brother. Instead, he recalled his father's behaviour immediately after the child's burial. The Rushe children kept some songbirds at the rear of the house in cages that were built by my grandfather. The birds had been supplied by my father's childhood friend Paddy Clarke, who had a passion for birds which he bred at his own family home nearby. As a result of the disruption and trauma caused to the Rushe family by Mikey's sudden illness and death, the feeding of the birds was overlooked and they died. In a rare and uncharacteristic display of anger, my grandfather reprimanded his children for neglecting the birds, refused permission for the procurement of replacements, and dismantled the cages.

Was my grandfather's action triggered by his grief at the sudden death of his son? My father's view was that my grandfather was partly driven by grief but was also teaching his children that they had obligations and responsibilities which should not have been neglected. Mikey's death was inevitable. The deaths of the birds should have been avoided.

In 1937, Mayo County Council built a number of houses at Convent Road, Claremorris and the Rushes successfully applied for one. They moved into number 58, a semi-detached house with two bedroom upstairs and a kitchen, sitting room and back-kitchen downstairs. In front of the house, there was a small lawn that soon featured a wooden garden seat made by Tom. At the rear, there was a long garden that was partly used for growing vegetables while allowing ample playing space for the four children.

Following Coleman's fourteenth birthday in 1938, he was eligible to leave Claremorris Boys' School. He had already completed sixth class, the final formal year of study in primary school. Because he was not going to attend secondary school, he as obliged by law to remain in the education system until his fourteenth birthday. In order to keep the boys engaged, the headmaster supplied them with books which he encouraged them to read and he obliged them to memorise some Shakespeare speeches. Throughout his life, my father enjoyed bemusing listeners by reciting from memory the opening speech by Antonio from "The Merchant Of Venice":

"In sooth, I know not why I am so sad:
It wearies me ; you say it wearies you ;
But how I caught it, found it, or came by it,
What stuff 'tis made of, whereof it is born,
I am to learn ;
And such a want-wit sadness makes of me,
That I have much ado to know myself."

My father invariably finished with a flourish by adding:
"Shakespeare. The Merchant of Venice. Act 1 - Scene 1."
Perhaps it was the encouragement of the teacher that stimulated my father's interest in books. He became a discerning reader at a young

age and I suspect that the guiding hand of the teacher was involved. He read incessantly in his youth and particularly admired the works of Mark Twain and Oscar Wilde.

Secondary education was not available locally in Claremorris in the 1930s. St. Colman's College, a boys' school that I later attended, was founded in 1945 and the Sisters of Mercy established a local secondary school for girls in 1940. Education in primary schools was free of charge but if you wanted to continue your studies at a higher level, fees had to be paid. Such a financial commitment was out of the range of most families. Wealthier parents could afford to send their children to boarding schools or, if there was a secondary school nearby, it was possible to attend as a day student. For people in the Claremorris area, there was the option to attend Ballinrobe Christian Brothers' School as a day pupil. Even for those who could afford the fees, the daily round trip of 28 miles by bicycle was impractical.

My father was clear thinking, articulate and intelligent. He compensated for his lack of formal education by reading books and newspapers and took a keen and often opinionated interest in national and world affairs. He would have benefited greatly from further education and clearly had to intellectual capacity to cope with it. His friend, Father Michael Keane, who attended the local school with him, later wrote: "what a pity it was in your day that there was such a lack of opportunity for further education for gifted children. You were … the smartest lad in the Claremorris Boys' School...you could have been anything you wanted to be, given half a chance".

This tribute from his childhood friend reveals a hint of regret at opportunities missed and at potential unrealised. But I never heard my father articulate any such remorse. In later life, he was determined that his own children should obtain a good education in order to give them more choices in life. However, in his youth in the late 1930s, he accepted that further education was not an option for somebody from his socio-economic background. While he valued formal education, he would argue that it was possible to have a fulfilled, productive life without it. Father Keane agreed ; "There are so many brainy and successful men who in their lifetime have not achieved what you and Kitty managed against such odds."

The Gleeson brothers, Paddy and Billy, lived next door to the Rushes at Convent Road. Paddy, the eldest, had a job at Ronaynes Brush factory, one of the few employers in the area. Enviably, Paddy always seemed to have enough money in his pocket to buy cigarettes and to go dancing regularly. Coleman spotted Mr Ronayne, the brush factory owner, as he walked past the Rushe's house on his way home from a race-meeting at the local racecourse. Without consulting his parents, Coleman approached Mr Ronayne and asked him for a job. Luckily, the employer was amenable to the unorthodox approach and my father commenced work in October 1938 at the age of fourteen.

Factory hours were from eight to six on Monday to Saturday. My father's basic wage was eleven shillings and nine pence for a sixty hour week. He handed ten shillings to his mother and kept the remainder for himself. At this time, average wages for an adult farm labourer in Ireland were less than fifteen shillings per week so that my fathers wage as an untrained factory boy does not seem unreasonable. Indeed, his bird-breeding friend, Paddy Clarke, later told me that he considered that my father was lucky to be in such a well paid job. After leaving school, Paddy worked as an assistant in a local drapery shop. He claimed that he was not paid formal wages but he got a new suit each year to a value of two pounds ten shillings. Effectively, Paddy worked for a shilling per week.

One of Coleman's first extravagances was to commence smoking. He also acquired a passion for music at about this time. Next-door neighbour, Billy Gleeson, his former schoolmate who had also recently obtained employment in the brush factory, had learned to play the trumpet under the tutelage of his uncle, Mick Moore. On the other side of the Rushe house, the Brennan brothers were also good musicians. When Johnny Brennan offered to give him fiddle lessons, Coleman identified a suitable instrument that was for sale at eleven shillings and sixpence. He started to put some money aside and hoped that the fiddle would not be sold before he had a chance to acquire it.

The Rushe family took occasional trips to Roscommon in order to visit the Mitchells, my grandfather's foster parents. When my father told Sarah Mitchell that he was saving to buy the fiddle, she immediately gave him a gift of the remainder of the purchase price. The fiddle was still available but, to his dismay, Coleman discovered that the price did not include a bow. His mother solved his problem by buying the bow for him.

Johnny Brennan kept his promise and provided some early fiddle lessons. Coleman practised and quickly became a competent musician who could read music and play well by ear. He was also the possessor of a fine baritone singing voice that was ideally suited to the kind of romantic ballads that were being popularised by Bing Crosby, whom he greatly admired.

Mick Moore, uncle and musical mentor of the Gleeson brothers, played trumpet with a local band that was led by Matt MacDonagh. Coleman went along to watch the band practising and sometimes sat in with the musicians. Moore was frustrated when Matt didn't immediately invite Coleman to join the band and he took matters into his own hands.

"Colie is coming with us on Saturday night", he told Matt. Coleman's activity as a working musician had commenced and would continue until the mid 1960s.

Matt's band was not the usual casual collection of musicians thrown together in the hope of earning some extra cash and catching the approving glances of the local girls. No, this was serious stuff. A photograph of the band shows a six-piece ensemble that would not look out of place at a supper dance in a fashionable hotel in Dublin or London. The female pianist, Matt's sister Chrissie, is wearing a modest but fashionable gown while the five men wear matching band jackets, white shirts and bow-ties. The jackets are tight-fitting, double-breasted with epaulettes, two rows of brass buttons, and piping in a pale colour around the lapels and cuffs. Across the front of the stage, seated behind their music stands, are the trumpet, saxophone, fiddle, and accordion players. The drummer and pianist are on the raised platform behind. The tall fair-haired trumpeter, who has an array of mutes on the floor near him, is Billy Gleeson who has replaced his uncle, Mick Moore, in the band. Matt McDonagh, the band leader, cradles his saxophone and has a clarinet resting on its stand. My father, disarmingly young and handsome, is seated next to Matt with fiddle poised. The sole microphone is at front centre of the stage between my father, the main vocalist, and Matt, who would sing a few sentimental ballads. The accordion player on the right looks slightly uncomfortable, possibly because his trousers, which he is trying to shield behind his music stand, are a slightly lighter shade than those of his colleagues. The well equipped drummer at the rear seems even younger than my father and Chrissie fingers the piano keys while giving a wistful sidelong gaze at the photographer. Above the piano and on top of an instrument case in the background are two small speakers on which somebody has carefully painted in white lettering "Mattie MacDonagh's Dance Band, Claremorris".

Before long, there were rumblings of dissatisfaction in the band. Some of the young musicians were becoming bored with the musical diet of ballads, waltzes and occasionally, Irish jigs and reels. Instead, they were attracted to the exciting and dangerous new music to be heard on the cinema screen and on radio. My father's lifelong passion for New Orleans music had taken root.

CHAPTER TWO

All That Jazz

The Evils of Jazz
Dear Irish colleens, hasten ye and crush
Jazz dancing, for it makes the Virgin Mary blush.
Rout out such vile creations from our sod,
Come, banish these modes, so displeasing to God.
Patriotic daughters, it's now up to you
To cease jazz dancing for the sake of Róisín Dhu.
- C. Bohan, Mohill.
Published 30th December 1934 in The Leitrim Observer newspaper.

Jazz was an emotive topic in Ireland in the 1930s and the music was rarely broadcast on Irish radio. While there was no official radio ban, the playing of jazz records was discouraged as was the broadcasting of performances by crooners and dance bands. To understand the reasons why, we have to examine Irish life in the 1920s and beyond.

Following the establishment of the Irish Free State in 1922, Irishness came to be defined as an essentially rural aesthetic. People were encouraged to identify with Irish music, culture, sports, and the Catholic moral code. Already, the Gaelic Athletic Association had been successful in establishing Gaelic football and hurling as the most popular sports. This was achieved by imposing a ban on members who played, watched or promoted "foreign games". The result was the virtual disappearance from rural Ireland of sports such as rugby, soccer, and cricket.

In the 1930s, foreign music, and jazz in particular, came to be perceived as the latest threat to the Irish way of life. In January 1934, a local priest, Father Confrey, organised a demonstration in Mohill,

County Leitrim. Three thousand people marched through the small west of Ireland town carrying banners which proclaimed "down with jazz" and "out with paganism". Father Confrey was concerned that the new music, that could sometimes be heard on the newly established Irish radio station, was resulting in immorality, lewd behaviour, and was "worse than drunkenness or landlordism".

The secretary of the Gaelic League, which had been established to preserve and promote the Gaelic lifestyle, addressed the crowd in Mohill and directed his wrath at the national radio service. He said that the Minister for Finance, Sean McEntee, had "a soul buried in jazz" and accused him of being more concerned about the money being received from sponsored radio programmes than the spiritual soul of the nation. The Gaelic League wrote to public bodies urging the members to lobby against the broadcasting of jazz and to boycott foreign dances. The response was mixed but the debate raged.

It is clear from contemporary newspaper coverage that the primary concern about jazz was the style of dancing with which it was associated. Irish dancing, with its minimal physical contact, was considered acceptable as was waltzing which encouraged "old fashioned thoughts". Jazz dancing, however, was seen as a by-product of uncivilised, pagan, and depraved "jungle music". Concern was expressed at a meeting of Dublin Corporation that people were "following the dances of Negroes". Women, in particular, were in danger. The Kilkenny People newspaper was concerned that "women were becoming fag smoking, jazz dancing, lip sticking flappers".

The success which had been achieved in replacing foreign games with Irish indigenous sport was not replicated in the music arena. Nevertheless, the furore did have some impact. Irish radio opted to ignore jazz and the airwaves were now dominated by traditional and classical music. BBC radio, which drifted across the Irish Sea from the UK, gave listeners the opportunity to hear jazz and dance music. Irish cinema goers were also flocking to see films featuring crooners such as Bing Crosby.

Dixieland jazz, characterised by its syncopated rhythms and danceability, had evolved in New Orleans but began to achieve wider acceptance and popularity through the recordings and performances of the Original Dixieland Jazz Band. In February 1917, this band made the first jazz recording and was at the forefront of the jazz craze which become a sensation in New York and later around the world. They were the first US jazz band to play in London where they repeated their New York success with performances at the London Hippodrome and a Royal Command performance at Buckingham Palace in 1919.

What was it about this music that made it so compelling to a group of teenagers in Mayo in the early 1940s? And why did Dixieland jazz have such an impact in Ireland that it quickly became viewed as a threat to the Irish way of life?

As we have seen, one cause for concern was the sometimes frenetic dancing that was associated with the jazz craze and which was seen as a threat to morality. There was also a racist element to much of the opposition. Another factor was fear that an unhealthy level of self expression was being encouraged. Improvisation was an integral part of the music and this freedom of expression was also viewed with suspicion, not just in Ireland. In the Soviet Union, jazz was suppressed and labeled a "bourgeois" music.

But it wasn't just about the music.

Jazz was espoused by young people, not only because the music appealed to them, but also because if afforded them an opportunity to rebel against the status quo and to establish their own identity. The jazzers were seen as a threat by their elders and by some of their contemporaries. Jazz fans encountered the same hostility that rock and rollers or punk rockers experienced in later generations... and they loved it.

In Mayo in the early forties, my father and a few friends craved a change of musical direction. Suddenly, events took their own course. Band leader Matt MacDonagh had a dispute with Mr Ronayne, the owner of the brush factory. Knowing that two of his employees, my father and Billy Gleeson, had ambitions to break away from Matt and to have a band of their own, Mr Ronayne approached them and offered them a loan of one hundred pounds to buy the necessary equipment. The boys jumped at the offer and enlisted Paddy Clarke, their bird-fancier friend, as drummer and another friend, Mick O'Loughlin as accordion player.

Many Mayo people, particularly those who lived in the countryside, liked to dance to Irish music with a few waltzes thrown into the mix. Some of the younger set, who lived in town, preferred the more heady mixture of jazz and standards. This was the repertoire played by the new band which was formed by my father and his friends with its novel line-up of trumpet, fiddle, drums and accordion. The result was an encouraging level of success in the south Mayo area and the quick repayment of Mr Ronayne's loan.

In later years, band member Paddy Clarke made a list of over fifty "joints" in the catchment area that designated themselves as ballrooms, and in which the band played regularly. He vividly described these venues.

"Most were lit by oil lamps which midway through the night became invisible owing to the dust from the floor. They usually had six lamps and after an hour or so if you could see two it was deemed very good."

He recalled the band frequenting "dim, dusty, cold, oil lamp lit, Palaise De Dances trying desperately to enlighten the masses to the joys of Jazz". They played from 10pm until 4am which made it difficult for them to get up for work in the morning. "Monday was not a good day" according to Paddy. But they loved the music and the money was good. "We usually got 6 or 7 pounds…. We would have stayed up all night for that much".

Paddy also described my father as being "not without (as you would expect) a sizeable following of the opposite, dare I say the word, sex. Being endowed with good looks and smoking a fag a la Robert Mitchum, many poor simple country girls, I'm sure, found themselves unable to resist."

There are three photographs from the 1940s that show my father with a cigarette dangling from his lower lip "a la Robert Mitchum". He was an avid cinema goer and it is apparent that he had studied and emulated Mitchum's smouldering, moody, intense pose. Two photographs show him with teenage friends and fellow musicians on an outing to the seaside. His friends are smiling and relaxed. He is maintaining his broody look, hair slightly unkempt, drooping cigarette glued to the left side of his lower lip. Another picture was taken a few years later. Now he is wearing spectacles and is jacket-less with shirt sleeves slightly rolled. The studied, uncompromising Mitchum look is again completed by the dangling cigarette.

I don't know why my father decided to abstain from alcohol although his mother's antipathy to hard drinking may have been a factor. My grandfather had an occasional social drink as did my grandmother. But she had a morbid fear of alcohol abuse, possibly because of the excesses of her eldest brother, Martin Reynolds. Perhaps his mother's hostility to excessive drinking persuaded my father to be a teetotaller. His non-drinking may also have been connected to his work as a musician. Many years later, when I began to play music in pubs, he advised me to avoid drinking. Too many musicians play for drinks and end up with alcohol problems, he explained.

By his late teens, when he met my mother, my father was already showing signs of the sometimes contradictory traits which would characterise his later life. His espousal of jazz, his decision to get a job without his parents' pre-approval, his non-drinking, and his studied, attention-seeking appearance imply a level of non-conformity and independence. Yet, he never rebelled against his parents and handed most of his earnings to his mother in order to help the family budget. For the rest of his life, he would regularly demonstrate a propensity for independent thought and a refusal to join the herd. Nevertheless, his overriding characteristic was loyalty to family which he would display in a multitude of ways over the following years.

Who was Kitty Ryan, newly arrived in Claremorris, who caught my father's eye in 1943? She was a long way from her birthplace which was about 150 miles to the south. Kitty was born in November 1925 in Cappamore, County Limerick and was the second child of Mick and Catherine Ryan, who raised their family on a small farm on the edge of town.

Kitty's mother was one of a large family, many of whom had emigrated to Australia and the USA. Mick Ryan, Kitty's father, never discussed his family or his origins with his children - yet another example of things not talked about. In later years, when I questioned my mother and my Ryan aunts and uncles, they said that my grandfather would not answer questions about his parents or any relatives. It was assumed that he was an only child who had lost his parents when he was young and the impression was given that he might have been raised for a time by his grandmother.

Following their marriage, Mick and Catherine Ryan inherited the small farm and, in order to supplement their modest farm income, Mick got a job at Cappamore Creamery where he continued to be employed for all his working life. My memory is of a slight, gentle, pipe smoker with a mischievous sense of humour. He loved teasing his grandchildren and seemed quite content to let Catherine, my grandmother, take charge. She was a fine, kind, energetic woman; very much the head of the family.

Michael and Catherine had their first child, Johnny, in late 1924 and my mother Kitty was born in November 1925. Further siblings followed. Kitty attended Cappamore national school and, unlike my father, went on to obtain secondary education at the nearby Convent of

Mercy. She enjoyed school and, having become quite proficient in the Irish language, she attended a summer course in the Irish-speaking area in Cork which she recalled fondly many years later. When I went to secondary school, and was struggling with French, she confounded me by recalling various French phrases and helping me with translation.

She finished school at the age of sixteen and immediately left home to take up a job as a waitress in Hayes' Hotel in Thurles, County Tipperary. She recalled that she felt proud, having acquired a job in such a prestigious hotel and achieved financial independence. Shortly after her arrival in Thurles, the manageress of the hotel, her boss, invited Kitty to join her on her habitual evening stroll around the town. All the passing gentlemen respectfully raised their hats in greeting as the two women walked by. Kitty's pride was somewhat dented the following evening when she walked alone. This time, the hats were unraised.

After some time in Thurles, she successfully applied for a catering job with Great Southern Railways, the company that controlled the railway network within Ireland. She was employed to work in the restaurants and bars at the larger railway stations. In the film "Brief Encounter", Leslie Howard and Celia Johnson had their clandestine meetings in the Refreshment Room at Carnforth railway station during WW2. I've always watched the film with interest because it gives me a glimpse into the life my mother led before she married my father. I imagine her preparing meals and serving food and drinks to the fleeting passengers during the war years. Such refreshment rooms, known in Ireland as "saloons" were located at railway junctions where passengers might while away a few hours as they waited for a connecting train. Meals were provided and the premises were licensed to sell alcohol. There was also an office and basic living accommodation for the workers.

Kitty's first posting was to the west of Ireland when she was dispatched to work at Claremorris railway station. She later described how, when they heard that she was to be stationed 150 miles away at Claremorris, her family and friends from Cappamore teased her and told her that she was going to "a terrible place".

In 1945, Claremorris was a small-town with a population of 1170. The main thoroughfare, which ran north/south, was comprised of James Street and its continuation, Church Street. Intersecting with this were two streets. You could travel west on Mount Street to reach

Convent Road and then onwards towards Castlebar, the principal town in Mayo. Going eastwards from the main street was Courthouse Road, also known as the Ballyhaunis Road. Adjacent to the intersection with Mount Street was a small town square. At the northern end of Church Street, the Catholic and Protestant churches eyed each other suspiciously from opposite sides of the road. Claremorris Boys' School nestled, both symbolically and physically, in the shadow of the Catholic Church. As if to maintain a discreet distance from this display of religion and learning, the more worldly buildings such as the two banks, the cinema, and the dancehall were all located in James Street, near the other end of the main thoroughfare. Opposite the town square and parallel to Mount Street was the short Station Road which provided access to the nearby railway station.

The growth of the town of Claremorris in the nineteenth century owed much to its location at a railway junction. The busy east-west track from Dublin to Westport intersected with the north-south Sligo to Limerick railway line. In addition, there was a further railway track from Claremorris to Ballinrobe. Claremorris was also the nearest railway station to Knock, the location of a reported apparition by the Blessed Virgin in 1879. Each summer Sunday, thousands of pilgrims alighted from special trains in Claremorris and were transported by bus on the seven mile journey to the Marian Shrine at Knock.

Diversion for the local population was provided by the Central Cinema, which showed films each night except Saturday, and the Savoy Dance Hall, better known to the locals as Isaac's, in deference to the owner, Isaac Gannon. There was no public library in the town in 1945 but Miss Downey of Church Street allowed locals to borrow her own books and she also lent books by arrangement with Kenny's Library in Galway. There was occasional horse racing at Claremorris racecourse and the town could also boast of a tennis club, a GAA football club (which did not yet own a playing field) and a billiards club at the Town Hall.

There were few opportunities for employment locally and many people emigrated to England or the USA. Those who were lucky enough to have jobs in 1945 worked at the Claremorris Bacon Company, at Ronayne's Brush Factory, at Hollybrook Farm Products Limited, which manufactured ice cream, or at the local railway station.

When Kitty Rushe first stepped off the train in Claremorris station in 1943, she was not yet eighteen years old.

CHAPTER THREE

Love And Marriage

After their first visit to the cinema, Kitty and Coleman began to go out together. In later years, she liked to poke fun at him by reminding him that she could be living a life of luxury if she had made a wiser choice. She claimed that she broke a date with a doctor to go dancing with my father.

"I left the poor unfortunate man standing by the corner at the Bank of Ireland" she would laugh. "I could be rubbing shoulders with big shots and instead of that, I went off dancing with your father. And look at me now!"

The relationship between Coleman and Kitty was progressing well. He had a steady job in the brush factory and the band was getting plenty of work. In 1945, their success was such that my father and the band members could afford to buy a car in order to travel to gigs. The car was a battered 1932 Morris that had been idle during the war years due to the shortage of petrol.

My mother loved her job at the railway station but changes were afoot. The Great Southern Railway Company was dissolved in 1945 and its assets were taken over by CIE, a new company which assumed responsibility for the national railway service. Having spent two years in Claremorris, Kitty was transferred to Rosslare, a seaport on the south-east tip of Ireland - about as far from Claremorris as it was possible for CIE to locate her. Coleman and Kitty were suddenly living almost 200 miles apart.

My father's youngest sister, Chris, had a similar job with CIE in Rosslare in the 1950s and described the work to me. Many Irish emigrants to Britain travelled by boat between Rosslare and Fishguard in Wales. Chris lived with two girls on the CIE premises at the port.

She remembers scrubbing bar stools which had to be spotless when the passengers arrived. One of the ferry staff would knock on the girls' window in the early morning and tell them the exact number of passengers on the incoming ship. If the numbers were small, the girls could steal an extra hour in bed. In any event, they had to be ready for the inflow of punters who would line up at the bar and drink heavily to celebrate their arrival in Ireland before departing by train for their homes.

Kitty and Coleman were cracked about one another by now and were determined not to allow their separation to halt their relationship. They kept in touch by letter and Kitty submitted a request to be transferred back to Mayo. A year later, in 1946, her request was granted by CIE and she again relocated to Claremorris. The reunited couple became engaged and planned to marry in June 1947.

In Ireland, at that time, a woman was obliged to give up any paid work outside the home when she married. This practice had its origins in 1933 with the introduction of a marriage bar which dictated that female school teachers were prohibited from working after they married. The restriction was later extended to the Civil Service and soon became the accepted norm in most parts of the private sector. The Irish Constitution, adopted in 1937, reinforced this attitude towards working women by stipulating that the state would "endeavour to ensure that mothers shall not be obliged by economic necessity to engage in labour to the neglect of their duties in the home".

The situation prevailed until 1957. Even then, the easing of the restriction was due to necessity rather than any change in the attitude towards women. A shortage of teaching staff resulted in the lifting of the marriage bar for primary teachers. Ireland's joining of the European Economic Community in the 1970s finally necessitated the abandonment of the marriage bar. Legislation was introduced to prohibit sex-based pay inequality and to outlaw gender discrimination in the workplace.

Marriage would entail a considerable adjustment in my mother's life. Since leaving school, she had worked in Thurles and with the railway company in Claremorris and Rosslare. Photographs taken during their courtship shows a confident, well dressed young woman, clearly comfortable in front of the camera. She valued her independent lifestyle and her relationships with co-workers and close friends. Marriage would inevitably result in a lessening of social contacts and the loss of her financial independence.

She had another disadvantage. The vast majority of women who married in the west of Ireland at that time tended to live in close proximity to their parents so that family support and assistance with child-care was readily available locally. But my mother's parents and siblings lived 150 miles away from Claremorris. On the plus side, she could rely upon the support of my father's family. As an only son and only brother, Coleman was idolised by mother and sisters. Some level of resentment at the intrusion of a fiancé would not be unexpected. But Kitty had already met the Rushes and they were immediately won over by her amiable and relaxed manner. For her part, she was instantly comfortable and felt welcomed in their company.

Marriage would bring about changes in Coleman's life too. He still handed most of his wages to his mother each week. With marriage, this would cease but his sisters were now starting to work and to contribute to the family budget so that his contribution would not be missed. From now on, Coleman would have to support himself and Kitty, and pay rental on a house, from his wages at the brush factory and his income as a musician. Both sources of income seemed secure and the couple were confident as they planned for their future together.

Their first priority was to find a home. A property in the town would have been their preference but they could not locate a suitable one. They heard about the availability of a rental house in Streamstown, about two miles outside the town. Coleman and Kitty went to Streamstown, inspected the property, and agreed to rent it. They were lucky to get such a good house. It was the only slated home in the village; the others had thatched roofs. Another benefit was its location on a quiet sandy road that was safe for children. The owners, the Moran family, lived in a thatched house next door.

The house had three small bedrooms and a kitchen/living room with a small porch. In front of the house was a small grassy area that sloped downwards towards the road. A low wall formed a boundary with the unpaved narrow roadway. A small gate and a few stone steps provided access to the front door. To the rear was a modest garden with a small shed that functioned as a toilet.

In 1947, Ireland was still recovering from the impact of World War Two. The Irish government had opted to remain neutral during The Emergency, as the war was referred to in Ireland. In reality, the neutral stance was the only viable one because of the political situation in Ireland. A decision to support the Allies in 1939 would, in effect, invite

British troops back into Ireland, albeit on a temporary basis. The reappearance of British troops on Irish soil would have been so divisive that there was a realistic fear of massive unrest possibly leading to a revival of the Civil War. The Irish government decided that the best option was to remain officially neutral but, behind the scenes, there was passive support for the Allied cause.

Despite the country's policy of neutrality, the war years had an impact on life in Ireland. There was rationing of butter, margarine, coal, firewood, gas, and matches. Fuel for heating and cooking was in short supply, resulting in increased reliance on turf-cutting. As the war progressed, fuel for private motoring was so scarce that most cars were taken off the roads and people began to rely upon horse-drawn vehicles.

In 1947 the post-war Irish economy had not yet recovered and rationing would continue for another two years. Emigration was high, especially from Mayo and the western counties, as Irish workers were in demand to rebuild English cities after the ravages of war. Health services in Ireland were poor and seemed powerless to cope with tuberculosis which was causing many deaths.

On the morning of Thursday 24 June, 1947 Coleman Rushe and Kitty Ryan were married in Cappamore, Kitty's home parish in County Limerick. He was just two months past his twenty-third birthday. She was twenty-one. Instead of the traditional white wedding dress, Kitty was dressed in a tailored, powder blue jacket and skirt with matching blue suede high heeled shoes. Her floral head-dress was augmented by a small veil also decorated with flowers. The outfit was completed by a matching flower on her left lapel and a leather handbag and gloves. Coleman opted for a dark grey, pin-striped, double-breasted suit with white shirt and dark tie.

In the afternoon, they took the train to Dublin where, in an effort to preserve their privacy, they had already booked bed and breakfast accommodation under their married name. They were confident that their subterfuge had worked until they came down for breakfast the following morning and, much to their embarrassment, were greeted with applause and congratulations by the owner and the other guests.

They spent a week sightseeing and enjoying themselves in Dublin. They photographed each other on a pebble beach on a cold and windy day. He is well wrapped up in an overcoat and seems to be wearing his wedding suit underneath. Because of her lack of skill with the camera, the top of his head is missing from the photograph. She is photographed standing on the beach, grimly and unsuccessfully trying to stop her coat and dress from flapping in the wind. A more light-hearted moment was captured by my mother later when my father fashioned some kind of elaborate head-dress and posed as a pirate in the rigging of a sail-boat. The photo is childish, playful, and optimistic.

One of their oft-repeated anecdotes in later years concerned their arrival at their new home in Streamstown following the honeymoon. They were broke, having spent all their money in Dublin. When they opened the front door, they found an envelope. It was sent by Coleman's uncle, Jack Reynolds, and contained a ten pound note. The delighted and relieved couple were able to live in comfort until Coleman received his next pay-packet.

The story of the generous gesture was regularly related to us children and to visitors in later years, mainly as a way of giving credit to Uncle Jack. We were not told about an earlier windfall. In June 1947, the Mayo News newspaper reported the wedding of Coleman and Kitty and added that "Coleman, who is a valued member of Messrs. Ronayne's staff, was presented with a wallet of notes by Mr. George Foley, manager, on behalf of Directors and staff".

It is likely that the gift from Coleman's fellow workers and employers was used to buy some essentials for the new home. Further assistance for the newly-weds was provided by their families. Tom Rushe, my grandfather, put his carpentry skills to use. As a wedding present, he made a bed, a wardrobe, and a kitchen dresser for the new home. Kitty's mother travelled to Mayo from Limerick to Mayo in order to visit the "terrible place" and purchased another bed.

In September, Coleman and Kitty opened a bank account at the National Bank branch in Claremorris. They were on their way towards making a new life together and starting a family. But almost immediately, things began to go wrong. Over the following fifteen years, the young married couple were to be confronted with an appalling sequence of set-backs and misfortunes.

CHAPTER FOUR

TB Blues

The future seemed bright for Tom and Mary Rushe, my grandparents, as 1948 dawned. They had a comfortable, semi-detached home on the outskirts of Claremorris and Tom had a relatively secure job. Since 1942, he had been working on the railway as a carpenter. Coleman, the only son, had married and left home but he and Kitty were living less that two miles away. Coleman invariably dropped in on his way home from work to visit his parents and his three sisters, who adored their only brother.

The eldest of the Rushe girls, Mary, was now twenty-one and was shy and reserved when compared to her sisters. Patsy, the middle sister, was eighteen and was the most energetic of the three. She liked dancing and staying out as late as her mother would allow. "She would burn the candle at both ends", my father would later say affectionately. Chris, still only fourteen, was cheerfully outgoing and the possessor of a razor-sharp wit.

Patsy developed a cough and, because of the fear of tuberculosis, was immediately brought to a local doctor. To the relief of the family, the doctor diagnosed a touch of bronchitis, prescribed some medication, and sent Patsy home. When her condition did not improve, her parents' growing concern overcame their reluctance to question the doctor's decision. They arranged to have her re-examined by another doctor who, to their dismay, immediately diagnosed that Patsy had contracted the dreaded tuberculosis. One of Patsy's lungs had already collapsed and the other was badly damaged. My grandfather was furious and had to be restrained from physically attacking the first doctor whom he blamed for the misdiagnosis and the consequent deterioration in Patsy's condition.

As a precaution, the rest of the family had to be tested for TB. Their worst fears were realised when it was discovered that the eldest daughter Mary also had a small shadow on her lung.

Irish people had a morbid fear of tuberculosis, commonly known as TB. In the 1940s, an estimated four thousand people per year were dying from the disease in Ireland. It could attack the spine, kidneys, lungs, or brain and was spread by coughing or sneezing. TB also prevented defence cells from functioning properly and the resultant chronic lung infection could be fatal. Unless diagnosed and treated at a very early stage, the disease usually necessitated a stay in a sanatorium for two to three years. Patients whose condition was untreatable were allowed to return home to die. In order to prevent the transmission of the disease to other family members, the patient was obliged to live in a chalet which was usually erected in the garden close to the family home. In the sanatorium, it was considered necessary for the patient to have as much fresh air as possible. As a result, beds were moved outdoors, usually on to a verandah. Sometimes, patients were even obliged to remain outdoors overnight.

In Ireland, a stigma, born of prejudice and misinformation, was associated with TB. The public reaction was similar to the initial response to AIDS in the early 1980s. It was mistakenly believed that uncleanliness was one of the primary causes of TB. It was true that overcrowding and poor diet could make one susceptible to the disease but many people who were affluent and lived in comfortable and spacious housing were also infected. TB was seldom discussed openly, however, because of the fear and prejudice surrounding it. Misconceptions and misinformation were rampant. There were even instances where people expressed disquiet at the location of a sanatorium in their town.

Patsy and Mary Rushe were first admitted to the County Hospital in Castlebar. Mary was to remain there for six months before she was declared free of TB and, to the delight and relief of her family, she was allowed to return home. Patsy, whose condition was much more advanced, was transferred to Saint Theresa's Sanatorium near Ballinrobe, about thirteen miles from her home. But it soon became apparent that she needed more specialist treatment and she was relocated to Castlerea Sanatorium in County Roscommon. At first, the treatment for TB patients consisted of long periods of bed-rest in well ventilated areas and often in the open air. In some cases, as part of the treatment, an operation was performed to remove some ribs. During the procedure, which often took ten hours, the patient had to make do with a local anaesthetic.

Most of the patients were young people and the boredom of bed-rest and hospital routine had to be countered by whatever means were available. Male and female patients were segregated but overcame this obstacle by sending messages and requests to each other on the hospital radio. Regular letter writing also helped to relieve the tedium. Visits from family and friends were sometimes restricted, depending upon the needs of individual patients.

The Castlerea sanatorium was twenty-five miles from Patsy's home in Claremorris. She was allowed regular family visits and, despite the stigma attached to TB and the fear of contracting the disease, some friends also cycled the fifty mile round trip to see her. The family and friends thought little of a two hour cycle trip to Castlerea and a similar journey home in the evening.

My father's band-mate and friend, Billy Gleeson, was especially fond of Patsy and visited often. Patsy also had another admirer and there was mutual jealousy between the men. Patsy, perhaps mischievously, declined to either encourage or discourage her two suitors. My father described the scene when both men visited at the same time. They sat on either side of the bed, each holding one of Patsy's hands, and refusing to speak directly to one another. The eighteen year old object of their admiration clearly relished the attention.

My father and mother in Streamstown and the Rushes in Claremorris were concerned at Patsy's condition. My father, in particular, was very worried about her; they were very fond of each other and exchanged letters regularly.

Some good news was needed in order to lift the gloom so that the revelation that my mother was pregnant and was expecting her first baby in June 1948 was a most welcome distraction. The prospect of a first grandchild for Tom and Mary Rushe, and a niece or nephew for the Rushe girls was exactly the morale boost they needed. The news was greeted with similar delight by the Ryans in Cappamore.

The pregnancy appeared to be progressing satisfactorily when suddenly, in early April, my mother went into shock and was rushed in a comatose state to the Mayo County Hospital in Castlebar. The exact reason for the coma is unclear but such pregnancy complications, while rare and sometimes fatal for mother or child, were not unknown.

A baby girl was born on April 6, two days after her father's twenty-fourth birthday. The child was two months premature and weighed only four pounds eleven ounces. Mother was recovering but there were concerns about the survival of the baby so that she was baptised immediately after birth. In a gesture designed to show love and support to the baby's Aunt Patsy and to boost her morale, Coleman and Kitty named the baby Patricia.

Mother and child remained in the hospital while Kitty recovered and baby Patricia gained her strength. When they were released from hospital, Coleman and Kitty brought the baby to the Church of the Holy Rosary in Castlebar for a blessing before heading home to Streamstown.

The jubilation at the arrival of the baby, who was fussed over by grandparents and especially by aunts, was overshadowed by the lack of improvement in Patsy's condition.

There was hope on the horizon for TB sufferers. Dr. Noel Browne had recently been appointed as Minister for Health. This maverick, left-leaning politician had switched political parties on a number of occasions and had a reputation for being difficult and intransigent. His own family had been devastated by poverty and by TB; both of his parents had died from the disease. As a consequence of his youthful intelligence and ability, he won a series of scholarships and, eventually, a benefactor provided the funds and support in order to put Brown through medical school. He also became involved in politics and was elected to the Dail. He was handed the Health portfolio and he immediately set himself the challenge of overhauling the health service. His first project was the TB Eradication Scheme, an attempt to counter the devastation being caused by the disease. Over the next few years, he introduced the most modern medical procedures and practises, used funds from the Hospital Sweepstake lottery to finance the sanatoriums, and purchased the new drugs which were now coming into use in the UK and the continent. Under his watch, drugs such as streptomycin were brought to the forefront of TB treatment in Ireland.

By the early 1950s, the incidence of TB in Ireland began to fall and increasing numbers of sufferers were surviving the disease. But Patsy Rushe's condition had deteriorated before the improved treatment regime began to have effect. Photographs of Patsy before she became ill show a healthy teenager, slightly heavier than her two slim sisters. Later photographs that were taken in the sanatorium confirm that she had lost weight. She had also aged; she would no longer pass for a teenager.

As Patsy's hospitalisation entered its second year, spirits were lifted by the news that my mother was pregnant again. In Ireland at that time, one in three births took place in the home, usually under the supervision of a local mid-wife. Nevertheless, it was decided that my mother would give birth in Castlebar Hospital. The decision was probably taken because she was expecting twins and also because of the complications which arose with her previous pregnancy.

On 10 April, 1949, Kitty Rushe gave birth to twins, a boy and a girl. The boy was named Michael after both of his grandfathers and the girl, Mary, was named after her Rushe grandmother. Both babies were pronounced healthy, as was the mother, and the good news was quickly conveyed to the Ryans in Cappamore and to Patsy Rushe at Castlerea Sanatorium.

The first photograph of the twins was taken outside the Streamstown house. When pictured, they seem to be about four months old. My mother is proudly and smilingly cradling one in each arm. The babies look healthy and contented. But tragedy had already struck by the time the photograph was taken.

Patsy's condition had been deteriorating despite various attempted treatments. On Monday 20th of May 1949, she wrote to my father.

Regional San.

Castlerea,

Monday

My dear Coleman,

Did you get home alright the last day. I hope so. I got a few more injections after that and I'm still getting them. I was down again today and I got my lung washed. I never expected to be going down again so soon. I got over it though. It wasn't the same doctor as the last day. Nurse gave me punch after.

The sister came down now to see how I was this evening and she told me the stuff for the washouts is very valuable. They are only after getting it and they hope it will do me good. It's newest on the market. She also said I had very nasty fluid on my chest and I would feel better of getting it off. I have to get them done twice weekly so please Coleman and Kitty pray for me to have the strength and nerve to go through it. I'll probably be done on Thursday again, please God. Brigid Mc Hale said a full Rosary and prayers for me when I was down today. She's great, God bless her. It's no wonder I was sick with that old stuff on my chest. The doctor said I was good again today to stick out. I hope God keeps me that way. Tell Mam and the others to pray for me, as if they aren't praying enough already I know. You are all wonderful. I hope Kitty and the twins are very well.

   Please excuse my writing, Colie, as I'm tired after the day.
   Your loving sis
   Patsy xxxx
   PS Write soon.
The letter was postmarked Tuesday, May 21, 1949.

Patsy died at Castlerea Sanatorium two days later. She had recently celebrated her twentieth birthday. Her remains were brought back home and she was buried in the graveyard at Crossboyne near Claremorris.

"You father never really got over Patsy, you know".

My mother had been listening as I was putting some questions to my father as part of my research into our family history. He answered my direct questions and smilingly added the anecdote about Patsy's hand-holding with her two admirers. He then went on to talk about his abhorrence of the public reaction to TB sufferers, and his life-long admiration for Dr. Noel Browne, whom he regarded as the man responsible for virtually eradicating the disease in Ireland.

I got the impression that he had deliberately changed the focus of our discussion into a more general talk about TB and Dr. Browne and I tried to redirect him by asking about the impact on the Rushe family of Patsy's death. He responded by pointing out that, as a result of Patsy's death, his mother became insistent that her children and later her grandchildren should get plenty of sleep, eat well, and never ignore coughs or other early warning signs of illness.

I guessed that he did not want to talk about the emotional impact on himself or the family and I did not press him. Shortly afterwards, when my father was out of the room, my mother quietly made the comment that he had never got over Patsy's death. I realised that she was explaining his reluctance to be candid about his feelings on the death of his sister.

It is clear from the tone of her last letter to him and from the warm and affectionate way in which he spoke about her, that my father was very close to Patsy. "Colie", as she pet-named him, was her only brother and, as the eldest in the family, was put on a pedestal by his sisters. Doubtless, he felt protective of her and this feeling would have been intensified when she became ill. The illness and death at such a young age was also a burden on the rest of the family. Coleman's parents were coping with conflicting emotions. Grief at the loss of a second child. Anger at the perceived failure of the doctor to detect the illness in time. Guilt that Patsy had somehow contracted TB and that they had not immediately sought a second diagnosis. Helplessness that there was nothing that they could do for her. As the eldest, Coleman, would have felt the obligation to help his parents and sisters to cope with the tragedy and to show a strong front. My mother's comment leads me to believe that, privately at home in Streamstown, she watched and supported him as he tried to come to terms with the loss. Her words made it clear to me that his conflicting emotions were never fully resolved.

As my parents struggled to come to terms with Patsy's death, they were about to receive another body blow.

CHAPTER FIVE

Little Grey Home In The West

The townland of Streamstown was approached by traversing the railway line at a manned, gated, crossing. The fairly straight road then passed by a few farm houses before swinging left towards open countryside. The last house on the right, just before this bend to the left, was the home occupied by the Rushes. As we have seen, the house, with its slated roof, was as dry and warm as any in the locality. Despite their modest household income, Kitty had made it as comfortable as possible. Throughout his life, my father marvelled at her ability to organise the household and to "make do" on very little.

"Kitty could make a home out of two sticks".

Yet, living conditions were primitive, by modern standards. In 1946, sixty-one percent of Irish houses did not have a piped water supply and only fifteen percent of all homes had a fixed bath or shower. The vast majority of dwellings with access to piped water were located in urban areas so that the percentage of houses in the countryside with running water was minimal. Some of the larger rural farmhouses had their own well or private pump but these were the exceptions. In Streamstown, drinking water was drawn by bucket from the local spring well. Rain water, which was used for cooking and washing, was collected in barrels or water-tanks.

Children were bathed, or "scrubbed", to use my mother's preferred expression, once a week. This ritual took place in a metal bath which was placed in front of the open fire. The children's enjoyment of this family ritual was only marred by the sting of soap in the eyes or by my mother's occasional insistence on rinsing the child's washed hair with a sudden and unexpected dousing of cold water. This was reputed to close the pores and keep colds away. Parents attended to their own bathing needs when children were safely tucked in bed.

Kitty did all cooking and baking on an open fire which was the focal point of the large kitchen and which also provided the only heat source for the house. In the recess of the fireplace, there was an iron crane which pivoted so that the arm could be swung outward in order to enable my mother to position cooking pots on a hook. The pot-hook was adjustable so that the kettle or other cooking vessel could be suspended at the most suitable height over the flames. Potatoes, vegetables, and meat were cooked in a cast-iron, round bottomed, three legged pot which was hung over the turf fire. A flat-bottomed pot, referred to by my mother as the oven, was used for baking bread and also for roasting. Water was boiled in a large heavy black kettle, also round bottomed with three legs. The other necessary cooking implements were a large frying pan and a teapot. In order to keep the tea warm, a few embers were removed from the fire, crushed and placed on the hearth. The flat bottomed teapot was then positioned on top of the embers.

The kitchen floor was bare concrete. The bedroom floors were overlaid with more welcoming linoleum but the open fire and cooking process rendered this floor-covering unsuitable for the kitchen.

Fuel for the fire consisted of peat, known as turf, which was cut and saved by my father in a bog just beyond our house. Electricity had not yet reached this rural area so that light was provided by lamps which were fuelled by pink paraffin oil.

Clothes were washed in a tub, with the aid of a washing board. Some items, such as babies nappies, had to be boil-washed over the fire. Clothes were hung out to dry on the clothes line if the weather permitted. In emergencies, essentials such as baby clothes had to be dried in the kitchen by hanging them in proximity to the open fire.

And toilet arrangements? In Streamstown, sanitation consisted of an outside toilet, known as the lavatory, in a shed behind the house. The shed contained a chemical toilet. Toilet paper consisted of rectangles of old newspaper through which a piece of string was threaded and which were hung on a nail. This provided that added bonus that the user could browse the newspaper cutting before putting it to the more essential use.

My father regularly emptied the toilet receptacle into a pit which he had dug in the remotest corner of the back garden, covering it with some earth or other garden waste. He then rinsed and disinfected the container thoroughly before relocating it in the shed.

During my youth, our lavatory did not have a lock on the door. A lock was superfluous. If the door was closed, you knew that somebody was in situ and you waited. When you departed the toilet, you left the door ajar. This had the dual benefit of signalling that the facility was unoccupied and of providing much needed ventilation.

The remaining link in the sanitation system in the house was provided by chamber pots. Over time, the old style ceramic pots were gradually replaced by enamel and later by plastic receptacles. A pot was positioned under each bed for use during the night in order to obviate the necessity of leaving the house. The pots were taken out and emptied into the toilet each morning and rinsed with water.

Early photographs of the house in Streamstown confirm that the Rushes, in common with most rural families, had acquired a flock of hens. They were housed at night in a crude wooden hen-house in the back garden, wandered freely during day-light hours, and provided eggs for the family needs.

Although she was busier following Patricia's arrival, my mother must have been lonely during the long days while my father was at work and especially at night if he was playing with the band. She occasionally exchanged greetings with neighbours when she passed their houses on her way to town. But the location of the house at the end of the village meant that there was rarely a passersby to break the monotony. Even the local scenery was bleak and uninteresting. Her pre-marriage life as a waitress and cook, bantering with customers and socialising with friends, had disappeared suddenly and now she was alone. She could cycle to town to do some shopping and to visit her parents-in-law but, since Patricia's arrival, even this distraction was more difficult to arrange. If the weather was suitable, she could put the baby in the pram and walk to her in-laws' house, a journey that would take less than half an hour.

The battery powered radio provided a welcome distraction and Kitty was an avid listener. Since the foundation in 1926 of 2RN, the Irish national broadcaster, radio listenership had gradually increased. The Athlone transmitter brought radio to a wider audience in 1933 and by 1949, three quarters of Irish households had radio coverage. Radio Eireann, as the station became known, was now broadcasting for about seven hours per day. There was afternoon coverage from 1pm until 2.30pm and evening broadcasts from 5.30 until 11pm. An hour long broadcast in the morning was eventually added in 1952. Listenership surveys undertaken by the Central Statistics Office indicate that two-thirds of houses which possessed a radio tuned in to listen to the news bulletin at 1.30pm.

The listener was not confined to Irish radio. In many parts of Ireland, one could tune into BBC radio which had longer broadcasting hours and a more eclectic selection of music. The radio in the Rushe household seemed to be switched on at all times. Without fail, Kitty listened to Mrs Dale's Diary, a soap opera that was broadcast on BBC each afternoon. At night, she and my father were regular radio listeners.

Apart from her avid radio listening, I recall two other activities of my mother that I now recognise as coping mechanisms in her effort to deal with her isolation. Each evening, when my father arrived from work and was having his dinner, he gave her a detailed report on his day. She listened attentively and, when necessary, prompted him as he set out a full account of the banter, the gossip, the intrigues, and happenings during his workday.

She also kept in touch with the outside world by reading the newspapers. My father unfailingly brought home the Irish Independent newspaper each evening. On that night or the following day, my mother read the paper from cover to cover. She did not browse through the pages in the usual way, scanning headlines and reading the detail of the occasional article that took her fancy. Instead, with the attention and diligence of a book reader, she started at the front page and read through the whole newspaper, column by column, article by article. As a result, she accumulated a tremendous amount of knowledge about a wide variety of subjects. The Sunday papers and the local weeklies were also devoured in a similar fashion. All through her life, she persevered with this meticulous consumption of newspapers.

CHAPTER SIX

Stand By Me

Mary didn't seem to be quite right. It must have been in late 1949, not long after Patsy's death, that my mother first sensed that something was not as it should be with her younger daughter. The twins were only a few months old and shared a large wooden cot which was the most recent item hand-made for the family by carpenter and grandfather, Tom Rushe. As she watched the babies in their cot, my mother noticed that Michael was much more active than his twin sister. She discussed her growing concern with my father and they tried to reassure themselves that children can show marked variations in their rates of early development. Nevertheless, Kitty was alarmed when she observed that Mary allowed Michael to crawl over her in order to be lifted from the cot in the morning. Mary was the same size as Michael and was as physically strong and healthy as her twin brother. This is borne out by early photographs in which it is difficult to differentiate between the babies. To my mother, Mary passivity seemed to indicate that something was amiss.

A local nurse offered reassurance that there was nothing to be worried about; the twins would develop but not at the same pace. Kitty continued to be concerned and brought Mary to the doctor. Again, she was told that it was far too early to draw any conclusions about the child's development. But as time went on, it became obvious that Kitty had been correct all along. Mary had learning difficulties. In the parlance of the day, she "wasn't right".

Modern Ireland has only recently commenced the process of coming to terms with its past failure to protect the vulnerable. The Irish government has latterly acknowledged the injustice and cruelty inflicted on unmarried mothers, their children, and those who were installed at industrial schools and other such institutions. As a nation, however, we have not yet engaged with our previously neglectful attitude to people with mental health problems or with learning difficulties.

There were two significant factors which rendered Ireland an unwelcoming place for people who were "not right". One was the absence of any educational support. The other was the attitude of society.

The Department of Education assumed responsibility for schools in Ireland in 1924. The Commission of Enquiry into the Reformatory and Industrial School System issued a report in 1936 which stipulated that children with special needs should not be educated alongside "normal" children, as they were described. It was felt that the presence of the special needs pupils would be detrimental to the learning of the other children. This attitude reflected the belief that responsibility for special needs children was a medical issue rather than an educational one.

As a result of parental pressure and also the work of some religious communities, there was a gradual push for a more enlightened approach to meeting the needs of these children. One result was the Report of Enquiry on Mental Handicap in 1965 which recognised that special schools were needed for some children with mental or physical handicap. The report also suggested that there should be classes for slow learners within mainstream schools.

At local level in the west of Ireland, services to support children with learning disability and their parents were non existent. In frustration, Johnny Mee, wrote to his local newspaper, the Connaught Telegraph, in January 1966. He highlighted the lack of local services for his own daughter, Mary, who had special needs. If she was to receive any specialised educational help, she would have to leave home and attend a centre in Cork or Dublin. Mr. Mee's letter called for the establishment of a local group comprising interested people who would raise funds, act as advocates for children with special needs, and provide support for their parents. The letter clearly struck a chord with Mayo people and the outcome was the formation of the Mayo Association of Parents and Friends of Mentally Handicapped Children. The fundraising and advocacy of this group resulted in the early establishment in the county of a special school and eventually in a full range of educational and training services including schools for mild, moderate, and severely handicapped children. Residential homes were also made available for some of the profoundly effected children.

But these developments in the late 1960s were much too late for children like my sister Mary who were born in less enlightened times. Education was not an option and County Clinics had the responsibility for assessing the children, who were often committed to institutions. Some were locked away for the rest of their lives and many were abandoned by their families and erased from the family history and memory. Many Irish children were never made aware of the existence of a sibling in an institution.

This combination of fear, embarrassment, and prejudice towards those with learning difficulties was not unique to Ireland. For example, in the UK and USA, many such people were locked away because it was believed that this was for the good of society. In Britain, the Mental Incapacity Act of 1913 legitimised the incarceration of an estimated 40,000 people.

Centuries before, in ancient Ireland, there had been a more enlightened view. The Brehon Laws, which applied in Ireland before the time of Julius Caesar and continued into the Elizabethan era, had provided some protection. The laws allowed for the imposition of heavy fines on anybody who mocked people with any form of learning difficulty. There were also legal obligations on the guardians of people with special needs. The guardians, who were usually close family members, were obligated by law to protect them against self injury. But, by the twentieth century, Ireland shared the view of the "civilised" world that those with learning difficulties should be hidden or locked away from public view.

I recall one such local man during the 1950s who was rarely allowed to leave the house. Although I knew the other members of the family well, I was not aware of this man's existence until I saw him working in a field and enquired about his identity. It was quietly explained to me that he was "not right" and was only allowed out occasionally to help with farm work. Even then, he was not permitted by his family to work in fields adjoining the road lest he be seen by passersby.

I was shocked by this casual callousness because my parents had taken a different attitude towards Mary's situation. They were determined from the outset that Mary, where possible, would be treated in exactly the same way as their other children. It was clear that she would not be able to attend school but little else was ruled out. If we were going out to play, to visit a neighbour's house, or to draw water from the well, Mary was brought along and we, as her siblings, had a duty to look after her. She accompanied us on family holidays to my mother's home place in Cappamore. Mary was included in our occasional family outings to the circus or the carnival and she appears on all family photographs.

The cause of Mary's disability was never officially established or diagnosed. It was just accepted by the family who, under my parents' guidance, developed strategies to deal with it. When I discussed Mary's condition with my father many years later, he expressed the view that she may have been temporarily deprived of oxygen at birth resulting in brain damage. Whatever the cause, the reality was that she had very limited intellectual ability and could not speak. She did not know the difference between right and wrong but she had a limited sense of danger. For example, she did not endanger herself by going near the fire and she did not walk out the gate in front of traffic.

She needed help when dressing and in the toilet. If my mother didn't bring her regularly to the toilet, there was a danger that she might have an "accident" but this rarely happened because of my mother's vigilance. As time went on, the rest of us children could read the changes in Mary's behaviour and arrange for her to avoid any embarrassment. One of the less avoidable side-effects was a bed-wetting condition which created much extra washing work for my mother.

Mary couldn't read but had no trouble passing the time contentedly. Sometimes, she sat for long periods, indoors or outdoors, in a little wooden chair which my grandfather lovingly crafted for her. She watched her brothers and sister at play but never joined in. At times, as an alternative to sitting, she was contented to stand, rocking gently from one foot to the other, and humming a tune while keeping time by clicking her fingernails on the metallic lid of a biscuit tin, that she carried around for this purpose.

Despite her inability to speak, she could cry aloud if disturbed and she could hum a tune. She obviously inherited my father's musical ability and she regularly astounded him by her ability to pick up a tune from the radio after only one hearing and to hum it repeatedly in perfect time and in perfect pitch. As a youngster, I prided myself in the speed with which I was able to memorise and repeat a tune. But, unlike me, Mary only needed one hearing before she was note-perfectly humming the latest Rosemary Clooney or Guy Mitchell hit.

Mary had a unique relationship with the family terrier. Blackie, a much loved but occasionally bad-tempered dog, was introduced to the family as a pet about the time the twins were born. He soon developed a fractious relationship with Sydney, the family cat, who was named after Sydney Greenstreet, one of my father's favourite film actors. Blackie quickly gave himself a life-long role as Mary's protector and companion. He sat at her feet or in her vicinity and adopted a loud and aggressive demeanour if anybody other than close family approached her. While Mary was seated outside in the summer sunshine of the garden, my mother could carry on with her housework in the confident knowledge that Blackie was on sentry duty.

The loyalty and protectiveness shown by Blackie to Mary would be easier to understand if she patted, stroked, fondled, and cuddled him as a child might be expected to do. On the contrary, she seemed to be oblivious to his existence and never favoured him with any display of affection. The rest of the family fussed over the dog, patted him and, of course, fed him regularly but never gained Blackie's attention and loyalty as Mary did. In every photograph of Mary taken at home, a watchful Blackie is to be seen nearby. The reasons for such a bond between child and dog are unclear. Animals seem to have an ability to sense when humans are ill or in need of support. Some children with autism and other learning difficulties can better interact with animals than with other people. It is thought that this may result from the tendency of such children to rely on nonverbal forms of communication as animals do. This may account for the affinity between Mary and Blackie.

Given the attitude towards people with learning difficulties at that time, it would not have been surprising if neighbours and friends disapproved of my parents insistence that Mary be seen publicly and, where feasible, should mix with other children. I have no memory of such a negative attitude and my parents never mentioned any problem to me. If any neighbours were uncomfortable with Mary's condition, they did not demonstrate it. Children can often unwittingly reveal the hidden prejudices of parents by repeating in public the unguarded comments and observations made in the privacy of the home. I never heard any such adverse comment regarding Mary or about my parents openness regarding her condition. Neighbouring children came to our house to play and we Rushes, often accompanied by Mary, visited other homes in the same way. Mary was treated with the same kindness and welcoming attitude as the rest of us.

The commendable ease and tolerance of our neighbours towards Mary was not replicated in the wider world. On one occasion, my mother was taking us by train for our summer trip to Cappamore to visit her parents. Upon seeing Mary, a woman passenger objected to her presence on the train.

"That girl should not be out", remonstrated the woman. "People should not have to look at her. She should be kept at home".

Years later, as she recalled the incident, my mother, by nature a placid woman, would display intense annoyance.

"You can be sure that I gave her a piece of my mind", she said darkly.

"How did she react?"

"She soon cleared off and sat somewhere else. And good riddance. The stupid woman."

CHAPTER SEVEN

A Day In The Life

In November 1950, my mother was about to give birth to me. It was decided that I would be born at home in Streamstown rather than at the hospital. Unusually, it was arranged that the doctor would be present in addition to the midwife who normally worked alone.

My father had taken a rare day off work. It was Friday 17th and he was at home when my mother asked him to fetch the doctor. He cycled quickly to town but was told by a friend that the doctor was playing golf at Claremorris Golf Club. Luckily, the friend had a car and drove Coleman to the golf club where he discovered that the doctor was out on the course. My father followed directions onto the golf course in order to intercept his quarry and he located the doctor who was close to finishing his round. The doctor calmly reassured my father and asked him to wait until he completed his golf match. They then headed for Streamstown where I was born shortly afterwards.

I can only surmise that my mother was already pregnant with me before the full implications of Mary's condition were apparent. Otherwise, she and my father might have waited to have another child. My theory is supported by a gap of five years after my birth before my mother had another child. Following my arrival in November 1950, my mother was taking full-time care of four children under the age of three. When one takes into account that one of the children had special needs and that the family were living in a remote location in the countryside without running water or electricity, the workload and responsibility seem daunting.

What was Kitty's typical day in the months following my arrival?

My father started work at 8am and my mother always got up to make his breakfast. The alarm clock was set for 6.45am at the latest. In order to ensure that they did not sleep through the alarm, the clock was placed in an enamel bowl which amplified the sound and rattled in response to the vibration.

Moving quietly in order not to disturb the children, my mother lit the fire from the embers of the previous night. The practise of raking the fire was common in Irish households. At night, ash was raked over the live embers which would still be glowing in the morning and would be used to revive the fire. It was not unusual to hear stories about households where the fire never went out, having been renewed each morning as a result of the raking process.

The kettle was quickly boiled to provide shaving water for my father and to make tea. While my father washed and shaved, my mother prepared breakfast. One of her non-negotiable convictions was that a hot breakfast was essential, irrespective of the weather or the time of year. This might consist of a boiled egg or porridge which she had prepared the night before and reheated in the morning.

They had breakfast together before he left at about 7.30 am to cycle to work. Already, the children would be stirring. Patricia, the eldest, was toilet trained by now but craved attention in the manner of three year-olds. My mother helped her to dress and wash before seating her at the table for breakfast.

Then attention had to be directed towards the three youngest. Bottles had to be filled and warmed. Three babies had to be lifted, fed, and winded and three nappies had to be changed. It is difficult to imagine how these tasks were accomplished. Did the most demanding and loudest baby get attended to first? Or perhaps the babies learned instinctively that they would be fed eventually and waited quietly.

My mother revealed that I was breast-fed as a baby and, as far as I know, I was the only one of her children whom she fed in this way. Perhaps it was a way of multi-tasking - could she feed me while giving a bottle to one of the twins? Let's move swiftly on.

Disposable nappies were not in general usage in Ireland at that time. Nappies, usually made from terrycloth towelling, had to be boil-washed after each usage. Assuming my mother had a dozen nappies for the babies, it was still necessary for her to do a boil-wash almost every day. Monday was the day designated for the larger family wash, provided the weather was favourable for drying clothes on the clothes-line. Otherwise, essentials such as baby clothes had to be dried by placing them near the fire.

When water was needed from the well, it was not feasible for my mother to leave the children alone or to bring them with her. I can only surmise that my father drew water in the evening after work or that he looked after the children while my mother escaped from the confines of the house for a much needed break. Trips to the well afforded an opportunity to meet and chat with neighbours on the same errand - an early form of social networking.

After the children were put in their cots for an afternoon nap, my mother had a little time to have some lunch and perhaps listen to the early afternoon news on the radio. But, as always, there were other chores to be attended to. Beds had to be made and baby milk bottles, which were made from glass, needed to be washed and sterilised. A fresh work-shirt had to be ironed for my father for the following morning. The metal shoes had to be heated on the fire and inserted into the box-iron before this chore could be completed.

By now, the children were restlessly stirring again and the lifting, changing, and feeding ritual had to be repeated.

The next chore was the preparation and cooking of dinner so that it would be ready when my father arrived home from work. Lamps had to be lit and, occasionally, it was necessary to trim the wicks, to refill the lamp wells with pink paraffin oil, and to clean the globes.

Following his arrival from work, my father washed himself and then amused and perhaps gave a bottle feed to the babies while my mother was getting the dinner on the table. Their chat over dinner mainly consisted of him telling her about his work. To my mother, the sound of an adult voice must have been a relief after the long day.

During the late spring to autumn my father usually spent the daylight evening hours in the garden sowing and tending to potatoes and vegetables which would supply the family needs for virtually all of the year. He also spent many hours in the nearby bog where he cut and saved turf which was brought home and used as fuel.

If the weather made it impossible for him to work in the garden or the bog, he might spend a few hours practising on his fiddle or quietly singing a new song in preparation for the band's next date.

After dinner and the washing-up, the children had to be settled for the night. As the children got slightly older, night prayers were taught, recited, and encouraged. But the chores were not yet finished. My father's lunch-box for the following morning had to be prepared. Also my mother might steep the porridge in water overnight which would make it bulkier and easier to cook for breakfast.

The late evening allowed a little time for relaxation: reading, chatting, or listening to the radio. But my mother also used this time for repairing our clothes by darning, sewing or patching. She also knitted a regular supply of gloves, scarves, jumpers, cardigans, and pullovers. In the winter nights, a hot water bottle was filled and placed in each bed. Then the lamps were quenched and the fire was raked. The children were "looked in on" and, if the night was cold, my father's overcoat was placed over them as an extra blanket. Finally, a sprinkle of holy water was flicked over their sleeping forms. Before my parents finally went to bed, the alarm clock was wound and positioned in the enamel basin as another long day wearily ticked to a close.

CHAPTER EIGHT

It's Over

My mother and father never spoke about these early days in Streamstown with anything other than nostalgic affection. As we were growing up, they gave no indication to us that their lives were difficult or stressful during this or any other period. As I write, I feel that I am appreciating for the first time the magnitude of the obstacles with which they were unflinchingly coping. They were showing great strength and fortitude in their handling of a difficult situation.

Perhaps they consoled themselves that better times were coming. It seems that no further additions to the family were planned until the children got older. Each year would lighten the workload slightly as the babies became less dependant on nappies and baby bottles. Patricia was already chattering to her mother and taking her food unaided. Surely it was only a matter of time before the others were following her lead. And who knew what to expect from Mary? Early signs were not good but there was hope that her speech might develop and that she might gradually become more self-sufficient.

But, instead of improving, the fortunes of Coleman, Kitty and their young family were about to encounter the next in a seemingly unending series of setbacks. "Trouble never comes unattended" was a commonly used local expression. My grandfather, Tom Rushe, had a wry variation on this pessimistic outlook: "When God closes one door, he shuts another".

I was only a few weeks old when my father got the first inkling that trouble was looming. The information was provided to him by a summons server whose duties included delivering writs which gave notice of pending legal action over unpaid debts. The debt in this case was not ours; my father had a strong aversion to borrowing. The summons server was a friend of the family and knew that my parents' financial situation was precarious. He approached my father and revealed confidentially that he had served a number of writs in respect of debts incurred by Ronayne's brush factory, my father's employers. The clear implication was that the factory was in financial difficulty. The summons server was of the opinion that the brush factory could be facing imminent closure.

My father was faced with a dilemma. He was not in a position to ask any questions at Ronayne's as he had been given the information confidentially. He was one of forty factory workers who might be made redundant simultaneously in a town where few alternative employment opportunities existed. There would be an unseemly scramble for any elusive local jobs but the vast majority of the workers would end up on the dole or would have to emigrate.

Should he wait and hope that the company's difficulty might be overcome? Or should he leave now and get a job before the local labour market became saturated by a horde of unemployed?

In 1951, a report was carried out on the Irish labour market with a view to predicting the future work expectations of young people who were about twenty-one years old at that time. Only ninety percent were expected to live beyond the age of fifty. It was estimated that thirty percent of males and forty percent of females would emigrate before they reached the age of thirty. Of the people who remained, the men could expect to be gainfully employed but few of the women would have paid jobs. Subsequent statistics have proved that the 1951 predictions were accurate, with the exception of the estimated percentage of females in the workplace which did not anticipate the eventual abolition of the marriage bar.

If the brush factory closed, employment prospects in Claremorris were going to be dismal. My father discussed the situation with my mother and they agreed that it would be better to take the initiative. He approached a local builder and was offered a job. He handed in his notice and left Ronayne's, where he had worked for over eleven years. His reference was signed by Sean Roynane, a son of the owner who had been approached by the fourteen year old on his way home from the races many years before. The letter, dated January 2, 1951, stated that my father was "an honest, trustworthy and excellent worker" and that he left the job "on his own accord".

A few months later, it must have seemed that the dire predictions about Ronayne's demise were unreliable. Or perhaps, as might be expected in a small town, the word about the financial difficulties had spread and more employees had left. Whatever the reason, my father must have been nonplussed when an advert appeared in a local newspaper on July 15.

"Wanted immediately, skilled workers in the Brush and Broom Trade, Bass and Hair Pan. Also machinists (male or female) for semi-automatic machines. Apply with reference to M. Ronayne & Sons Ltd. Claremorris."

It is not clear whether new workers were ever taken on or if the advert was a ploy in order to deflect attention and reassure creditors. Whatever the motivation for the advert, the display of optimism did not presage a change of fortune for the company. The factory finally closed in 1952 with massive loss of employment opportunities in Claremorris.

Other changes were taking place also. Bill Gleeson, my father's boyhood friend, band mate, and fellow worker at Ronayne's, emigrated to London. Bill had contracted TB but luckily, it was diagnosed at an early stage and he recovered after spending some time in a sanatorium. As an indication of his close friendship with my parents, Bill was selected by them to be my godfather when I was christened in late 1950.

As a result of his illness, Bill had to give up playing the trumpet. The demise of the four-piece band was inevitable when their other childhood friend, Paddy Clarke, decided to emigrate to the USA. Paddy's childhood fascination with birds resulted in his employment at Bronx Zoo where he worked as an aviculturalist from 1953 until his retirement in 1990.

Despite their geographical locations, the three childhood friends remained in close contact. They visited one another and regularly exchanged letters for the rest of their lives.

CHAPTER NINE

Beyond The Sea

My father did not read Ronayne's final job advert in the local newspaper. By the time it was published, he was already in London. The local builder, for whom he had worked following his departure from the brush factory, was "between jobs" and laid off his workers until the next contract materialised. Being unable to find other work, my father had two choices. He could claim a meagre level of unemployment assistance which would have been insufficient to provide a reasonable living for the family. Alternatively, he could travel to England where employment prospects were good.

During the Second World War, emigration of Irish workers to England had all but ceased. At home, some people joined the armed forces or obtained work on the land. The demand for food during the "Emergency" resulted in job creation in the labour intensive agricultural sector in Ireland. But as soon as the war was over, emigration resumed. The Irish government introduced a series of deflationary budgets that resulted in serious economic recession and the large surplus in the Irish labour force was soon exported to England.

There were two strands of emigration to England from the west of Ireland at that time. Some people left and eventually made permanent homes in England. Many intended to return home when the economic situation improved but such aspirations gradually faded as they married, purchased homes, and started families. Their children were soon attending school and making friends in England and had no interest in living in Ireland. The parents' aspiration to relocate to the old country gradually dissipated.

The second strand of emigration, which might more accurately be termed migration, comprised of fathers from rural Ireland who spent most of the year in England while their wives and children remained at home. Many owned small farms in Ireland and returned home for a few months during the summer when they were most needed for farm work. Others came home for Christmas and remained until their money ran out.

At first, my parents did not envisage that my father's move to England would be a permanent one. My grandfather promised to keep a close watch on the local job market and immediately inform my father if any employment opportunity arose. Bill Gleeson, now based in London, provided reassurance that work and accommodation was available. My father took the train to Dublin, the mail boat to Holyhead, and the train to London.

The impact of this sudden separation of a father from his wife and four infant children, combined with the uncertainty about their future as a family, must have been traumatic. My father was facing a solitary existence in a new country. His parents were accustomed to his daily visit on his way home from work and this was his first separation from them. More crucially, he was carrying the guilt of leaving his wife alone to cope with four demanding little children.

But the issues facing my mother seemed immeasurably more difficult. Patricia was now three years old and the twins, Michael and Mary, had just celebrated their second birthday. I was less than a year old. The situation sounds unmanageable and probably would have been had it not been for the support of both sets of grandparents.

The Rushe grandparents and Mary and Chris, my father's sisters, waded in with assistance. Patricia began to spend a lot of time with her grandparents in Claremorris, regularly staying overnight. Chris and Mary helped with child-minding in Streamstown, enabling my mother to cycle to town to do the shopping and to visit her parents-in-law.

My mother's family in County Limerick also helped. Fifteen year old Philomena, my mother's youngest sister, was dispatched from Cappamore to stay for periods in Streamstown in order to help with the children. During this time also, Mary, my sister, was brought to Cappamore for a few months and was cared for by Granny Ryan and her family so that my mother could get some respite.

When, many years later, I asked my mother about her feelings at that time, she smilingly shrugged off my concerns and adroitly deflected any opportunity for self-pity or regret.

"Sure your father was on great money and sending home every

penny. We were never better off money-wise than we were at that time."

As with their other difficulties, I never heard my parents complaining about their enforced separation or even discussing it in the presence of us children. I don't know whether this was a conscious decision or an instinctive one but it resulted in the Red Lemonade Syndrome which I mentioned earlier. The children were not burdened with such concerns and blithely carried on with their lives, oblivious to the impact of the various set-backs.

Upon arrival in England, my father found accommodation in the London area with the help of Bill Gleeson and got a job at Hayes, Middlesex in a factory which manufactured television sets. He found the noise to be unbearable and, I suspect, worried about potential hearing difficulties which would cause him problems as a musician. Having left the job after one week, he found work in a linoleum factory in Staines, also in Middlesex. Wages were good and lots of overtime was available. Each week, having paid his landlady for lodgings and retained a pittance for pocket-money, he was able to send a sizeable sum home to Streamstown.

My father was less reticent than my mother in taking about this period of their lives. He didn't elaborate on his feelings at being separated from the family but he shared anecdotes about his activities in London. He worked as much overtime as he possibly could so that his only free time was at weekends.

The pub, the usual refuge of the Irish emigrant, was not an option for him because he was a non-drinker. Instead, he indulged in one of his passions - a love of old buildings. At weekends, he traversed the greater London area, sometimes by public transport and often on foot, visiting stately homes, castles, churches, cathedrals and, of course, the British Museum. He took guided tours and devoured brochures and leaflets in order to enlighten himself on the historical and architectural significance of the buildings.

"It was too good an opportunity to waste. Sure, what else would I be doing?"

After the passing of a few months, there still seemed no prospect of obtaining work at home. My father's thoughts began to turn towards the possibility that he might have to make his life in London. But he was adamant that he was not going to be separated from his wife and children so that, in their letters, he and my mother began to discuss the possibility of moving the family to England.

As a first step, he began to keep watch for more suitable employment and spotted an advert for a job as a sound engineer with Decca Recording Company. He filled out a job application and was called for interview. In later years, he often used the experience as a cautionary tale for his children.

He felt that the interview was progressing well and he was getting a positive response until he was asked a seemingly casual question.

"Do you know anything about art?"

Thoughts raced through his mind.

Art? Paintings? Art galleries? In Claremorris?! Are you joking? Still, though. I could have gone to the National Gallery in Dublin when we were on our honeymoon? Never mind. Can't be helped. Better be truthful and not try to bluff.

"No. I don't really know anything about art."

He recognised that, following his response to the question about art, the interviewer seemed to lose interest in him and they parted shortly afterwards. As he sat on the top deck of the bus on his way back to his digs, he mused about what had happened.

Art? I don't know anything about paintings. Didn't see that question coming. I expected him to ask me about music. Anyway, what connection is there between paintings, art galleries and working in a recording studio? Now, if he asked me about music, I could have impressed him; not only about pop but all kinds of music. And about the great musicians...

He suddenly understood what had just happened. He had missed the point. When art was mentioned, he had thought solely of paintings. He was a singer and jazz musician who had been steeped in music all his life. He could spend hours discoursing on the art of Stéfane Grappelli, Jascha Heifetz, and Sean Maguire and would argue cogently that these jazz, classical, and Irish traditional fiddlers were equals in terms of artistic merit. He was a voracious reader of literature with a special admiration for he works of Oscar Wilde, O Henry, and Mark Twain. He had been an ardent cinema goer since childhood. His passion for old buildings also provided evidence of an artistic sensibility. He could even recite Antonio's opening speech from The Merchant of Venice, for God's sake!

No. He had missed the point. He heard "paintings" when the interviewer said "art" and he knew nothing about paintings. Ironically, in later years he developed a keen interest in the visual arts, with a special enthusiasm for the work of Carravaggio and the expressionistic paintings of Jack B Yeats.

My father did not harbour any resentment about his lack of success at the interview but, in later years, he often mentioned the experience in a self-deprecating manner to his children. He believed that, if he had been better educated, he might have recognised the opportunity in the question. He saw the event as an example of the need to prepare for an interview, to put yourself in the shoes of the interviewer, and to "see the bigger picture".

CHAPTER TEN

Friendly Persuasion

My parents were encountering a dilemma that was not uncommon in Irish households. They wanted to bring up their family in Ireland but instead, they were faced with two choices. They could either move the family to England or my father could continue indefinitely as a migrating worker, spending less time with his wife and children. This latter option was becoming increasingly unpalatable to my parents but they knew that emigration would result in great upheaval in the young Rushe family. Decision time was looming.

It seems appropriate to pause here to discuss how our family decisions were made. To do this, we need to understand the relationship between my parents and also their individual behaviours and characteristics. A superficial glance would lead one to believe that my father, as head of the household, made the decisions, having consulted with my mother but ultimately having the final say. In reality, the situation was more complex and, as individual decisions are examined, my mother's influence becomes much more apparent.

My father was opinionated; he wasn't slow to offer his views and advice on various subjects. As he demonstrated in the interview situation when he was asked about art, he was quite willing to admit his lack of knowledge in certain areas. But on subjects about which he knew a lot, or thought that he knew a lot, he was not slow to offer opinions and to argue his corner. He also had a tendency to become defensive when one disagreed with him.

My father saw himself as a self-taught working man. One of his idols, Mark Twain, was not enamoured with this subsection of humanity. He wrote: "The self taught man seldom knows anything accurately, and he does not know a tenth as much as he could have known if he had worked under teachers, and besides, he brags, and is the means of fooling other thoughtless people into going and doing as he himself has done."

Ouch!

Twain, it seems, had issues. But his words articulate the often unvoiced contempt of the elite towards the less well educated who do not know their place.

In my opinion, my father's occasional propensity towards dogmatism and intransigence arose from a feeling of inferiority resulting from his lack of formal education. He was not ashamed of his working class background which dictated that further education was not an option for him. But he tried to compensate for his lack of formal education by reading widely and he took a questioning interest in what was happening in the world. But I think that he sometimes felt compelled to show that his relative lack of schooling was not an impediment and he overcompensated occasionally by parading his knowledge.

His tendency to become defensive when questioned or challenged could easily be taken as a unwillingness to listen. On the contrary, he listened carefully and, over time, reflected on what had been said. This sometimes resulted in a revision of his previously held position. One such example arose from our shared interest in music which resulted in many discussions about the relative merits of various musicians and musical genres.

"There are only two kinds of music, good music and bad music."

My father was fond of quoting this statement which he attributed to one of his heroes, Louis Armstrong, but which has also been ascribed to Duke Ellington. After accepting this mantra for many years, I began to question it as I got older and when some variances in musical taste arose between me and my father. As an example, I pointed out that some of the more maudlin examples of the Irish hybrid of American country music were almost universally dismissed as "bad music" by those with more elite tastes. But, as demonstrated by rural local radio playlists, this music can resonates with and touch the emotions of many listeners, even when the musicianship is of a questionable standard. I argued that any two people might disagree on whether a specific piece of music is "good" or "bad" depending on their preferences.

"There are only two kinds of music, music you like and music you don't like", I argued.

He good-naturedly but firmly disagreed with my questioning of his well-worn mantra. I was being argumentative and pedantic. I was misunderstanding or misinterpreting what Louis Armstrong had said or meant. We left it there.

A few months later, during one of my visits home, we happened to be talking about music and musicians with a visitor. The guest admitted that Irish traditional music held no attraction for him. He thought that it was boringly repetitive and, more often than not, badly played. My father casually interjected: "As Colman is fond of saying, there are only two kinds of music, music you like and music you don't like".

My father was not lacking in self confidence but balanced this with the occasional need, as he saw it, to defer to others. In the manner of the times, he saluted or lifted his cap to a passing priest and showed deference to teachers, doctors, policemen, and politicians as if to acknowledge that such people merited a gesture of respect because of their education or position.

My mother lacked my father's volubility and was much less likely to be outspoken on any subject. When friends or relatives paid a more formal visit, she contributed confidently to the conversation without putting forward strong opinions. Conversely, in relaxed conversation, my mother was the talkative one. She could chat casually and at length with neighbours, with old friends whom she might meet while shopping in town, and even to strangers with whom circumstance might throw her into contact. She possessed an extraordinary empathy so that people would reveal intimate family information to her. Even strangers seemed to sense that she treated their revelations with unyielding discretion. For his part, my father was quite happy to let my mother do the chatting - he had little inclination to partake in what he termed "gossip and chit-chat". As we shall see, circumstances were to change this approach in their later years.

My mother's unwillingness to involve herself in opinionated discourse, in the manner of my father, did not reflect a lack of education or knowledge. As we have seen, she received more formal education than he did. Moreover, in my opinion, she was even more intelligent than him and was more learned as a result of her habit of devouring the newspapers. But, probably in deference to my father's sensitivity about his lack of formal education, she hid her intelligence and never contradicted or undermined him publicly.

How did they make a decision? Did my father usually get his way as a result of his opinionatedness? Or did my mother have to "fight her corner" before they reached a consensus?

In his book Pulphead, John Jeremiah Sullivan puts forward what he describes as a useful principle for all couples: "Don't try to change each other. Study and subvert each other." As I read Sullivan's words, I immediately recognised my mother's strategy. Perhaps it is best demonstrated by the process of deciding whether our family should acquire a TV set.

The Irish TV service was introduced in the early 1960s and, over the following few years, TV aerials slowly began to sprout on roofs in the neighbourhood. My father regularly articulated his firmly-held conviction that TV was an unreasonable distraction for school-going children. He argued that they could not be expected to do their homework while such an attraction lurked invitingly in the corner of the room. He concluded that a TV set would not be allowed in our house until the children had finished their schooling. A quick calculation revealed that, based upon this decision, it would by 1980 before the "new medium" would reach the Rushe household.

My mother, who was at least as committed to the education of the children as her husband, chose not to disagree with him. To do so would only serve to undermine him in front of the children and would not result in a change of the decision. A strategy of study and subversion was the alternative.

By 1966, about half the homes in Ireland had a TV set. We children were allowed to visit Conroys' house for about an hour each week to watch a music show and occasionally a Gaelic football match. When next door neighbour, Mrs Glynn, had a TV installed, she invited my parents to visit each Saturday night in order to watch the "Late, Late Show", a mix of current affairs, arts, and entertainment which had quite a cutting-edge reputation at that time. My mother, or Mrs Glynn at her behest, occasionally suggested to my father that he drop by during the week to view a particular forthcoming programme that might be of interest to him. I clearly remember his delight and enthusiasm when speaking about the showing of "The Importance of being Oscar", a celebrated one-man show by Micheal Mac Liammoir, which comprised excerpts from Wilde's writings. Other plays and educational programmes followed.

The coup de grace was the 'Our World" TV programme in June 1967. It was the first, live, international satellite TV broadcast and is now remembered because it featured the Beatles premiering "All You

Need Is Love". It comprised segments from many countries and time-zones around the world and had an estimated world-wide audience of 400 million viewers.

My father was fascinated by the programme. Now he was talking passionately about the innovation, and the educational and artistic value of television for children and adults. The dangers of distraction from homework were still a concern but my mother, who shared his conviction about the over-riding importance of education, was confident that viewing by the children could be rationed and managed as necessary. A decision was made that a TV would be rented on a trial basis so it could be returned if the experiment didn't work.

I see my mother's fingerprints all over this decision and many others over the years that seemed, on the surface, to be made by my father. She didn't undermine or unduly manipulate him. She merely provided the necessary information and time in order to allow him to reassess his position and reach a different conclusion. A benign strategy of study and subversion.

The interaction between my parents when making decisions was not always apparent, at least to me. When speaking to me about their relationship in his last years, my father said that he regretted that he left the decisions about our education to my mother. He indicated that he was fully in agreement with choices which were made about schools or other options but he felt that he should have been much more supportive when decisions were necessary. Instead, he left the burden for my mother to deal with. I was taken aback. I had always assumed that the decisions were taken by both, with my father having the final say. They were certainly communicated to us children as having been agreed jointly.

Perhaps the interaction of good parents is best exemplified by the hands of a pianist. They are performing complementary and essential functions, fingering different notes in different positions but each aware of and making allowance for the other, in order to achieve something which could not be accomplished individually. Or perhaps, a violin player is a more apt example; the left hand delicately and precisely fingering the strings while the broad strokes of the bow in the right hand produce and amplify the sweet sound of the music.

CHAPTER ELEVEN

It's Now Or Never

"Daddy! Daddy! Daddy!

Patricia and Michael and I were on the look-out. We were waiting impatiently on the road outside our house in Streamstown when we spotted the approaching figure on his bicycle with the large suitcase secured on the carrier. Yelling with excitement, Patricia and Michael raced up the road to meet him and quickly left me in their wake as I tottered behind, vainly trying to keep up.

"I'm home! Hello Patricia! Hello Michael! Careful! Not too close to the pedals!" he laughed.

Turning to join him, my brother and sister skipped and danced on either side of the bike as all three came back along the road to where I was now standing. My father, now cycling at a snail's pace, looked quizzically at me and said:

"Whose child is that? I don't know who he is. He's definitely not one of ours."

I was crestfallen as he slowly cycled by. Patricia and Mike were laughing wildly and yelling at him:

"Daddy! That's Coleman. That's our Coleman!"

Now they had reached our front gate and he dismounted, leaning the bike against the front wall. With Patricia and Michael now climbing over him, he stretched out his arms towards me as I tottered towards him.

"Come here, Coleman"

He grabbed me in his arms.

"I didn't know you, you got so big. You were only a baby when I left."

I have a clear memory of this sequence of events on the occasion of my father's homecoming from England. Or I think that I do. But I was not yet two years old when it happened.

There has been research to demonstrate that children can remember events which occurred when they were two years old. Many believe that babies can sometimes recall happenings from much earlier. It can also be demonstrated, however, that young children have the capacity to fabricate memories based upon the stories later told by adults. As a result, testimony that is based on early childhood memory is often disqualified in a court of law.

Half a century later, I asked my father if he could recall his arrival home and his failure to recognise me.

"I can't remember it but it sounds about right."

"What about not recognising me? Do you recall anything like that?"

He looked at me questioningly.

"No. I'd certainly remember if anything like that happened. Sure, who else would you have been but you? There were no other children living down at that end of Streamstown. But it sounds just like something I'd do, teasing Patricia and Michael by pretending I didn't know you."

His rationale made perfect sense to me when he explained it. Such teasing was part of his armoury in dealing with us as small children. My childhood impression that I was not recognised was a result of my innocent failure to pick up the nuance of my father's humour.

My father's return was as unexpected as it was welcomed. While in London, he received a letter from my grandfather, Tom Rushe, who had promised to keep watch for any work opportunity at home. Granda was working as a carpenter with CIE, the railway company, and wrote to his son that a temporary job on the railway was available. It would probably be short term but at least my father could hope to be reunited with his family for a few months. He handed in his notice at the linoleum factory and took the train to Holyhead to catch the mail boat home to Ireland.

My father was uncertain about the future of the family in Claremorris. He and my mother had discussed the options in their letters and a decision had been made. They were resolved that the family would not be apart again. If he had to return to England, the entire family would go with him to embark on a new life.

A few months later, my parents' worst fears seemed to be realised. CIE announced that, because of cutbacks, seven hundred railway workers were being made redundant nationwide. My father was laid off work again. Luckily, he got a labouring job with a local builder but shortly afterwards, a few days before Christmas 1952, he was unexpectedly made redundant again. He was bemused because all the workers were laid off even though there seemed to be enough work on hands to keep them employed for longer. One of his fellow workers quietly told my father that he could apply for the job again after the Christmas break. It was explained to him that, by laying off the workers, the builder could avoid having to pay them for two days holiday over Christmas.

My father was furious at what he interpreted as sleight of hand by the employer and he re-examined his options. He had heard that, following the lay-offs of permanent workers by CIE, there were occasional requirements for part-time staff. He called to the railway station and found that there was a temporary vacancy for a lorry-driver's helper. Although the job was only expected to last for a few weeks, he accepted the CIE offer and rejected the builder who got in touch with him after Christmas in the expectation that he would return to his old position.

When his spell as a driver's assistant ended, he feared redundancy again but was relieved to be reallocated by CIE to other jobs, mainly providing cover for workers who were on leave for various reasons. Some months later, in May 1953, he was offered a full-time job by CIE. He was to remain with the company until his retirement in 1989.

During this period of uncertainty, my parents shielded their children completely, ensuring that they were unaware that anything unusual was afoot. We only became aware as adults that emigration of the family to England was only narrowly averted. Mike and I were still very young but Patricia, as a five year old, could easily have become upset and unsettled if she sensed that her parents were undergoing a period of stress and uncertainty. As we grew older and the family ship encountered much more turbulent waters, this pattern of protectiveness was repeated. Every effort was made by the parents to buffer the children and to make their lives as normal as possible.

CHAPTER TWELVE

Family Affair

"Who are you? What's your name?"

"Coleman."

"No. Not my name. Your name. What are you called?"

"I'm Coleman, Daddy!".

"No. That can't be right. My name is Coleman. So you can't be Coleman."

"But I am, Daddy!"

"No. Coleman is an unusual name. There can't be two Colemans. That's silly. Sure, we wouldn't know who Mammy was shouting at if there were two Colemans in the house."

"Daddy stop! I'm Coleman, too!"

"Are you me? If you're Coleman, maybe you're me."

"What? ...... That's silly, Daddy."

"If you're Coleman, and I'm Coleman, maybe you're me and I'm talking to myself. Am I?"

"Daddy. Stop it!"

"We'd better get up or we'll be in the dog-house. Mammy will be home shortly."

This conversation or a variation of it, is another delightful early memory. I was probably about three years old. On Sunday mornings, my mother departed for Mass in Claremorris, accompanied by Patricia, Mary, and Michael. Before leaving, she switched me from my cot into the bed beside my sleeping father. She then dropped off Mary and Michael at Granny Rushe's house while she and Patricia attended Mass at 9.30am. Afterwards, she collected the children and returned home.

My father worked from Monday to Friday and a half-day on

Saturday. Consequently, Sunday morning was his only opportunity to have a lie-in. My mother tried to ensure that I slept for a while after joining my father but her efforts met with mixed results. I can never recall even the slightest sign of impatience when I inevitably woke him from his Sunday morning slumber. His invariable response was to look at me in feigned surprise and say:

"Who are you? What's your name".

He then proceeded to tease and confuse me by tying me up in verbal knots regarding our sharing of the same name. The fun would only cease when it was time for him to get up, to wash, and to shave while my mother, who had now arrived home, cooked the customary Sunday morning fried breakfast. He then cycled to 11.30 am Mass in Claremorris where he was a member of the church choir.

Another family ritual was my father's return from Mass when he produced from his pocket a bag of Scots Clan sweets. The chocolate-covered toffees were rationed to us with the warning:

"Don't be greedy now. Save some for later or you'll spoil your dinner."

Family life had settled back to normal since my father's return from England. Mary had come home from Cappamore and it was now becoming clear that her capacity was going to be quite limited and that she would require constant care. Patricia was about to commence attending school. Her grandparents had become very attached to her during my father's sojourn in London and it seems likely that her chattering presence in the house in Claremorris helped to mitigate the pain caused by the absence of Patsy, after whom she had been named. It was decided that Patricia would remain overnight with her grandparents during the week and would attend school at the nearby Saint Michael's Convent. Each Friday evening, she would be collected by my father and carried on his bike back home to Streamstown. He would drop her off at her grandparents' house again on Monday mornings. This rota of four nights with her grandparents and three nights at home was to continue through her childhood and teenage years until her schooling was completed and she left home to work in Dublin in 1965.

My father was not earning nearly as much as he had while in London but he had resumed his part-time work as a musician in order to supplement the family income. He played, usually on Sunday nights, with Matt MacDonagh, his first band-leader, and also with bands led by Johnny Brady and Mick O'Loughlin. His versatile fiddle playing was in demand as was his singing. He had expanded his repertoire to include songs popularised by Frank Sinatra, Nat King Cole, Perry Como, Guy Mitchell and Frankie Laine, as well as old stand-by, Bing Crosby. A particular favourite of his from this era was "The Tennessee Waltz" which had been popularised in 1950 by Patti Page and remained in my father's repertoire for the rest of his life. Another less worthy Patti Page song from 1953, "(How Much Is) That Doggy In The Window" became a special favourite of us children and was sung loudly and, I suspect, tunelessly, to unfortunate visitors.

In the evenings, when he wasn't busily tending to the vegetable garden or cutting and saving turf in the bog, my father sat in the kitchen practising his fiddle playing or his singing while wife and four children swirled around him, paying him little attention. He sometimes placed a mute on the bridge of the fiddle which dampened the sound of the strings. He also muted his voice by cupping his hands over his mouth in the fashion of a harmonica player and singing through them, occasionally fluttering one hand against the other to give a tremolo effect. I suspect that he did this in order to mute his vocals but it may also have served to improve or manipulate his breathing technique. From our adult conversations, I know that he was certainly conscious of the impact which breathing and phrasing can have on a song. He was especially impressed by Frank Sinatra's mastery in this aspect of singing, which the vocalist had refined by studying the seamlessly effortless trombone-playing of Tommy Dorsey.

Apart from emptying and cleaning the chemical toilet, and occasionally cradling and feeding a baby in the early years, my father, in the fashion of the times, did not do any housework. Circumstances were to change this in later life but, while the children were growing up, he went to work each day and, while at home, took responsibility for the vegetable garden and the turf as well as any necessary repairs, painting, and decorating. Both parents seemed to be happy with this division of labour. Of course, as we children got older, we were expected to help indoors and outdoors and we were allocated chores and duties.

My mother worked ceaselessly and uncomplainingly in the house as well as occasionally helping in the garden and the bog during particularly busy times. In my memory, she seemed to be constantly cooking or washing; her hands pale and shrivelled from the watery detergent, and her knuckles red from the friction with the wash-board. She was particularly conscious of the close connection between health and household cleanliness so that floors and cupboards were constantly being washed. The kitchen, which was the family living area, saw most of the traffic and the bare concrete floor required regular scrubbing.

The bedrooms were gradually furnished with linoleum floor covering which my mother polished and then buffed to a dull gleam. There was a common belief, shared by my parents, that safeguarding children completely from germs was counterproductive because it deprived them of the opportunity to build up resistance to infections. As a result, we were allowed and encouraged to creep and crawl around the kitchen floor and to play in the sometimes muddy front garden. One outcome may have been a healthy resistance to infections and germs. Another less welcome result was a further addition to the clothes washing workload.

The apron, an item of clothing which is seldom seen in modern homes, was my mother's ever-present work uniform and remained so for the rest of her life. Apart from protecting her clothes, the apron performed numerous other functions. It dried children's tears and cleaned dirty faces. It wiped work surfaces, dried hands, and operated as a kind of oven mitt when lifting or removing the lids from hot pots and pans. By grasping and holding up the bottom of the apron, my mother could use it as a receptacle for collecting eggs or for carrying small sods of turf indoors for the fire.

If visitors arrived unexpectedly, there would be a flourish as my mother whipped off her old apron and replace it with a fresh one. In the event that callers were expected, she might wear her clean apron underneath the old one in order that she could perform the transition even more efficiently. For the children, her aprons became our comfort blanket. Our protective shield against the outside world.

As young children, we were not allowed to venture far from the house into the surrounding countryside. One adventure that was available to us was to go to the top of a field behind the house in order to watch wide-eyed through the fence as the train to Westport steamed and hissed by with an occasional blast of the whistle. My father explained to us that the old familiar steam engines were being replaced by new-fangled diesel locomotives which were faster, more powerful, and more reliable. He told us that the first ever locomotive on the Westport line would pass by that afternoon and we took our vantage point at the appointed time. I recall the excitement as the new, sleek, powerful, noisy engine barrelled by. The wonder was tempered by a sense of disappointment at the absence of the whistle, the plume of smoke, and that distinctive steam train smell which settled over us and reminded us of summer holiday train trips to Cappamore.

Another earlier memory is of sitting on the wall, watching the arrival and operation of a thresher in a field directly opposite our house. The machine, powered by a strap affixed to a steam powered tractor, resembled a mysterious, hungry, headless giant as it nestled impatiently among stacks of oats. The oats from the stacks was tossed on top of the thresher by fork-wielding farmers. The sheaves of oats were loosened and fed through the roof of the thresher by some fearless men, unworried by the noise and the vibration. After noisily digesting the offering, the giant disgorged the spent straw through its neck while the grain was collected by sacks affixed to the rear. The bulging sacks were removed, and stacked nearby for storage and possibly sale.

Further diversion and excitement was provided by the occasional discovery of a rat in the oats stacks. The disturbed rat would make a burst for freedom amid shouts, thrown farm implements, and the howling of local dogs who would chase it, usually unsuccessfully, through the nearby fields. After a futile few minutes of barking, circling, and scratching impatiently at the dry stone wall where the elusive rat had taken refuge, the dogs would reluctantly return to the haggard hoping for better luck with the next escapee.

When I revisited Streamstown after a gap of over half a century, I was disconcerted to note that there was no haggard opposite our house. As I gazed on a large open field, I began to doubt my childhood recollection of the threshing. Was it an acquired memory, assembled from a combination of later events? I questioned my father. He assured me that the haggard had existed and we worked out that the particular harvest that I remember happened in 1954 at the latest, when I was not yet four years old.

Christmas at Streamstown also brings back snatches of warm, comforting memory. In the traditional way, we were encouraged to hang our stockings at the end of our beds on Christmas Eve and to anticipate the visit of Santa Claus while we slept. We never failed to get an abundance of presents which, I only realised in later years, were sent to my parents by our aunts and uncles from both sides on the family. The Rushe and Ryans had become even closer as a result of the marriage in 1953 of Johnny Ryan, my mother's brother, to Mary Rushe, my father's sister.

Extra Christmas magic was provided by my mother's practise of waiting until the children were sleeping on Christmas Eve before she put up the tree and decorations. As soon as they heard our first sounds of activity on Christmas morning, my mother and father would join us as we excitedly opened and examined presents which we found at the foot of each bed. But my most vivid and abiding memory is of walking from the bedroom into the living area. The kitchen, which had been familiar and ordinary when I left for bed some hours earlier, was transformed into a magical wonderland, illuminated by lamps and candles. Christmas cards were on display on all available surfaces. Colourful and sparkling decorations and balloons draped from the ceiling. Berried holly festooned pictures and wall hangings. A crib showing the Nativity scene was illuminated by a table lamp. The curtains in the front window were tied safely back so that a centrally placed large candle could be visible from the road. The tree, which I had last seen tied to my father's bike when he arrived from town, was now studded with ornaments, baubles, and trinkets and strewn with sparkling tinsel. Snow seemed to have lodged on some of the branches until closer examination revealed that the "snow" was comprised of artfully placed clumps of white cotton wool. The lights on the tree were candle holders which clipped onto the branches. The candles and lamps had been carefully lit by my mother before we left our bedrooms so that we children encountered the whole magical vista as we entered the kitchen on Christmas morning.

CHAPTER THIRTEEN

You Better Move On

I was a curious four years old, standing by our front gate when a man, whom I did not recognise, approached, smiled kindly and spoke.

"Is this Moran's house?"

I looked at him belligerently.

"No. It's ours!"

Chastened and no doubt amused, the enquirer retreated in the face of such innocent logic. The man, who later told my father about the episode, was a visitor from the USA and was a friend of the co-owner of the house. My innocent and defensive response to the question is ironic in the light of subsequent events.

In 1954, it seemed that the Rushes' run of bad luck had come to an end. My father was now settled into his new job on the railway and was no longer regarded as a temporary worker. He and my mother were gradually making the home in Streamstown more comfortable for the family. Patricia, now a six year old, was contentedly attending school in Claremorris and sleeping over with her grandparents before returning home at weekends.

It had gradually become apparent that Mary's condition would not improve but my mother seemed to be able to manage her effortlessly and insisted in involving her fully in family life. To Mary's siblings, it all seemed perfectly natural. We were a normal family and Mary was just a sister; a slightly different kind of sister, perhaps. Just as Patricia and Michael were expected to make allowances for me when I was too small to run fast or to climb over walls, we were all expected to make allowances for Mary. It was that simple.

Michael was now a curious and adventurous five-year old and was ready to start school in Claremorris in September. This was going to create its own problem. The school was two miles away and, as was the norm in rural Ireland, walking to school was the only option. My mother would have to walk with Michael each morning to the home of a neighbour who had older school-going children. These children would tend to Michael who would walk to school with them. My mother would pick him up again in the evening and this routine would continue until he was old enough to make his own way home. Mary and I would have to accompany my mother on these daily trips as we could not be left at home alone.

I was not yet four and was vying for attention and trying to compete with the others. Although I never raised the subject with them in later years, it's clear that my parents wisely decided, after I was born, that having more children in the short term was unrealistic or even irresponsible. Apart from the cost of feeding and clothing a family of four children and two adults, they also had to consider the extra workload and pressure on my mother as a result of Mary's condition. With the help of the grandparents who were caring for Patricia during the week, the young family had found its feet.

Then the solicitor's letter arrived.

It was completely unexpected and my parents were dumbfounded. Notice was served on the Rushe family to vacate the house in Streamstown.

Michael Moran and his brother in the USA co-owned the house in which we were living. Michael and his family lived in a thatched house next-door to the modern, slate roofed house occupied by the Rushes. The older Moran house was in need of major refurbishment and, because of the prohibitive cost of renovating and re-roofing their old property, the Morans realised that it made more financial sense to reclaim the much better house next door. Mr. Moran approached his solicitor in order to ascertain his legal position. He was told that he had no grounds for removing the Rushes because their rent was fully up to date and they were maintaining the property. The solicitor said that he would write to the Rushes and request them to vacate the property.

Although they were shocked by the letter, my parents, who had a good relationship with the Morans, recognised their dilemma, and found it difficult to argue with their logic. Michael Moran was obviously uncomfortable with the situation that had arisen. Clearly, he received legal advice that he should not get involved in any potential dispute with the Rushes and that the matter should be handled by his solicitor.

My father immediately took the letter to another local solicitor and enquired about his options. He received legal advice that our family could not be forcibly evicted while the rent was being paid. Nevertheless, it was clear it would be best if the Rushes started looking for another house. The solicitor responded in writing to the notice to quit, stating that his clients had a legal entitlement to remain in the property but that they were exploring other alternatives and would be in touch if and when they were successful.

The Irish housing market in the forties and fifties had a significant rented sector. According to Central Statistics Office figures, just over half of houses in Ireland in 1946 were owner occupied. The rented sector comprised 280,000 units but the vast majority of these were in the cities and larger urban areas. This was to change. Over the following half century, there was rapid change in Ireland resulting in owner occupancy of 80% by the 90s.

Enquiries by my parents revealed, as they feared, that a suitable rented house for a family would be extremely difficult to locate in the Claremorris area. Would they consider living further away, possibly in another town? Ideally, my father needed to live within cycling distance of Claremorris railway station, where he was based. He could manage if the family moved to another town that had a railway station. But such a move would mean that the Rushe grandparents would no longer be nearby and their help and support was much valued.

The first decision which my parents made was to delay Michael's start at school until the situation became clearer. Otherwise, he ran the risk of enrolling for school in Claremorris and then facing the disruption of changing school at a young age.

Following an unfruitful trawl of auctioneers and estate agents, my parents approached the Mayo County Council and enquired about the availability of a local authority house but again without success. The fact that we were in a house to which we had an entitlement probably meant that we were not a priority for the Council. My father spread the word among his friends in the church choir, his workmates on the railway, and his bandmates. My grandfather similarly made enquiries. But to no avail.

As the months passed and another winter approached, the only development was the occasional arrival of a letter from my parent's solicitor seeking an update so that he could reply to the latest enquiry from the Moran's lawyer. When we talked about this period many years later, my father was at pains to point out that the Morans never displayed any hint of impatience despite the lack of progress and the passage of time. Clearly, Michael Moran knew that the Rushes were trying to find an alternative home and accepted that they would move as soon as they could. If he and his family were eager to take possession of the house, they displayed no hint of this and their forbearance was much appreciated.

My parents gave no indication to their children that anything was amiss. As far as the children were concerned, life went on as normal. Although we were still young, Patricia and Michael, at six and five years of age, could easily have become aware of the pressure caused by the dilemma which my parents were enduring. Such an unsettling upheaval and threat to their childhood security could have resulted in behavioural or other problems. In my adulthood, when they talked about the loss of the house, it became clear to me that this was a period of frustration and powerlessness for my parents. They knew that they would have to move sooner or later but they could not find a suitable house for a family of six.

Suddenly, a possible option presented itself. My parents heard that a Mrs Smyth, a widow who lived a few miles away in Murneen, had been trying unsuccessfully to dispose of a house for some time. My parents were not optimistic. If Mrs Smith couldn't get anybody to take the house despite the local housing shortage, there must be a problem. My father went to see Mrs Smyth and a sad and more complex story emerged.

Nell Smyth lived in the Murneen countryside with her husband Jackie and their teenage children. Their house was a local authority cottage on one acre of land and the Smyths had a rental purchase agreement with the Council. As purchasing tenants, they were making rental payments and also had an entitlement to purchase the full ownership of the property in the future.

Jackie Smyth contracted tuberculosis in the mid forties when the disease was virtually untreatable. Because of the fear that the infection would spread to the other family members, a chalet was built for him in the garden about thirty metres from the house. He was cared for by the family in his deteriorating condition and he died in August 1946.

As the Smith children reached adulthood during the following few years, they emigrated to the USA. Nell Smyth decided to join her children but she encountered problems when she tried to sell her interest in the property. The stigma and irrational fear associated with tuberculosis was still prevalent in Ireland in the 1950s. Although Jackie

Smyth had not spent his last months inside the house, prospective buyers were unwilling to consider living there. Some may have harboured fears that they might contract the disease. Others may have accepted that such a risk didn't exist but were concerned that they would be talked about by the less enlightened. Following Jackie's death, the chalet in which he died had been demolished and the house had been fumigated. As was standard practise, the rest of the Smyth family were medically examined and found to be clear of the disease. Eight years had passed since Jackie's death. Despite this, no buyer could be found.

Because of their experience of Patsy Rushe's illness and death, my parents were knowledgeable about the risks associated with tuberculosis. They also had strong views on the stigma which existed; my father was particularly derisive of the prejudice displayed by some people regarding the disease. They both cycled to Murneen to inspect the house and they decided to acquire it. They reached an agreement with Nell Smyth who was willing to transfer her interest in the property to my father for thirty pounds. I do not know how my parents raised this amount in 1954; the equivalent today is about 800 euros. They may have accumulated some savings as a result of my father's period of work in England. Alternatively, it might have been borrowed from my grandparents.

A complication soon presented itself. When my father went to notify the County Council that he was now the new purchasing tenant of the property, he was told that this was not the case. The prior approval of the County Council should have been obtained before the deal was done. The matter was rectified on 15th of October 1954, when a formal document was signed by my father, by Mrs Smyth, and by a Mr Cafferkey, representing the Council. This confirmed the payment of thirty pounds and the resultant transfer of Mrs Smyth's interest in the property to Coleman Rushe, who was now the new purchasing tenant.

It was to be some months yet before Nell Smyth got her affairs in order. She finally vacated the house in the following summer. The Rushes hired Andy Creighton who loaded all the family possessions onto his lorry. My mother and we four children piled into the cab with the driver and we left the house in Streamstown which had been our home for eight years.

Murneen South, the location of our new home, is about five miles north of Claremorris. Whereas Streamstown, as the name implies, was pock-marked with streams and ponds at every turn, the higher land in Murneen was much dryer and more fertile. An unpaved, gravel road lazily undulated downwards from Barnacarroll, at an elevation of 126 metres, on the busy Claremorris to Knock road where it intersected with the Claremorris to Balla thoroughfare. Much of County Mayo is flat; its name in Irish is *Maigh Eo* which translates as "Plain of Yew Trees". Although our new house was only about 100 metres above sea level, the vantage point provided a view across the Mayo plain to the pyramid shaped, holy mountain of Croagh Patrick, known as "The Reek", which was thirty miles to the west. The peaks of the Twelve Bens mountain range, forty miles to the south-west were also visible. A short walk down the road opened up another vista across the plain to the Nephin mountains, thirty miles away in a north-westerly direction.

We had listened excitedly as my mother explained to us that we were moving to a new house in a nice area. She promised that we would have lots of other children as neighbours and Michael and I could go to school locally. No mention was made about the real reason for the relocation.

Now the day had finally arrived and the lorry, laden with all the family belongings, rumbled uphill until the gravel road levelled off for a few hundred metres. My mother pointed ahead to a large copper beech tree at a spot just before the road began to climb again.

"Our house is just across the road from that tree."

A woman was walking up the road ahead and turned enquiringly when she heard the approaching lorry. My mother waved to her and the woman smiled and waved back.

"Who is that?"

"That's my friend, Mrs. Glynn."

While I do not recollect much of the detail of the day, I can clearly remember my reaction to that comment by my mother. I was happy that she had already made a new friend during an earlier visit to the house. Perhaps I sensed that she was isolated and house-bound in Streamstown while we were babies and toddlers. Now that we, with the exception of Mary, would be going to school, she would have more time to interact with friends and neighbours.

Such was our childish delight when we saw our new house that I was quite taken aback when, years later, I found a photograph which was taken at about the time we moved in. In the photo, the house looks dark, unkempt, and uninviting. The grey-black walls are streaked and discoloured by the weather and the wooden frames of the sash-windows and the solid wood door are painted a depressingly dark colour. A well trodden, narrow, sandy path leads from the front door to the wide, five-bar iron gate which is suspended on two large pillars set in a rough, uneven, dry-stone wall. Other boundaries are either stone walls or earthen ditches dotted by an occasional scrawny tree. The one acre site is carpeted with tangled, over-grown grass.

The house was solidly constructed and had a tiled roof. As in Streamstown, there was no electricity or running water. There were four rooms: three bedrooms and a kitchen/living-room. The house lacked a front porch and, unusually, a back door. Immediately inside the front door was the "hall", a narrow corridor which had doors leading to the kitchen and two bedrooms. To get to the remaining bedroom, it was necessary to walk through the kitchen. The largest bedroom could accommodate two double beds. A double or a single bed together with a child's cot could fit in each of the other bedrooms. As well as the large open fire in the kitchen, there were smaller fireplaces in two of the bedrooms.

A small shed behind the house was divided into two sections, with separate external doors. One section housed the chemical toilet while the other was intended for fuel storage. Attached to the back of the house was a large, concrete, water tank which collected rain water from the gutters on the roof.

Water for drinking had to carried in buckets and cans from local spring wells. One was located on Mullaneys' land, less than a half mile away. The other necessitated a walk of about one mile through the fields and was located beside church ruins and an abandoned graveyard at Kilcolman.

We soon discovered that, within a half mile radius, there were eighteen houses and about half of them were the homes of school-going children. With the exception of Mrs. Glynn, who lived next door with her son and daughter in a Council cottage virtually identical to ours, all the other neighbours lived on small farms.

CHAPTER FOURTEEN

Friends And Neighbours

"It takes a village to raise a child".
 - African proverb.

When we moved to Murneen in the mid 50s, daily life in the rural west of Ireland had changed little for centuries. Some of the newer houses were solidly built with slate or tiled roofs but the countryside around Murneen was still dotted with older, white-washed, thatched farmhouses. Since the foundation of the Irish state, new laws and regulations had been introduced regarding the ownership of land. There were no longer any tenant land-holders, as in the nineteenth century. Farmers were now the owners of their land and some had acquired additional acreage when untenanted estates were compulsorily purchased and divided among local families.

However, the farming methods and practices had remained unchanged for centuries. Horse drawn ploughs and harrows were used to till the ground. On the smaller farms, crops of hay and oats were cut by scythe unless a horse-drawn mowing machine was available for hire. The open fires in the homes were fuelled by peat, known locally as turf, which was cut from the bogs with a slane, a spade-like implement. The turf was spread to dry and was saved by hand. Farm produce was sold or bartered at local weekly markets. Pigs were either slaughtered on the farm for food or were sold with fattened cattle and sheep to provide family income.

Local people grew most of their own food. Surplus milk was churned in the farmhouses to produce butter and the residual butter-milk was used for baking or as a thirst-quenching drink. Flour was purchased in large sacks so that bread could be home baked. "Cake bread", as the home-baked variety was known, was by far the most commonly used. Occasionally, for variety, "loaf bread" from the bakery was purchased.

Two travelling shops circulated in the Murneen area. These were modified lorries which had designated stopping points and times when locals could buy and sometimes sell goods. The shops were known colloquially as "egglers" because, as well as selling groceries and household wares, they also purchased surplus farm eggs for resale. Such transactions were almost invariably carried out by farmers' wives who guarded the "egg money" as their only source of independent personal income. Walsh's lorry stopped each Tuesday at Mike Conroy's gate, a few hundred yards away and Staunton's lorry had its designated stop directly across the road from our house each Thursday.

The local post-man, Jim Morley, cycled through the village each day. As well as delivering the post, he brought news about happenings and events which he picked up on his travels. A most discreet and ethical man, he only revealed general information. Jim Connor had just started mowing the top field. There were signs of potato blight in Rockfield. The Yanks had just arrived at Prendergasts. But Jim was discreet. As a daily deliverer of much good and bad news, he must have been aware of intimate and private information which he never disclosed or discussed on his rounds.

Visits to the locality by a doctor or vet were rare. Mrs Gavin was the first port of call for anybody suffering from an injury or ailment. She had trained and worked as a nurse in England before returning home to marry and start a family. She carried out an appraisal of the wound or illness and, if she considered that professional expertise was necessary, would suggest a visit to the doctor in Claremorris. Usually, she was satisfied to deal with the problem herself by applying poultices or lancing infected wounds or boils. There were hot poultices, sometimes containing bread and milk, to bring infections to a head so that they could be lanced. Then she applied cold poultices of Epsom salts and castor oil to drain all the infected matter from the wound.

Her treatments and remedies were much respected locally, even if they were sometimes unorthodox. On my way home from school, I tripped on a road which had just been been resurfaced with rough stone chippings. My knee was badly cut and some skin was removed. Mrs Gavin cleaned the wound thoroughly and she applied some ointment and a bandage. When she re-examined my knee a day or two later, the wound was still raw and she was not happy that the area where the skin had been removed would heal properly.

"Did you ever see a dog licking at a sore on his leg?", she asked.

"Yes. It's disgusting!"

"He does it because he can cure himself. Dog's saliva protects the wound and helps it to heal. Do you know what saliva is?"

"Yeah. Spit."

As she talked, she gently spread a liberal amount of soft, home-made butter on my short-trousered knee and instructed me to sit on the doorstep and not to move. She watched and encouraged me to be brave as the family sheepdog approached warily, sniffed at the butter, and began to lick my knee vigorously. Even after the last trace of butter was removed, his long coarse tongue slobbered on my knee until, to my relief, the dog became bored and wandered off.

"Don't touch it. Keep it clean and let the sun get at it. And don't pick at the scab! 'Cos if you do, your leg might fall off!"

The gummy saliva gradually hardened into a crusty scab which disappeared over the next few days to reveal new delicate pink skin underneath.

Even more primitive remedies and cures were common. Mrs Celia Conroy lived directly across from our house in the shade of the copper beach tree which had been our first landmark upon our arrival in Murneen. She was in her seventies and lived with her husband, Peter and their unmarried daughter, Monica.

Mrs Conroy pointed to a cluster of warts which had appeared around my left knee.

"Merciful hour! You'll want to get rid of them boyos."

"Ah. They're no trouble, Mrs Conroy. Sure I don't even notice them."

She was a stern, humourless woman whose scrutiny made me uncomfortable. I was anxious to escape. She held my gaze.

"They're no good for you. There could be badness in them."

I didn't know how to respond. She pointed up towards Mullaney's hill, a rocky mound at the rear of our house.

"Did you ever notice how a shower of rain leaves small pools of water lodged in cracks and dimples in them rocks?"

"I did."

"The next time it rains, wait for an hour after and then go up the hill. Dip your fingers in the rain-water that's lodged in a rock and rub plenty of it on them ladeens, the warts. After a few times, they'll be gone."

"Right, so. Mrs Conroy."

Despite my young age, I was sceptical of Mrs Conroy's suggestion. After all, this was a woman who regularly talked about the "old people", her ancestors, who believed in fairies. These spirits, known as "the little people" could prove to be mischievous and even dangerous. Mrs Conroy explained that some of them lived in the ring fort in Noone's field and that they stole or switched babies if people weren't vigilant. The little people were also prone to dispensing illnesses to humans and animals and would curse with misfortune anybody who incurred their wrath. Of course, locals were either incredulous or at least highly sceptical of such claims. Yet there was an underlying, unspoken consensus that it might be unwise to do anything which might antagonise or disrespect the fairies, just in case they did exist. This ambiguity was best illustrated by a number of "fairy trees" in the neighbourhood. These trees usually stood alone in the middle of a field and remained unmolested despite providing an obstacle to tillage or hay-making. To fell or damage a fairy tree was reputed to bring bad luck to the perpetrator and to the farm. Many such trees still remain undisturbed in the twenty-first century.

When somebody expresses a view or does something which is considered outlandish, people say that he or she is "away with the fairies". I thought that Mrs Conroy was away with the fairies when she gave me her instructions. Furthermore, I would be judged to be away with the fairies if I was seen to be following her advice.

It was my fear of facing her disapproval rather than any concern about the fairies which motivated me to climb Mullaney's hill after a rainy morning. I located deposits of rain water in depressions and crevices in the rocks and rubbed the water liberally on to the warts, allowing my knee to dry naturally, as Mrs Conroy had instructed. Even as early as my second climb to repeat the ablution, I noticed a change. As I vigorously rubbed in the rain-water, I noticed that some of the warts had loosened and were about to detach and fall away from my knee. After a few repeats of the remedy, the warts had disappeared.

No doubt, there is a scientific explanation for what happened. The rocks were limestone and perhaps the interaction of the rain with the lime gave some mildly toxic quality to the rain-water. Or perhaps clear pure rainwater alone is sufficient. In Islamic and Chinese medicine, the curative power of rain-water is much revered. But let's not tempt fate.

Let's wait until we have empirical evidence before discarding the possibility that the fairies had something to do with my disappearing warts. No point in chopping down fairy trees, even metaphorical ones? Or perhaps I'm away with the fairies…

Local cures and remedies, as an alternative to a consultation with a professional, were not confined to humans. When an animal showed signs of sickness, the vet was not immediately called. Tommy Keane, a local farmer was regarded as having special expertise with animal ailments. He was regularly asked to examine a sick animal and to provide or suggest a remedy. His diagnostic tactics included visual and tactile examination with special attention to eyes and mouth; feeling and applying pressure to test the animals response. The beast would also be thoroughly examined for ticks or other parasites. By stroking or massaging, Tommy could force the animal to involuntarily pass urine which he would examined and smell. If he satisfied himself that he could deal with the situation and that a visit by a veterinarian was not necessary, he mixed a potion for the animal. The dosage was applied by using a large whiskey bottle. Tommy held the bottle in his left hand and poured the contents down the animal's throat while using his right hand to grip the nostrils and prise open the animal's mouth.

Tommy's expertise was also in demand when cows were having difficulty delivering a calf or when an animal had fallen and wedged itself in a drain. He responded to all such demands for his service with cheerful good humour and disarming irreverence. A mischievous single man who lived with his ageing mother, he flirted harmlessly with the farmer's wife while refusing a cash payment but accepting a glass of whiskey or a bottle of porter after his work was done.

The Oatses' farm bordered Tommy Keane's land. (Arising from a linguistic quirk often heard in the rural west of Ireland, some people have a difficulty in pronouncing the plural of words that have "t" as the final consonant. So, breakfasts become "breakfastses", texts become "textses" and the Oates sisters were invariable referred to collectively as the "Oatses".) The three unmarried sisters were approaching their 60s and lived together in a two roomed, thatched, farmhouse without running water or electricity. Oatses' Road, the lane where their house was situated, formed a shortcut which people passed through on their way to town. Although the sisters possessed different personalities and traits, they were all hospitable and friendly women who were especially kind to and gentle with children. Teresa, the youngest, was strong, straight-backed, and sturdy, and had the dominant role in the household. She cycled to town each week to do the shopping and directed operations on the farm where her sisters shared the workload. Teresa took responsibility for their dry cattle and tended them daily. She sought and was given the assistance of neighbour, Tommy Keane, when buying or selling livestock. Quiet, reserved Mary Ellen, the eldest sister, was in charge of the housework, taking responsibility for cooking and cleaning. She only left the farmhouse to attend weekly Mass. Delia, the middle sister, was the more social and eccentric of the three. While Teresa was serious minded and Mary Ellen seemed shy and reclusive, Delia was a chatterer. She bantered with Tommy Keane, regularly emerged from the house to have a chat with a passer-by or, to Teresa's exasperation, neglected her farm work in order to lean over the fence and share the latest gossip.

Delia had another endearing eccentricity. Each year she accumulated a collection of the most colourful sweet wrappers she could find. She waited until all the leaves had fallen from one particular bush that was situated across the lane from their house. Then she painstakingly decorated the bush by twisting and folding the sweet wrappers and fixing them to the branches. I can recall the startling impact each winter as I entered the lane and was caught off-guard by the flash of colour in the distance. While all around was grim wintry greyness, the first impression on the viewer was of unseasonal flowers blooming in the bush. Then all became clear. Delia had done it again. The spirits were lifted by the magical vision. Delia had made her annual gift to the world.

Mike and Bill Fallon were brothers who lived and farmed together. Like the Oatses, each had his role in the household. Bill was quiet and seldom appeared in public apart from occasional visits to Sunday mass. He took responsibility for the household chores and all the cooking and he helped Mike on the farm. Mike was much more outgoing; he went to town to do the shopping and visited neighbours' houses at night. On the fair day each month, Mike had a rigid routine. He habitually travelled to Claremorris in his donkey-drawn cart, even if he had no livestock to buy or sell. He purchased the groceries and the provisions for the farm and loaded them onto the cart. Then he visited a nearby pub and drink more than his fair share while the donkey patiently waited outside in the falling darkness. At closing time, Mike climbed unsteadily into the cart, flicked the reins, started towards home, lay down in the bed of the cart, and promptly fell asleep. The donkey pulled the cart, with the recumbent Mike, for the five mile journey through the quiet, dark, roads to Fallon's house. In the pitch blackness of a moonless winter night, one might hear the faint jingling of harness or the gentle clop of a dainty donkey hoof as Mike's unlit homeward bound cart rolled by. Bill would have ensured that the five-bar gate was left fully ajar so that the donkey could enter and pull his cargo into the shelter of the hay-shed. Mike sometimes remained asleep in the cart until roused by Bill for breakfast in the morning.

Pake Mortimer was a reserved, unmarried man who lived alone and who was a mysterious figure to us children. He was the kind of man whom my mother might describe, not unkindly, as an "oddity". Each afternoon, Pake ceased his farm work, cleaned himself up, and donned his best clothes before cycling the three and a half mile journey to Claremorris railway station. He waited on the platform for the arrival of the afternoon train and discreetly but carefully scrutinised the alighting passengers before departing for home, changing his clothes, and resuming his farm work. As children, we idly wondered what motivated Pake to follow this daily ritual which involved a round trip of seven miles. Questions to my parents did not elicit any helpful information.

"The man is minding his own business and you should do the same. He's a bit of an oddity but he's not doing harm to anybody. And don't let me hear you making fun of him or of anybody else for that matter..."

I still do not know the reason, if any, for Pake's obsessive behaviour.

The requirement to treat neighbours with respect, no matter how unusual or eccentric their actions, was constantly being impressed on us by my parents.

"We don't have many rules in this house... but one is that you have to show respect to older people and you do not make fun of anybody, no matter what they do."

All married people had to be respectfully referred to by us as Mister or Missus. While other children in the neighbourhood would talk about Joe Gavin or John Healy, we were obliged to refer to them unfailingly as Mr. Gavin and Mr. Healy. Any confusion resulting from having two Conroy families in the neighbourhood was avoided by referring to the eldest, Peter Conroy, as Mr Conroy. The other man, Mike Conroy, was referred to as Mr Mike and his wife as Mrs Mike. We were not expected to be as formal when we spoke to people who were not married. It was considered acceptable for us to use their first and second names when we interacted with older unmarried people in the neighbourhood.

Relationships between people and households in the locality were good - there was no overt antipathy or rivalry between any of the families. The manner in which people interacted varied depending upon the personalities and habits of the individuals. My mother regularly dropped in on Mrs Glynn or Mrs Gavin for a cup of tea and a chat and both women would similarly call to our house. Mrs Conroy from across the road did not visit neighbours although her daughter, Monica, was a regular caller. Mr Conroy might call to us at night to while away an hour. In fascination, we watched his slow, solemn ritual; unfolding his penknife, paring slivers from his plug of tobacco, kneading it in his palm, filling his pipe, tamping down the tobacco with his thumb, holding a lighted match over the bowl of the pipe, and sucking on the stem so that the match flame bowed gently to ignite the tobacco.

Whether or not they visited each others houses, neighbours regularly encountered one another while drawing water from the well in the evening. When passing by a farmer working in the fields, it was customary to say "God bless the work" and to pause for a chat. "God bless all here" was the standard term of address when entering the home of a neighbour.

If a family was in distress due to bereavement or illness or for any other reason, all neighbours rallied round, even those who rarely socialised. This was partly the result of an innate desire to help but it also reflected an investment in good will which could be drawn upon if misfortune struck in the future. If somebody had a field of unsaved hay that was in danger of being lost as a result of impending bad weather, the word went out and a *meitheal* was assembled. All able-bodied neighbours arrived with their hay-forks and rakes and set to work until the crop was saved. Many of the women worked in the field with the men while others helped to prepare food for the volunteers. I can recall one such *meitheal* in Conroys, across the road. It was memorable because, as the workers sat at tables in the kitchen having their dinner, Mrs Conroy, the woman who cured my warts, sat on the front doorstep in the sunlight and entertained the diners by playing lilting tunes on a battered, old melodeon.

Most of the families in the locality who had school-going children in the 1950s are still represented in the area today and continue to be a vibrant community. However, the unmarried people who lived in the other fifty percent of the houses have left no trace apart from gravestone inscriptions in nearby Barnacarroll cemetery. The magical, winter-flowering, bush tended by Delia Oates is a fading memory although the old house in which the sisters lived has been wonderfully restored by a relative. Nobody replaced Pake Mortimer as the sentinel of the afternoon train. There is no ghostly jingle of harness from Mike Fallon's donkey as he trudged homewards in the early-morning darkness. There is no *meitheal* to be entertained by Mrs Conroy's lilting melodeon.

A visit to Barnacarroll cemetery provides another insight which, in death, reflects the closeness and interdependence of these people in life. Many of them did not survive their co-dwellers for long. Mike Fallon and his brother Bill died within two years of one another. Mary Ellen and Delia Oates died within an eight month period; Teresa survived for another three years. Two other cohabiting sisters, Kate Ann and Winnie Caulfield also died with a twelve month period. Mrs Keane, mother of Tommy, the unofficial local veterinarian, died in August 1981. Tommy, alone for the first time in his life, only survived her by two years.

CHAPTER FIFTEEN

Blinded By The Light

The replacement of the steam engine by the powerful diesel locomotive was an early indication that modernity was gradually coming to the rural west. But another change was to have a more immediate impact on our family and the wider community.

On our first drive to Murneen, we had seen giant pylons stalking the distant fields, shouldering cables which, as my father explained, transported electricity from a generator on the Shannon river to local transformer stations. He pointed out some recently erected wooden poles that would relay the power from the transformer stations to homes. Yes, he answered. We would be getting electricity in the new house. It was 1955 and the Rural Electrification Scheme was finally impacting on the rural west.

"When, Daddy, When?"

"Soon, please God."

Soon. A hate-word for children. The great indeterminater. The great frustrater. The great obfuscater. We wanted it to happen now. Not soon.

The reason for my father's equivocal response did not become apparent until later. Before our arrival, the people in Murneen had already been canvassed and had either opted out or given a commitment to install electricity in their homes. It transpired that Mrs Smyth, the previous owner of our house, had opted out. My father got in touch with the electricity company but was told that we had missed our opportunity; we would have to wait until the area was being revisited. Nobody could give a commitment or even an estimation of when that might happen. It seemed that the other houses in the area would be connected but we would have to wait.

There was much talk and discussion among the local people who harboured a mix of optimism and apprehension about the arrival of electricity. I recall accompanying my mother to Gavin's house, soon after our arrival in Murneen. While the dog with healing powers slept before the fire, I listened as Mrs Gavin spoke to my mother about the impending arrival of "the light", as electricity was colloquially known.

"I believe that the new light bulbs are so strong that you can sit anywhere in the room and read a book. It will be just as bright in the far corner as if you were sitting under the bulb itself."

Despite my young age, I remember being highly sceptical of such exalted expectations. Because I was usually not slow in articulating my opinions, I had been forewarned by my mother to remain silent and I heeded her instructions. But I knew from experience that, when reading, it was necessary to sit close to the oil lamp or to a candle. It did not make sense to me that a whole room could be illuminated by a single bulb.

My mother and Mrs Gavin discussed concerns about "the units" which would be used and which would determine the extent of the "light bill" to be paid at the end of the month. Lights could be switched off and the electricity used sparingly. But the new Sacred Heart light, which would replace the old oil lamp, was a particular cause of concern. The dim red bulb would obviously have to remain lit permanently. It would be burning units for twenty-four hours a day, seven days a week. There was no way to avoid it. Heads were shaken in resignation at the prospective expense.

Within a few weeks of our arrival in Murneen, the wooden poles were being sunk and local electricians were wiring our neighbours' houses in anticipation of their connection to the grid. My father spoke to one of the busy electricians about the failure to get our house included in the list for connection. The electrician, who understood the machinations of the electricity company, suggested a stratagem. He advised my father to notify the electricity company that, before he was aware that Mrs Smyth had opted out, he had already made arrangements for the house to be wired. Now, that the house was ready, could our name be added to the list of Murneen houses which would receive power? My father was uncomfortable with the subterfuge but went ahead with the ploy. The electrician was correct. Approval was given on the understanding that the house was already wired. Which, of course, it wasn't.

My father contacted the electrician and asked him to wire the house as quickly as possible because the power was due to be connected any day. The man was busy but agreed to call and do the job a few evenings later. Sooner than expected and to my father's dismay, the electricity company workers arrived to connect the Murneen houses. Was this God's way of punishing him for his dishonesty? He had no option but to approach the foreman of the connection crew and explain his dilemma. Luckily, the foreman took a benign view and agreed that he would run the power line onto the roof of our house. The electrician, whom the foreman knew and trusted, could then wire the house and connect the power.

The electrician finally arrived. Patricia, Michael, Mary and I watched in fascination as modernity crept into our lives through a hole drilled in the wooden frame of the front door. Soon, mysterious sounds emanated from the cramped attic space where the electrician was crouched. Flakes of plaster fluttered from the centre of the ceiling of each room as a drill-bit peeked through followed by a naked wire. Light fittings were attached and my mother carefully unwrapped and handed over new lamp shades and bulbs. Wires, encased in wooden conduits, were run down the walls of the kitchen to the Sacred Heart lamp and also to the single wall socket. Dire warnings were issued to the children about the dangers of interfering with the socket, which, with the exception of the light switches, was the sole electrical fitting or wire which was within our reach.

At last, the magic moment. The red bulb of the Sacred Heart lamp glowed dimly to signal that the power was connected. We raced from room to room as light switches were flicked. This was no gradual build-up of brightness which we had been accustomed to from our oil lamps. Instantaneously, each room was bathed in bright light. And Mrs Gavin was correct. Wondrously, the light seemed to be evenly distributed over the whole room.

We took turns switching the light on and off, encouraging Mary to become involved. As was her way, she didn't quite catch the excitement of the occasion. She wasn't interested in using the light switches but watched enquiringly as the bulbs glowed and faded.

Something was happening in the kitchen. We dashed back only to be asked whether we had switched off the bedroom lights. Money didn't grow on trees, after all. We sheepishly returned to do our duty. Back in the kitchen, my father had taken down two large packages from the top of the kitchen dresser. One was unwrapped to reveal a gleaming copper electric kettle. We watched as it was partly filled with spring water - it was essential to cover the element, we were instructed. The kettle was plugged into the socket and we waited.

"A watched kettle never boils", said my father with a grin.

"This one does", said the electrician. "And faster than God ever intended when he invented the open fire."

Already, the kettle was wheezing and hissing and soon the steam was puffing through the spout and rattling the lid.

"We'll all have a nice cup of tea to mark the occasion", said my mother, reaching for the tea-pot.

My father winked at the electrician as we excitedly eyed the second, larger package.

"We're not finished yet."

He unwrapped a gleaming, wood-encased, Bush radio which he positioned on the kitchen table.

"Granda is making a wooden shelf and brackets so that the radio will be up on the wall out of harm's way", he explained.

He plugged the radio cable into the socket. The dial lit up but nothing happened.

"Not to worry. It takes a few seconds for the valves to heat up."

Suddenly, disembodied voices and static burst from the radio as my father adjusted the volume, and turned the dial to the "Athlone" setting. Immediately, we were listening to music and speech from Radio Eireann.

"Thanks, Mrs Rushe", said the electrician as my mother handed him a cup of tea and offered a slice of bread and jam. "No more need to be sparing and heating batteries for the wireless. And you can make a cup of tea and boil an egg in the morning or even give Coleman some hot shaving-water without having to light the fire."

"Please God. Still, it's nice to get the fire going first thing."

The electrician sipped his tea and nodded in agreement.

"The electric is great but you could get carried away. People are losing the run of themselves with the stuff they're buying. There's a fortune being spent of cookers and heaters and the like. And it's all on tick. The instalments are added to your bill every month."

"There'll be a lot more heat generated in some houses when the light bills begin to arrive", said my father. "Still, if it makes life a bit easier for people and they can afford it, fair play to them."

The electrician nodded in agreement.

"I suppose that anything that would take the drudgery for women out of washing clothes would be welcome. I hear there's some class of an electrical machine for washing clothes but it's fierce expensive. And of course, you'd want to be living in town because you'd need running water."

"Washing is all part of a day's work", said my mother. "It's trying to dry clothes in bad weather that would break your heart. And trying to press clothes with a box-iron is a nuisance when you have to be always reheating the metal shoes in the fire. It's a heart-scald."

"We might stretch to getting an electric iron", said my father. "We're talking about it anyway."

Study and subversion. Soon afterwards, the new iron completed the collection of electrical implements in the Rushe household.

Adjusting to the usage of the new appliances was not without its confusions. For example, it seemed perfectly logical to use the electric kettle to boil eggs for breakfast. If the kettle could boil water for the tea in a fraction of the time when compared to using the old system, surely it could produce a boiled egg in, say, a minute compared to four minutes as previously? In practise, the electric kettle boiled the water quickly but, for some unexplained reason, it couldn't speed up the process of boiling an egg. Also, the eggs came into contact with the element of the kettle and were prone to cracking when the boiling water began to bubble. Gradually, the experiment ceased and people drifted back to the old method.

The electricity bill, known colloquially as the "light bill", and referred to by my father as the "charge of the light brigade", soon ceased to be a topic of concern or discussion.

Shortly after the arrival of electricity to Murneen, there were rumours of another welcome infrastructural change. Our gravel road was designated for upgrading. The news that we were going to have a tar road was generally welcomed but there were some reservations. Vehicular traffic on the road was sparse because car and lorry drivers preferred to avoid gravel roads. Would our new tar road attract more road users which might make it dangerous for children who were unaccustomed to traffic?

When was it going to be tarred?

Soon!

The first firm indicator of progress was the arrival of a stone crusher at the bottom of Day's hill, near our house. Large rocks were delivered in County Council lorries and fed into the thunderously powerful, belt-driven, crusher to be broken into more manageable stones which were suitable for use as hard-core for the road. The incessant noise from the crusher and the clouds of dust had to be accepted as a necessary evil for the duration of the work. Steam rollers slowly trundled by as the hard core was compressed in readiness for the new surface. Mounds of stone chippings were placed at regular intervals along the roadside. Finally, the massive black, steaming, tarring machine with it's overpowering smell, approached slowly, depositing a thick film of hot tar. A swarm of workmen followed, quickly shovelling an even layer of chippings onto the still hot surface. They were followed by a trundling steam roller which levelled and sealed the top layer.

Good things happen in threes. First the electricity. Then the tarring of the road. Sean was the third.

The novelty of the arrival of electricity and the upgrading of the road was soon surpassed by the unexpected addition to the family on 28th May 1955. Unexpected by me, that is. The arrival by train of my aunt Philomena, my mother's youngest sister, should have signalled that something was afoot. I assumed that her visit was connected to Patricia's First Communion which was about to take place. I was blissfully unaware that anything unusual was about to happen until, one morning, my mother was installed in the back bedroom, the doctor was on his way, and Philomena packed us of to a neighbour's house for the afternoon.

We arrived back later to be informed that the doctor had delivered a new baby brother for us. I was not naive. I was almost five years old and I was not fooled by grown-ups when they told me that babies were carried by a stork or were found under a head of cabbage. No. The doctor delivered babies. I had overheard somebody saying so. That made sense. He arrived with a big brown leather bag which obviously contained the new baby. I hadn't yet quite figured out where he got the babies from.

On the same day that this excitement was happening in Murneen, Patricia was receiving her First Communion. May Keane, formerly May Tighe, my mothers old friend from her early days in Claremorris, dressed Patricia for her big day and accompanied her to the ceremony before allowing her to dash home to Murneen in order to welcome the baby.

Our newest brother was named Sean and he was the first addition to the family in almost five years. A chubby, red faced baby who, it seemed to me, screamed from morning to night, just for the fun of it. "Yes. Sean liked the sound of his own voice", my mother said affectionately many years later when I verified my recollection with her.

When Sean was still a baby, we had one of our occasional visits by my father's uncle, Martin Reynolds. This was the elder brother of Granny Rushe. He hailed from Meelickroe in County Roscommon and led a colourful and nomadic lifestyle. He was a hard drinker who did some casual work for farmers during the summer. Martin had also lived for a while on a farm with his younger brother Jack. But mainly, he moved around the countryside in the west of Ireland, staying for a few weeks at a time with relatives and friends until he became bored or wore out his welcome. He was accepted as a guest in many houses because of his reputation as a singer, storyteller, and composer of ballads.

Martin's lifestyle resembled that of the ancient Irish bards who enjoyed the patronage of the owners of the landed estates. In return, the bards composed poems and songs about local and national events and in praise of their hosts. In 1938, a sample of Martin's work was collected for its archives by the Department of Irish Folklore. In 1963, he composed a song about the visit of John F Kennedy to Ireland and received an acknowledgement from the White House. Presumably he, or somebody on his behalf, sent the song to JFK and received the standard letter of thanks.

In his later years, Martin admitted himself to the County Home each winter. When the workhouses ceased to function in the 1920's, local County Councils provided accommodation, known as the County Home, for the care of the elderly, the homeless, and others who were unable to fit into society.

There was a tension between my grandmother and her eldest brother Martin. In all other respects she was a most gentle, kind, and good-hearted woman who liked and helped people. She was devout and religious also and it must have pained her to be unable to love and cherish her brother as her Christian principles would dictate. But for reasons "not talked about", she harboured a strong antagonism towards Martin. She did not allow him to stay in her house or to visit. I wondered whether her distaste for Martin reflected her strong disapproval of his drinking and lifestyle. She was also proud and protective of what she called "the Reynolds name". She may have felt that Martin was dishonouring it and was determined that the reputation of the family should be unblemished.

My father took a more benign view of his errant uncle and Martin was welcome to stay in our house. My brother Michael and I would share a bed so that Uncle Martin could take the other one in the big bedroom. But he had to behave responsibly while he was staying with us. In reality, this meant that he had to stay sober which cannot have been easy for him. One of his methods of alleviating the boredom was backing horses. He once sat me in front of a list of runners and riders in the Irish Independent newspaper and asked me to select three names. Afterwards, he headed for town to place bets on my selections, and probably stopped for a drink on the way. I was not invited to repeat my selection skills so that I assume that our joint venture was not financially successful.

On another occasion when Uncle Martin was staying with us, Sean was crying as usual despite having just been fed and changed by my mother. She was going to the clothes-line in the back garden and Martin agreed to keep an eye on the baby for a few minutes. As my mother went out the front door with her washing, Martin was gently trying to comfort Sean.

"There, there. What's the matter? Who's a nice little boy?"

Walking around the side of the house to reach the clothes-line, my mother passed an open window. To her amusement, she could clearly hear the addled child-minder trying a different approach.

"Will you shut up, you little bastard?"

Enforced sobriety and possibly Sean's volubility ensured that Martin's visits only lasted for a few days.

Martin's story had a sad but inevitable conclusion. At my father's suggestion, Martin had nominated him as the person to be contacted if he became ill or needed help. In January 1973, a health official from Roscommon phoned my father to notify him that Martin had died suddenly at the County Home in Castlerea. Rather than have him buried in Castlerea, my father thought that Uncle Martin should be buried with the family. The graveyard in Roscommon where Martin's parents were buried and where my father's younger brother was interred, was now closed. Maintaining her vendetta against her older brother even in death, my grandmother refused to allow Martin to be buried in the Rushe plot in Crossboyne graveyard where Patsy Rushe was buried.

I travelled with my father to Castlerea when he arranged to claim the body and to have Martin's remains brought to Claremorris.

"We have to look after our own", my father told me during our drive to Castlerea.

He and my mother purchased a plot for the Rushe's in Barnacarroll cemetery not far from our home in Murneen. Martin Reynolds was the first to be buried in the Rushe grave. His only sister, my grandmother, refused to attend the funeral.

CHAPTER SIXTEEN

Sticks And Stones

Wallop, whack, whip, smack, slap, sceilp, strick, stroke, strike, reef, root, rap, rattle, mill, paste, peg, puck, poke, plaster, clobber, clatter, clock, clout, clip, crack, kick, lick, lash, leadóg, dig, flake, bang, blow, boot, belt, butt, banjo, dudóg, nudge, thump, hammer, softener, straightener, flattener, loosener, beldizer, haymaker, trimming...

According to the oft-cited trope, the Inuit people have one hundred words for snow. This is attributed to snow's ubiquity and its pervasive impact on their daily lives. Irish writer Brian O'Nolan, in his comic writings under his Myles na gCopaleen pseudonym, playfully suggested that drunkenness is as inextricably linked to the Irish as snow is to the Inuits. To illustrate his point, he listed about forty words or phrases that are in common usage in Irish speech to describe varying states of inebriation. O'Nolan, a man who was himself partial to a regular tipple, was poking fun at both our inventive usage of language and our dysfunctional relationship with alcohol.

It seems reasonable to suggest that the number of words or phrases in regular usage about a particular subject is proportional to its omnipresence in daily life. Idly, I began to list words in daily usage in my youth to describe the action of one person striking another and, to my surprise, was soon approaching a count of fifty. I confined myself to single words. If I had listed phrases, my collection would be much larger.

Interestingly, each of the words which I have cited has a subtly different meaning. The choice of word could depend on such variables as the nature or severity of the blow, its intent, or its impact on the victim. For example, mention of a nudge or a poke would indicate relatively light contact intended as a warning. If unheeded, a clip or, more severely, a clatter might follow. A haymaker would be held in reserve until it was clear that a serious altercation was taking place and a flattener might even be appropriate to bring the matter to a conclusion. The word selected by the assailant to describe his actions would also give an indication of his attitude. A perpetrator who says: "I gave him a dig" is in honest but apologetic mode. Alternatively, if he selects the word "beldizer" or "loosener", he is revealing himself as a braggart and a bully.

Was my childhood world a violent place? The word violence is an emotive one, particularly when utilised in relation to children. Dictionaries describe violence as physical force intended to hurt, damage, and intimidate. Attitudes towards beating children have changed enormously in recent decades. "Corporal punishment", which was the name used to describe violence against children in the home and in schools, had been outmoded so that now it is considered unacceptable to administer an admonishing "smack" to a child. For what it's worth, I have over time become fully convinced that it is both wrong and unnecessary to smack a child as a method of imposing discipline. It should also be admitted that, while my generation abandoned our former reliance on corporal punishment and discouraged or pressurised others to follow suit, we failed miserably to equip the next generation with alternative tools and strategies for disciplining their children.

The reality was that, for most of us who were children in the 1950s and 1960s, corporal punishment was deemed necessary and obligatory in the home and in the schoolroom. "Spare the rod and spoil the child" was the salutary warning issued to parents whose children were considered to be displaying signs of indiscipline.

In Ireland, the Minister for Education banned the use of corporal punishment in schools in 1982 and it became a criminal offence in 1996. Nevertheless, it was still not illegal in the home. A limited defence of "reasonable chastisement" still existed under Irish law until 2015. It was abolished following repeated calls for change from child welfare groups inside the country and from bodies such as the United Nations. The Irish state has successfully taken action in high profile cases where excessive or unreasonable force was used against children. The Department of Children has also carried out research which shows that corporal punishment in the home is now relatively rare in Ireland.

In the Rushe household, physical chastisement was seldom used but was seen as a necessary element in the raising of children. Indeed, it might be argued that its relatively scarce and benign usage in the home resulted in a lack of adequate preparation for the severity of the corporal punishment which we were to encounter in the school system.

The usual miscreants who were in need of correction were Michael and myself. Mary, of course, was never punished and Patricia seldom got into trouble when she was with us at weekends. Granny Rushe imposed tight discipline on her during the school week.

A light slap on the bare arm or, for more serious misdemeanours, on the back of the legs was occasionally administered by my mother as an "on the spot" punishment for misbehaviour when we were aged from about four upwards. But, more often that not, a verbal warning by my mother that a slap was her next option was sufficient to restore order. My mother's array of verbal admonishments, which now seem ominous as I write them down, were delivered in such a casual, matter-of-fact tone that they took the heat out of any situation.

"I'll cut the legs off you", was a favourite.

There were other variations.

"I'll kill you stone dead."

"I'll knock you into the middle of next week."

"I'll wipe the floor with you."

"I'll soon soften your cough."

As an unwelcome accompaniment to the threat, the culprit would then be handed a bucket or a tin can and instructed to traipse off to the well for water. Alternatively, a spell of weeding in the detested vegetable garden was imposed as a punishment.

A higher level of indiscipline might warrant production of "the stick". My mother sometimes kept a leafy twig which could be seen protruding from the rear of the framed picture of the Sacred Heart on the mantle-piece. In order to restore order, it was usually sufficient for my mother to warn us not to force her to "take down the stick". On the rare occasions that use of the stick was considered necessary, a light swish on the back of the legs was all she could bring herself to inflict.

A more comedic element was introduced if the stick was missing. As punishment, the culprit was dispatched outside with instructions to "bring in a good stick until I beat the daylights out of you." The embarrassing process of selection of a suitable stick was usually deliberately prolonged. First of all, a light and leafy stick had to be selected so that it would cause the least discomfort but it had to be strong enough to pass inspection by my mother. There was the added vain hope that a delay might result in the misdemeanour being forgotten as other household duties distracted my mother. More often than not, she administered a swish in the general direction of the culprit's legs before ostentatiously placing the stick behind the picture of the Sacred Heart.

"The next time, it'll be there waiting for you."

My mother knew that the real punishment which she was imposing was the guilt which she knew we felt when we disappointed her. We realised that she was far more lenient with us than other parents were with their children and that she only used physical punishment as a last resort. She trusted us to behave correctly both inside and outside the home and felt let down by us when we failed to meet her expectations. If we did something which she regarded as serious misbehaviour, she imposed the ultimate sanction.

"Wait until Daddy gets home. He'll have to hear about this."

There followed the agonising wait until my father arrived from work on his bicycle. The tension would be prolonged because she delayed telling him about the misdemeanour until he had finished his dinner. My father preferred to let my mother deal with disciplinary matters and seldom became involved. But, when he was obliged by my mother to intervene, his strategy was to firmly explain how and why our conduct was unacceptable and that both he and my mother were disappointed and felt let down by us. The feeling of guilt and shame was sometimes compounded if he later took the culprit to one side and quietly pointed out that Mammy was working very hard and had a difficult job to do "keeping the house together". He might also mention her workload with Mary and our obligation not to damage the reputation of the family. Our mother deserved our support and should not have to be troubled by our misbehaviour.

"We don't have many rules in this house but..." was my father's standard and slightly apologetic preface to a lecture on our obligations. I think that this wording led to a false but comforting perception in our minds that discipline was not as rigidly imposed in our household as in others. In reality, behavioural standards were imposed and boundaries were established and observed. As a result, corporal punishment was only sparingly utilised in our home. Sadly, this was not the case in the school system, as I was soon to find out.

CHAPTER SEVENTEEN

What's Wrong With Me?

"Authority is the mask of violence".
 - Ralph Steadman.

I didn't realise that there was something wrong with me until I went to school.

By the summer of 1955, when we moved to Murneen, I was not yet five years old but Michael was just passed his sixth birthday. But for the uncertainty surrounding our house move, Mike would have started school a year earlier. Now it was decided that both of us should commence attending school at the same time despite the eighteen month difference in our ages.

We were kitted out with shiny new raincoats and rain-hats. Our mother knitted woollen mittens and scarves for us and the ensemble was completed by the addition of two new schoolbags. In September, when the school year resumed after the summer break, we were entrusted to the care of some older children from the neighbourhood and we set off on the two mile walk to Ballyfarna National School. A trickle of about a dozen school-going children passed our house each morning. This soon became a stream as we were gradually joined by tributaries of children from byroads and boreens as we got closer to the school.

There were fifteen pupils in our "low infants" class: nine boys and six girls. The ninety-four schoolchildren in Ballyfarna National School in 1955 were housed in the standard two-room school building. It was, in fact, one large room divided by a retractable wooden and glass partition. The four lower classes comprising fifty-six pupils were under the stewardship of Mrs O'Leary while, on the other side of the dividing boundary, her husband Mr O'Leary taught the remaining thirty-eight children of the four senior classes.

The O'Learys had been teaching in the school since the 1920s and were now in their 60s. They had a good reputation in the locality and had taught the parents of most of our fellow pupils. Mr O'Leary, referred to as "The Master" was a kindly man who rarely resorted to corporal punishment. Ominously, there were mutterings among the older children about "The Missus". It was important not to get on the wrong side of Mrs O'Leary, a strict disciplinarian who, we were warned, wielded a wooden ruler with relish on all miscreants.

"Don't draw attention to yourselves."

Mike and I understood the reason for our mother's admonishment as she entrusted us to the care of the older school-goers. We were outsiders who had recently arrived in a closely-knit community. Almost all of the other children were from farming families that had lived in the locality for generations. Our father didn't work on the land and, almost uniquely among our new neighbours, was the recipient of a weekly wage. Financially, we were no better or no worse off than our neighbours. But difference can be seized upon by children and can lead to bullying or ostracisation. Hence our mother's advice to blend in and avoid displaying any airs and graces which might irritate teachers or fellow pupils.

Despite any real or perceived differences, Michael and I were quickly accepted and befriended by our fellow scholars. I attribute this to the innate openness and hospitality of the local people and also to my mother's efforts in preparing us for our integration into the new community. The necessity for good behaviour was being constantly impressed upon us as was the need to be aware of how our actions might be perceived by our new neighbours. We had soon blended in comfortably in the neighbourhood. There was no reason to assume that our transition in the schoolroom would not be just as smooth.

Or so it seemed.

Until I discovered that there was something wrong with me.

It may have been on my first day in school. Michael and I were seated side by side at our ink-stained wooden desk. We were being taught how to write. As instructed, our new, lined, copy books were open in front of us. Pencils were poised to copy out some letters which Mrs O'Leary had chalked on the blackboard. She had already set some writing tasks for the other three classes and could now direct her full attention on the new arrivals. She chalked horizontal red and green lines on the blackboard to mirror the lines on our copy books and then, with white chalk, she showed us how to write a, b, and c, pointing out the necessity of keeping within the borders of the red and green lines. Under her watchful eye, we began to painstakingly copy her work.

"Wait! You! Step out here!".

Startled, we looked up. She was glaring at me and pointing her finger in my direction.

"Yes. You!" she repeated, continuing to point at me as her eye roved over the rest of the class. "And you! You too!"

Two girls were also singled out.

"Come on! The three of you! Step out here this instant!"

She pointed to an area in front of the blackboard as we confusedly left our desks and approached her.

"Bring your copy books and pencils with you. And your schoolbags."

We scrambled back to retrieve our belongings. Three confused and frightened children soon stood in trepidation before our angry teacher.

"I'll have no *ciotóg*s in this class! Is that clear? It won't be tolerated."

I was confused. I knew what a *ciotóg* was. It had been pointed out to me at an early age that I was left-handed. But what was the problem? If my parents didn't mind, why should anybody else? I said nothing. One look at Mrs O'Leary's face was enough to convince me that this was not a subject for negotiation.

It has long been accepted in various cultures that left handedness is an undesirable trait. This is reflected in the manner in which many languages deal with the subject. The right hand is seen as positive, but the left has negative connotations. In English, the word "left" is a derivation of the Anglo-Saxon word "lyft" meaning "weak". The Italian "sinistra" and the old Spanish "siniestro", both meaning "left", have the same root as the English "sinister", reflecting the belief that there was something menacing and ominous about left-handed people. In French, the word for left is "gauche", a word also used to describe a person lacking ease or grace, or one who is unsophisticated and socially awkward.

In the Irish language, the word for "right" is "*deas*" which also means nice or attractive. Left is "*clé*" which also means awkward, sinister or wicked. The Irish word for a left handed person, *ciotóg*, is derived from *ciotach* meaning awkward.

Perhaps Mrs O'Leary considered that we would be better equipped socially if we were no longer left-handed. Alternatively, she may have shared some of the superstition and prejudice about left-handed people.

"Move back and take their places!"

She directed three children from the two front desks to leave their positions and to sit in the seats which we unlucky three had just vacated.

"*Suígi síos ansin*! Take those seats and sit down there where I can keep an eye on you. Anybody I see using their left hand will feel this ruler. *Ar aghaidh libh!* Carry on with your work!"

We took our places in front of the teacher. To my dismay, I was no longer sitting beside Michael and, to make matters worse, I was sharing a desk with a girl. In a daze of confusion and embarrassment, I opened my copybook and picked up my pencil. Immediately, I received a stinging rap across the knuckles of my left hand from Mrs O'Leary's wooden ruler. The floodgates opened. Through my tears, I chokingly tried to explain that I was just picking up the pencil with my left hand and was going to write with my right hand. She gave me a second rap on the knuckles and warned me not to "talk back" and to use only my right hand as I had been told. I looked back towards Michael for reassurance and observed that he was dismayed when he saw me being punished.

Thus began the nightmare which was to blight my first weeks in school and which continued to have an impact for many years. With the benefit of hindsight, I think that I developed at that early stage a feeling of victimhood which was to persist throughout my schooldays. Being physically punished by a teacher, or indeed by a parent, was an accepted unpleasantness for a child of that era. Most children endured and accepted the punishment as a necessary and unavoidable aspect of their upbringing and emerged from the ordeal as reasonably well adjusted human beings.

However, if the child believed that the punishment was undeserved or, worse still, that there was nothing which could be done to remedy the situation, the sense of injustice and frustration could be quite traumatic. My abiding memory of that early experience is an overwhelming feeling of helplessness and victimisation.

Of course, I quickly learned to hold the pencil in my right hand and began tentatively to copy the letters on the blackboard. Unsurprisingly, I had very limited control and found it impossible to keep the letters between the red and green lines as directed. This resulted in further slaps with the ruler on the palm of the hand. When I used a rubber to erase some of my wayward pencil strokes, I often unthinkingly and instinctively used my left hand resulting in further blows on the knuckles. Even when I used my right hand exclusively, I was still in trouble. If I wrote as quickly as the other children, my handwriting was almost illegible. If I slowed down to write carefully, I fell far behind and the blackboard was wiped clean before I was finished. In either event, further slaps of the ruler followed.

Michael looked on in dismay.

CHAPTER EIGHTEEN

Michael

A few years ago, Mike, as my older brother became known in adulthood, came to visit us in our home in Spain. A friend of my wife's later mentioned that she met and spoke to "Colman's brother" in the local market.

"What did you think of him?", asked my wife, who is extremely fond of Mike.

The reply was warm and heartfelt.

"He's a lovely, lovely man."

A few days later, when I was paying the bill at the counter of a local cafe, the waiter leaned towards me in a conspiratorial manner and, pointing to Mike who was out of earshot, said:

"Very, very good person."

From childhood, Michael has always had a cheerfulness and openness which immediately endeared him to people. By comparison, I was less adorable. Two of the earliest family photographs that show us together, are revealing. In the first, taken just after our arrival in Murneen, we are standing on the road in front of the house with our two sisters and Philomena, our aunt. Michael is gazing at the camera with an open, friendly, and enquiring expression. I have my hands clasped together in front of my half-smiling face as if in contemplation. My expression is of a scheming child who is deciding whether it is safe to carry out some mischievous act.

The second photograph, which is professionally taken, is of Patricia, Michael and me on the day of our Confirmation. Patricia is smiling proudly in her new costume. Michael looks enquiringly at the camera and seems like the happiest, friendliest, and most cheerfull child in the world at that moment. I am trying to smile, probably because I've been told to do so, but the result is a slightly sideways, frowning, half-smile which seems to say, "For goodness sake, can we get this over with?"

Michael was helpful and generous with people, displayed no hint of malice, and became a favourite with friends and neighbours. Half a century later, he is still the first one of our family whose health and wellbeing neighbours in Murneen enquire about. This is not to imply that the rest of the Rushe children were unpopular or disliked; we are all warmly greeted and welcomed when we return to our native place. But there is a special warmth and affection which locals unwittingly reveal when Michael's name is mentioned.

As I look back, I wonder whether I am due a modicum of credit for Michael's popularity. It is easier to recognise and appreciate a great painting in an art gallery if it is hung between other less accomplished works. You can immediately distinguish the Caravaggio from the assembled works of his pupils. I am not implying that I was a trouble-maker who made my brother look good by comparison - my mother would soon have put paid to that. But while Michael was uncomplicated and open, I was sometimes what my mother called a "smart alec". I discovered at an early age that, when somebody made a comment, I could think on my feet and come up with a riposte which I thought was clever and amusing. A quick-witted person can be a welcome and diverting companion if blessed with tact and discretion. As a child, I did not yet have the awareness or judgement to know when to speak and when to hold my counsel.

Michael was no saint. But even his misbehaviour was somehow endearing. Just a week or two after we arrived in Murneen, Michael unexpectedly announced one Sunday morning that he was not going to Mass that day or in future. He explained to my aghast parents that the Mass was boring. It was exactly the same every Sunday, and he saw no point in endlessly repeating the exercise. Been there, done that. He was quickly made aware that attendance was not a matter for negotiation and he very reluctantly acquiesced.

Some months later, when he decided that he wanted a break from school, he tried a fresh tactic. One morning, we had only walked a few hundred yards from our house when Michael turned and headed back home. He told my mother that he was sick and couldn't go to school.

"I felt sick and I vomited over the wall into Oatses field."

"Come with me", said my mother. "Show me where it happened."

She walked him up the road to Oatses field and he pointed vaguely over the wall.

"I can't see anything", said my mother.

"That's because I covered it with grass."

He was dispatched to school in some embarrassment.

The zenith of his misbehaviour was reached when we had been at school for two or three years. Ann Connor, who was in a class three years ahead of us, was one of the children with whom we walked home from school. As one of the oldest children on our route, she was the type of girl who would be relied upon by parents to supervise the younger schoolchildren. Unlike other children with such a role, Ann was not a bully and indeed would intervene if she saw any evidence of such behaviour.

Her kindness did not cut any ice with Michael. He became annoyed by Ann's occasional tendency to sermonise on various subjects to her fellow scholars. On the fateful day, she was standing on a raised earthen ditch beside the road as she pointed to and pontificated about some object or activity in the distance. When her back was turned, Michael stepped up behind her and gently pushed her into the muddy and knee-deep water of the dyke which was alongside the ditch. Michael's audacious action and the sight of muddy and wet Ann as she scrambled from the dyke were greeted by a combination of disbelief, shock, and hilarity by the other children. Even Ann's brothers took no action in her defence. Michael laughingly ran towards home as Ann called after him that he was in big trouble.

The seriousness of his impulsive action soon dawned on Michael. By the following day, he had been severely reprimanded by the school-teacher but our parents had not yet heard about the incident. We had to pass Connor's house on our route to school and the following evening, Jim Connor, Ann's father, was waiting. Before Mr Connor could say anything, Michael took the initiative.

"Mr. Connor! If you as much as lay a hand on me, I'll call the Guards on you."

Jim Connor had no intention of laying a hand on Michael and merely wanted to give him a telling off.

"I'll be talking to your father about this when I see him at Mass on Sunday."

Jim Connor turned and went back into his house. He was a wise and prudent man. I'm sure that he realised that Michael would have a few agonising days and possibly sleepless nights as he worried about my father's reaction to the news. He was correct. Both Michael and I waited in trepidation for our father to arrive home from Mass the following Sunday and were thrown into a further state of confusion when nothing happened. Was Mr Connor at Mass, we wondered? Did he not see or meet Daddy? The dreaded apprehension was prolonged for another week - and then another...

Jim Connor finally recounted the anecdote to my father many years later. He explained that he had barely been able to suppress his laughter when Michael threatened to "call the Guards". Despite Michael's display of bravado, Mr Connor was wise enough to recognise that the lesson had been learned.

I shudder to think about what would have been the outcome if I had been the culprit in any of these escapades. But Michael possessed such innocent charm and innate kindness that his misdemeanours quickly became endearing anecdotes whereas with me, they would have been cautionary tales. Interestingly, his ability to escape serious censure and his popularity never resulted in resentment or hostility on my part. I attribute this to the kindness and elder-brotherly protectiveness he always demonstrated towards me. Another factor was Michael's similarity to our mother. While I had many of my father's qualities, Michael had more of our mother's kindness, empathy, and generosity. To dislike or resent him would be as unthinkable as to dislike or resent her.

Michael and I had the expected inconsequential sibling disputes as children but they were never long-lasting. We formed a strong bond so that, because we were in the same class at school and of similar size, we were sometimes mistaken for twins. One of the outcomes of this bond was that we did not tell tales on one another. If anything happened at school which, we thought, reflected badly on one of us, the other could be relied upon not to tell our mother and father when we got home. For example, information about the Ann Connor incident did not reach our mother. The same code of silence was maintained even if one of us did something which was praised or rewarded by a teacher. If one brother was seen to be forging ahead, our parents might wonder why the other brother was falling behind, we surmised. So we said nothing.

As I look back, I realise that this omertà had its downside. My mother knew that Mrs O'Leary was obliging me to use my right hand but she had no idea that the changeover was causing me such difficulty and was resulting in almost daily punishment which was upsetting both Michael and me. I toyed with the idea of telling her but never seriously contemplated doing so. She was not a confrontational person and, in any event, I did not relish the prospect of a dispute between her and the teacher which might quickly become local knowledge. I would be teased incessantly for "running home crying to my Mammy".

"Colman Rushe is a tell-tattle!"

Michael and I - we were in this together - unwisely did not tell our mother about our problem. I was becoming overwhelmed by a feeling of victimisation and hopelessness but Michael knew that something must be done. He decided that practise was the answer. In order to avoid our mother's scrutiny and inevitable questions, he proposed that we work outside the house. He placed my copybook on an orange box under a tree in the front garden and seated me on a butter box. While our mother assumed that we were playing at being shopkeepers, Michael supervised me as I practised writing with my right hand. He explained the necessity of keeping within the lines and writing neatly and clearly. He persuaded me that I could only achieve this if I wrote slowly and painstakingly. Without the fear of a painful blow on the knuckles, I began to relax and to train my right hand to write satisfactorily. On subsequent evenings, he would encourage me to repeat the exercise and, this time, to see whether I could do it a little faster. If we saw that speed was causing a deterioration in quality, he encouraged me to slow down again and to practise some more.

Despite our efforts, matters in school were not improving. I found that, in order to keep up with the class, I had to write at a speed which resulted in poor handwriting. If Mrs O'Leary recognised any marginal improvement in my performance, she doubtless attributed this to her use of the ruler and she persisted with the punishment. The other *ciotógs* were also experiencing varying levels of difficulty in adjusting. If we had a bad day, the punishment did not just involve the stinging slaps on the palm or painful raps on the knuckles. When writing class was over and we switched to reading, we three pariahs were obliged to stand with our reading books for the duration of the class while the remainder of the class were seated.

A hiatus of sorts was soon to occur. The Missus decided that, as homework, we should practise our writing by copying a short paragraph from our reading book. We had to hand up our copybooks to Mrs O'Leary the following morning. She corrected the homework as we worked on some simple addition sums which she had written on the blackboard.

"Cóilin O'Rúis! Step up here!"

I still give an involuntary shudder when I hear the Irish version of my name. Mrs O'Leary seemed to use it only when she was particularly angry with me.

"Hold out your hand!"

She administered three stinging slaps with the ruler.

"What's that for. Ma'am?" I queried tearfully.

"You know what it's for. You wrote this with your left hand. *Feach ar sin!*". She held the copy so that the class could see.

"But I didn't. I swear. I only used my right hand."

"Don't lie to me. Hold out your other hand."

There was a scuffle of feet from a few rows back and a clap of wood on cast-iron as a seat was suddenly raised.

"He only used his right hand, Ma'am."

Sound was drained from the room. Mrs O'Leary paused with her ruler poised over my outstretched hand.

"I watched him every minute, so I did. He never used his left hand."

There were gasps from the rapt onlookers. The teacher glared at Michael who was now standing in the aisle beside his seat.

"Now we have not one liar but two", she said. "I've seen enough to know that he cannot write like that. Either he used his left hand, against my firm instructions, or maybe you wrote it for him. Either way, both of you will now be punished. Step out here this instant."

She paused uncertainly and frowned.

"I expected more from you, Michael Rushe."

MIchael stepped forward.

"No ma'am. I can prove it. Coleman wrote it. He can show you."

He stopped beside me.

"Go on. Show the Missus the way you wrote it."

He reached out, took the copybook which Mrs O'Leary had placed on her table and handed it to me as I looked at him open-mouthed. He nodded towards my desk.

"You'll need to sit down."

I rubbed my still stinging palm before taking up the pencil and painstakingly commenced to write.

"It takes him a while, Ma'am. He has to write fairly slow."

It seemed to me that he emphasised the word "slow" as a warning to me and I forced myself to be as accurate as possible. Mrs O'Leary glanced towards the other pupils who were watching in wide-eyed curiosity. She gave a rap on the blackboard with her ruler.

"Ar aghaidh libh! Pay attention to your work."

There was a flurry of rustling pages and the scratching of pens and pencils. Meanwhile, Michael was now leaning over my shoulder and watching me as I worked. We were back home again, under the tree in the front garden. I could do this.

By the time I had painstakingly finished the first line, Mrs O'Leary had seen enough. She calmly took the copybook from in front of me. Her former hostility had evaporated.

"He can only do it if he takes his time, ma'am," Michael said quietly as she examined my work. "He's trying to speed up but I'm not letting him until he can do it right."

"*Maith an buachall, a Mhicheál.* You have the making of a fine teacher. I'm relying on you to keep him at it."

My problems as a result of the forced usage of my right hand were not yet ended but, from then on, they were lessened. The trade off between speed and legibility continued to require regular reevaluation and readjustment. Mrs O'Leary was now more manageable, or perhaps she became more efficient in managing me.

I still abhor the practise of obliging children to use only the right hand for writing and the reliance on corporal punishment as enforcement. However, I realise that Mrs O'Leary was carrying out the perceived best practise at that time and she saw no other alternative. I sometimes wonder whether Michael's intervention resulted in any change in her method for dealing with ciotógs in subsequent years. I like to think that it did.

My left-handedness was disguised but not "cured". In the mid 1970s, I was about to do my driving test in Galway city. The examiner sat in the passenger seat and, before we set off on our drive around the city streets, he explained that he would give me verbal directions from time to time. I hesitated.

"I hope this isn't a problem for you but I have a difficulty with left and right............"

He nodded and smiled.

"Ah. You were forcibly changed as well? Was it a teacher or at home?"

"At school", I replied with relief.

He told me that he would place his hand, as appropriate, on the left or right of the dashboard when he called out the directions. I passed the test.

The driving test examiner understood. I didn't have to explain. Of course, I can differentiate between my left and right. But it takes me a second or two to figure it out and, by then, it can be too late. When I'm driving and somebody tells me to turn left, I do not instinctively go left as most people do. My brain clicks into action. Let me figure this out. I bless myself with this hand. Therefore this is my right side and the other is my left. Now I know. But in the fraction of time taken up by this thought process, I've driven past the turn-off, or at a minimum, I'm in the wrong lane and haven't flicked the indicator yet.

"Dad doesn't even know his left from his right!"

My discomfort is a source of high hilarity for my wife and children but sometimes causes other nervous passengers to look at me strangely. It is only one of many outcomes of my enforced realignment by Mrs O'Leary. Forcing a naturally left-handed child to use the right hand can, in some rare cases, result in learning difficulties, dyslexia, and speech disorders. There can also sometimes be benefits. In a paper called "Can Left-Handedness be Switched? Insights from an Early Switch of Handwriting" published in the Journal of Neuroscience in 2007, it is suggested that "attempts to switch handedness by educational training far from weakening the functional expression of left handedness in higher-order motor areas of the (dominant) right hemisphere in fact enhance it." In other words, the conversion will result in increased activity in the non-dominant left hemisphere of the brain but, intriguingly, there will also be higher activity in the dominant right hemisphere.

Rather than realigning me so that I would become a fully functioning right-handed person, Mrs O'Leary's efforts resulted in a confused ambidexterity. (Even that word, which derives from the root *dexter*, meaning *right*, reflects bias in that it implies that the solution is to equip the left-handed person with two right hands.) But the conversion had quite a few consequences for me, apart from the one mentioned above. I myself became aware of some idiosyncrasies and a few additional instinctive behaviours were pointed out to me by other people.

I shave with my left hand. When eating, I hold a knife in my right hand and a fork in my left, in the European fashion. When using a spoon for soup or dessert, however, I invariably use the left hand. If cutting bread or preparing food for cooking with a large or chef's knife, I again use my left hand.

I throw darts right-handed. When playing games such as cricket, hurling or tennis, I hold the bat, hurley, or racquet in my right hand or use a right-handed grip. I throw or bowl a ball with my left hand only but, if attempting a one-handed catch, will instinctively use my right.

When I started playing football at an early age, I favoured my right foot to kick from the ground or from the hand. In my teens, as I was becoming skilled as a goalkeeper playing Gaelic football, I realised that astute forwards quickly identified a one-footed kicker. This made it easier for them to block a kick from the hand or to turn the goalkeeper onto his less favoured side, making a clearance difficult. I soon taught myself to kick equally effectively with either foot.

Another advantage arises when holding a paintbrush. When I dabble at oil painting, I grip the brush in the right hand. If decorating a wall or ceiling, I tend to start with the brush in my right hand but can switch effortlessly to my left if my arm gets tired or to enable me to more easily get access to that awkward corner.

I play guitar right handed although I attribute the dexterity (that bias again) of my left hand on the fingerboard to my latent propensity to left-handedness.

There are two other possible legacies from the enforced change or, more specifically, from the violence that was associated with it. It marked the beginning of a conflicted relationship with schooling and with some teachers which was to continue into secondary school. I have some happy memories of my schooldays and derived much benefit from the education which I received. But my over-riding recollection is one of unhappiness, resentment, and a perception of victimisation.

I am not sure whether another legacy was a result of my early experiences in school. I cannot say for certain when my bed-wetting habit started but my best recollection is that it was about the time I started school. It is quite possible that it was a problem long beforehand but that I only became conscious that it was unusual so that I grew guilty and embarrassed as I reached school-going age.

Despite the extra workload which my habit caused for her, my mother's response was supportive, encouraging, and understanding as she tried various means to help me deal with the problem. These included prohibiting me from drinking in the few hours before I went to bed and, on one occasion, taking me for an examination by the doctor in order to check whether there was an underlying physical problem. The doctor could only offer reassurance that the problem would disappear as I grew older. Regulating my liquid intake sometimes resulted in temporary cessations but, inevitably, after a few days or weeks, there would be a resumption. Such unwelcome recurrences were the only time when my mother would betray her disappointment. Her frustration is easy to understand when one takes into account that she already had to deal with the reality of Mary's constant bed-wetting which was one of the consequences of her condition. In both our cases, rubber under-sheets, known as "oil sheets" contained the problem by protecting mattresses but daily washing of bed-sheets was an unwelcome fact of life for my mother.

It is now thought that most child bed-wetting is caused by developmental delay rather than by medical or emotional issues. Conversely, psychological problems in the child can be a consequence of pressure, punishment, and shaming by parents or carers. My mother's attitude ensured that I did not suffer such a fate. I think that heavy sleeping was a factor in the problem. I have always been and continue to be a heavy sleeper. My mother would joke that the house could fall down and I would sleep on, blissfully aware of any problem.

Bed-wetting remained an intermittent problem and frustration for me until I was about eleven years old when I stumbled on a self-help remedy. I was reading a newspaper or magazine article about the ability of some people to wake at a specific time without relying upon an alarm clock. It was suggested, for example, that if you bang your head seven times on the pillow at night, you will wake at seven o'clock in the morning. It was also claimed that, by concentrating hard on a specific time, you will wake at that time the following morning. The piece went on to ponder the mysterious power of the mind and of the sub-conscious.

I wondered whether I could persuade my mind to get me to wake up when I was about to wet the bed. But, I thought, why not go the whole hog? What if I could overcome the urge to urinate and wait until morning, thereby obviating the necessity of getting out of my warm bed? I decided to try this strategy first. For some reason, probably boyish innocence, I was quite optimistic that it would be successful. Just before falling asleep, I concentrated hard on not wetting the bed that night. It worked. And the following night? It worked again.

I gradually dropped the practise of carrying out my concentration exercise before sleeping but my dry nights continued and the problem finally disappeared from my life.

CHAPTER NINETEEN

Satellite Of Love

It was October 1957. There was an air of excitement and anticipation in the Rushe household. Two and a half years after Sean's birth, my mother was expecting another baby. While Sean's arrival had come as a complete surprise to me, this time I was aware that an addition to the family was imminent. Patricia, who gave the good news to me and Michael, was hopeful that another sister was on the way.

But this was not the main reason for our excitement. Incredibly, or so it seemed to me and Michael, the news had just broken that the Russians had put something called a satellite into space. Instantly, we were glued to the radio for more information. We learned that Sputnik was circling the earth once every ninety minutes, travelling at over five miles per second. But the most exciting news was that it was visible in the night sky, provided that there was no cloud cover. We learned from the newspaper the approximate time that it was due to pass over Ireland.

Our prayers were answered by a cloudless night and we stood with our father beside the house, scanning the northern sky high over Mullaney's hill. We bombarded our father with questions.

If, as he said, the satellite was slightly smaller than Sean's pram, and it was hundreds of miles away, how could we possibly see it?

Because it was as shiny as a mirror and would reflect the sun's rays so that it would look like a star.

Would it not look like all the other stars? How would we know which bright light was the satellite?

Because, unlike the other stars, it would be moving quickly across the sky.

Could it crash into one of the stars, Daddy?

No. You see the stars are far......

"Look! There it is!"

"Where. I can't .... ooh! Look...!"

We watched in wonder as the pin-point of light slid slowly across the night sky. It seemed that a barrier had been broken. We were living in our own small world where electric light was still a novelty and where we were still drawing our water from a well. The occasional drone of a propeller-powered aircraft drew our eyes skyward and we wondered vaguely what it would feel like to travel by plane. But somewhere out there, the world was entering a new era filled with previously unimagined possibilities. There was talk of putting a man in space and even travelling as far as the moon. In the past, such predictions would have seemed ridiculous but now, suddenly, it seemed that anything was possible.

As the object of our attention arced slowly towards the horizon, what were we viewing? Russian insiders, who were actively involved in launching and monitoring the Sputnik, now say that the satellite was invisible to the naked eye from earth. They contend that we were watching the spent booster rocket's second stage which was in roughly the same orbit as the satellite. It doesn't matter. We were gazing wide-eyed into the future.

A few weeks later, another Sputnik was circling in space. This one, we were told, carried a dog so that scientists could monitor his condition with a view to predicting how a human being would cope outside the earth's atmosphere. I realise now that there was much controversy arising from fears that the dog would not survive the journey. I cannot recall any such qualms or concerns in our household even though we had the well loved Blackie as part of the family. Ours was a rural and harsh world where the death and killing of animals was part of everyday life. Pigs, chickens, geese, ducks, and turkeys were killed on the farms for food. Sheep and lambs were killed or mutilated by marauding dogs. Cattle were fattened for the slaughterhouse and even faithful family dogs were sometimes shot when they were no longer of use on the farm. We were unconcerned about the fate of the dog on the satellite. Our minds were focussed on previously unimagined possibilities. We may have been in the gutter but we were looking at the stars.

Just a few weeks later, on November 19, the doctor arrived with his brown leather bag. This time, we knew what to expect as we were sent off to play with the neighbouring children. When we returned, a new baby brother was waiting for us. Kieran arrival brought the number of children in the family to six.

After delivering the baby, the doctor handed him to my father and said:

"This boy could grow up to be the first man to walk on the moon."

My fathers scepticism could best be summarised by the title of the current hit by Buddy Holly and the Crickets, "That'll Be The Day!" In 1969, when the first man walked on the moon and Kieran was only ten years old, my father admitted that the doctor's prediction had seemed utterly implausible. He had considered it unlikely that a moon landing would happen during his own lifetime but was willing to concede that Kieran might live to see it.

Music was an integral part of our family life during this period. My father continued to practise his fiddle-playing and his singing in the house and he played in dance-halls or marquees every weekend. We children sometimes waited on the road on Sunday evenings, keeping watch for the car, usually driven by Matt MacDonagh or Johnny Brady, that would collect my father and the other band members. The unmistakable shape of the double-bass, covered in canvas and secured to the roof-rack, enabled us to identify the car as it crossed Drumineen railway bridge, one and a half miles away as the crow flies. We excitedly dashed inside to warn my father that the car would arrive in a few minutes before scrambling to establish which one of us would be lucky enough to carry his fiddle case to the front gate.

If the dance-hall was in one of the local Mayo towns, he would not be picked up until after teatime. But the band often secured dates in far away locations such as Croom in Limerick or Stranorlar in Donegal. These venues were over one hundred miles away so that the band had to leave in the mid afternoon. Six or seven musicians were wedged into a large car or station wagon together with musical instruments and some basic amplification. The journey to the dance venue could take up to four hours because of the weight of the laden vehicle, the poor state of the road system, and the need to drive at a crawl through endless towns and villages en route. After the dance finished in the early morning hours, the car had to be reloaded. A quick meal or sandwiches provided by the promoter was consumed before the band set out on another four-hour homeward trek. Sometimes, a vehicle break-down or a puncture resulted in further delays.

My father had to be at work at 8 am on Monday morning. On quite a few occasions, I recall him arriving home at 7am, hurriedly having breakfast, and changing into his work clothes before cycling off to work.

Why did he put himself through this?

The main motivation was the opportunity to earn extra money. His wages as a railway labourer were low, especially when overtime was unavailable. There were now eight mouths to feed and, as my father would say with a smile "These growing children would eat you out of house and home".

But the additional family income from music was not the only attraction for my father. Playing music provided him with a means of recreation; a contrast to the physical work during the day. The camaraderie with other musicians as they played and travelled was also a bonus. But most of all, he loved performing on stage, displaying his musicianship and his singing ability.

The Bush radio, glowing softly and nestling on the wooden shelf crafted by my grandfather, seemed to be permanently tuned to some music programme. Mary softly hummed along, her fingernails clicking in time on her biscuit-tin lid. Patricia, Michael, and I were also interested in music as a result of our father's musicianship and our mother's love of the radio. There wasn't much on radio to catch our childish attention apart from the odd novelty song such as "The Yellow Rose of Texas" by Mitch Miller or energetic songs such as Lonnie Donegan's "Rock Island Line" and "This Ole House" by Rosemary Clooney. Guy Mitchell singing "She Wears Red Feathers", Doris Day's "Secret Love" or Ruby Murray with "Softly, Softly" were aimed at a grown-up, even middle-aged radio listenership. My father practised singing songs by Sinatra, Tony Bennett or Dean Martin but "Three Coins in a Fountain", "Stranger in Paradise" or "Memories Are Made Of This" were not destined to attract our childish imagination.

All was about to change. Suddenly, there was a different kind of music on the radio and, more interestingly, arguments and disagreements about it. A new vocabulary filtered through the airwaves: "juvenile delinquency", "rock and roll", "Bill Haley and the Comets", "Elvis Presley".

Although aged six or seven, I was already interested in pop music and was constantly listening for new songs on the radio. Gradually, the new talked-about music began to filter through, mainly on the sponsored programmes and was often introduced with a disapproving tone by presenters. I quite liked "Shake, Rattle and Roll" and "Rock Around the Clock" by Bill Haley and The Comets. I distinctly remember being unimpressed by my first hearing of Elvis Presley, who was garnering much comment on the radio. Unlike the Bill Haley hits, which were reminiscent of earlier songs such as "This Ole House", "Heartbreak Hotel" was unlike anything I'd heard before. Perhaps because of the primal sound and the staccato arrangement, the song didn't hold any attraction for me. In fact, I found it a little disturbing. I wondered what all the fuss was about until "Hound Dog" burst over the airwaves soon afterwards. I was hooked. "All Shook Up", "Blue Suede Shoes", "Don't Be Cruel", "Don't" followed. Elvis was my hero.

I realise now that my father's response to rock and roll had a major influence on my developing taste. Unlike most grown-ups, he was very taken by the new music. He listened to it and talked to us about what he called "the backing" which encompassed the arrangements, musicianship and the sound of the recordings. He soon knew that Scotty Moore was the guitarist on the Presley records and he also had great admiration for the background vocal contributions of the Jordanaires.

I wasn't blindly following my father's lead. The half-singing, half-screaming of Little Richard on "Lucille" and "Tutti Frutti" didn't particularly appeal to him but I loved it. He revised his view later when, Pat Boone, whom he disliked, had hits with songs previously popularised by Little Richard.

"I'm inclined to forgive that Little Richard fellow when I listen to that other *amadán.*"

Perhaps inevitably, it was music emanating from New Orleans that made the greatest impact on my father at this time. Fats Domino dominated the radio waves in the autumn of 1956 with "Blueberry Hill".

"Shush! Let Daddy hear the radio."

A hush fell on the household as Domino's distinctive piano style, accompanied by the fat sound of his backing band filled the room. That lazy, warm voice added to the intoxicating mixture and drove the song along but the best part was still to come. After a verse and chorus, there was almost invariably eight bars of a melodic, inventive, and utterly appropriate tenor sax solo. The power of the solo was such that it redefined what had gone before. When Fat's vocal resumed, it was as if you were listening to the song anew.

Of course, when I first began to listen to Fats Domino, I didn't know or care why his music appealed to me. I just knew that I loved it and that was enough. It was only in later years, when I analysed the music and discussed it at length with my father, that I began to appreciate its complex simplicity. By then, we knew that the Dave Bartholemew Band, which contained some of the foremost New Orleans musicians, was the backing band for the recording sessions. The timeless sax solos, models of economy and melodic inventiveness, were played by Lee Allen and, more often, by Herb Hardesty. In addition to the better known hits, we listened to, discussed, and bonded over such lesser known Fats recordings as "Blue Monday" and "When My Dreamboat Comes Home".

The new music was soon having an impact on the Irish dance scene. The days of the old style dance-bands were numbered even before rock and roll emerged. Previously, the musicians played while seated, attired in tuxedos or band uniforms. The Clipper Carlton were the band credited with the innovation of standing and moving on stage as they played. They also endeavoured to provide more entertainment and variety in their act. Showbands, as the new ensembles were called, were soon in demand around the country and the older style bands were forced to adapt or go out of business.

Standing still on stage and playing the old tunes was not enough any longer. Dancers were demanding the new music and the traditional line-up of double-bass, drums, brass section and either a piano or an accordion was ill-equipped to cope adequately. There were few guitars and even fewer electric basses in the west of Ireland in the mid 1950s. My father recognised that, while he could still rely on getting work as a vocalist, his violin playing was almost inaudible, even when he played close to the microphone. He decided to innovate by electrifying his fiddle. He discussed his options with Johnny Reidy, a local man who sold and repaired radio sets. The result was a combined amplifier and speaker, built and designed by Johnny Reidy. My father acquired a pick-up which he attached to the fiddle.

The fiddle shrieked and whistled in protest as my father struggled with feedback, one of the perils of amplified music. There were experiments with changing my fathers position relative to the placement of the amplifier and with raising and lowering the volume. Johnny Reidy also made some technical adjustments which helped to manage the problem. My father appreciated the additional volume and the options which it provided. He was unhappy with the tone that emanated from the speaker but realised that he would have to compromise on this. Soon, dancers were twirling around the floor to the sound of the electrified fiddle.

One of the unforeseen benefits of the change was that Michael and I no longer had to squabble about who carried the fiddle to the front gate. Now one of us toted the fiddle and the other proudly carried the new amplifier.

CHAPTER TWENTY

Green Onions

The acre of land, on which the Murneen house was situated, should have been ideal for growing potatoes and vegetables for the family table. However, doubts were soon raised regarding the feasibility of producing adequate crops from the thin layer of tired, sandy soil. Mr Conroy provided neighbourly advice to my father that, because of a lack of crop rotation and fertiliser in the past, the potato yields would be poor. Spreading farmyard manure on the land and resting it for a year would go some way towards remedying the situation, he suggested. He advised my father to speak to Tommy Keane, who owned the largest farm in the locality and, as we have seen, was regularly consulted by neighbouring farmers for assistance and advice on livestock ailments. Tommy was always anxious to get rid of some of the copious amount of farmyard manure which was a by-product of his cattle fattening operation.

Tommy was sceptical when he heard my father's plan.

"You're wasting your time with that garden, Coleman. You can take away all the manure you want - I'll be glad to get rid of it - but your heart will be broken trying to scrape a few spuds out of that place. My advice would be to let it go to grass for a few years at least. You could mow it and save the hay. There's many a local farmer would be glad to buy it from you at the back end of the year if the weather is bad and fodder is scarce. You could get your missus to pray for a bit of frost or snow. That'll get the selling price up, if God is willing."

This was our first introduction to Tommy Keane, who would have a telling impact on our lives in Murneen. He was unmarried man, aged about fifty, who lived with his mother on their farm of over one hundred acres downhill from our house. In an area where the average farm comprised fewer than twenty acres, Keane's farm size was quite unusual. Tommy was popular in the neighbourhood and not just because of his animal husbandry skills. His plain-spoken, irreverent, and witty demeanour made a positive first impression. As one got to know him better, he revealed himself as a voracious reader with an enquiring intellect.

"Tommy Keane was the first man I ever heard talking about the Common Market", my father would say many years later. "He was telling me about the advantages for Irish farmers of selling all over Europe and not just to England. It wasn't even being talked about on the radio at that time but he used to read the Farmers Journal from cover to cover."

Another of Tommy's qualities was his popularity with women. He combined an old style, respectful, courtesy with a vaguely flirtatious, roguish *plámás* which never failed to illicit a smile. He would pause from his work to greet a farmer's wife as she passed by his hay field, carrying her filled water-bucket from the well on a summer evening.

"God bless the work, Tommy."

He fractionally raise his ever-present hat in salute as he responded.

"Isn't it wonderful what the fine weather does? Sure, doesn't everything look its best when the sun is shining?"

Was he talking about her in her summer dress or about the countryside? Did it matter? She walked on with a smile as Tommy contentedly returned to his work.

When he discouraged my father from sowing potatoes in our back garden, Tommy had a ready solution. At his bidding, the two men walked a few hundred yards down the Kilcolman road, a boreen near Keane's house.

"It's called the Gosling Garden", he said, pointing to a plot of ground comprising about a quarter of an acre adjacent to a duck-pond. It was bound on three sides by bushy fences while the fourth side opened on to the pond. Nearby, there was a farmhouse in which the relatively reclusive Delia Keane, a distant relative of Tommy, lived with her brother, Joe.

"Delia used to keep a rake of geese and ducks who spent their days swimming in the pond or scratching around and doing their business in the garden. It's the best fertilised piece of land in the parish and it was never tilled, as far as I know."

Much to my father's discomfort, Tommy flatly refused to accept an offer of a rental payment.

"You'll be doing me a favour so keep your money in your pocket. You'll need it to buy some wooden stakes and wire so that you can fence off this open side unless you want to provide free winter feed for Joe Keane's cattle, and God knows the poor creatures could do with it!"

The garden was soon fenced and my father was breaking the soil using Tommy's horse and plough.

"You'll be doing me a favour if you borrow the horse. That ould beast isn't getting half enough exercise as it is. And take as much of that manure as you can use. It's only cluttering up the yard. As I say, you'll be doing me a favour…"

The soil was deep, rich, and easy to work with. It yielded excellent crops and was to fulfil most of our family needs for vegetables over the following decade. Ridges of potatoes were soon sown in half of the garden and the remainder was planted with vegetables so that, in subsequent years, the crops could be rotated. Months later, there would be an abundance of cabbage, lettuce, carrots, parsnips, beetroot, spring onions for salads and large onions for cooking.

The garden soon became a focus for my father. He spent many of his Saturdays sowing, spraying, weeding, or harvesting the crops. When the evenings lengthened, he had a quick dinner after he returned from work before heading down to spend an hour or two in the Gosling Garden which was almost one mile away from our house. As we grew a little older, Michael and I were also dispatched after school to weed the potato and vegetable patches. When our father was digging the potatoes in the autumn, we trailed behind him with buckets, collecting the unearthed potatoes and placing them in a pit. The potatoes were then carefully covered with rushes and a thick outer layer of clay in order to protect the crop from winter frost and scavenging rats.

If properly stored and protected, potatoes and large onions would last for the full year. Carrots and parsnips could be preserved by leaving them in the ground for as long as possible. Cabbage would also be left in the ground to be cut when needed for the table. Some varieties were quite frost resistant while others needed more protection. Lettuce and spring onions would be harvested as needed but would have to be consumed before the autumn.

Another by-product of our involvement with Gosling Garden was the exposure of myself and Michael to the work practises on local farms. We quickly learned to differentiate between a plough, a scuffler, a harrow, and a grubber. We could tackle a horse or donkey and hitch the animal correctly to a cart. Our vocabulary expanded to encompass words for parts of the horse's tackle such as halter, bridle, bit, collar, hames, straddle, belly-band, britchel. We could deftly get Tommy Keane's horse into position, connect the traces to a swingle which was in turn hitched to the scuffler, and hand the reins to our father. We watched carefully as wide-legged, he held and steadied the handles of the scuffler, applied his weight and flicked the reins so that the horse leant forward, took the strain, and moved slowly along the furrow between the ridges. The scuffler bit deeply into the compacted earth resulting in an ample supply of soft rich clay which could later be shovelled to mould the potato ridges. Many years later, when I read Seamus Heaney's poem "Follower" in which he describes his father ploughing, I immediately recognised my own father in the Gosling Garden. "His shoulders globed like a full sail strung between the shafts and the furrow. The horse strained at his clicking tongue."

My father's job as a railwayman was reasonably secure but the trade-off was a low wage so that his supplementary earnings as a musician were essential. His other contribution towards helping the family finances was to reduce the weekly outlay on groceries. As a result of his efforts in the evenings and at weekends, we were meeting most of the family's vegetable requirements from the Gosling Garden. Following Kieran's arrival, there were eight mouths to feed in the Rushe household and, as we children were becoming bigger and stronger, our appetites expanded in proportion. Apart from the luxury of an occasional packet of cigarettes, my father's wages were available in full towards the family budget.

I now realise that my mother and father struggled to make ends meet but, at the time, we children were oblivious to their problems. The Red Lemonade Syndrome again. It did not occur to us that we were poor. Therefore, we were not poor. In fact, my childish perception was that we were better off than some of the children with whom we attended school. Poverty is relative. One can only be rich or poor in comparison to somebody else. If other local children were no better off than we were, then we did not perceive that we were poor.

My fathers weekly wage provided a steady stream of income throughout the year while other families had to rely upon the sporadic cash flow from the sale of farm and dairy produce and sometimes from the farmers' dole, a Government payment designed to offset the low earning potential of many small farms. Some farmers also took casual seasonal work to help out with the family finances. In our family, the reliability of a regular wage packet provided the illusion of prosperity but, in fact, our household income was smaller than that of many local families.

Children in the rural west of Ireland in the 1950s had few if any shop-bought toys. Pocket money was not given to children. To a child, the only real measures of economic comparison between families were food and clothing. Some children came to school with clothes which were in a poor state of disrepair. Often, the garments were either too large or too small for the wearer, having been handed down from older brothers and sisters. Other children were more fortunate. If cattle prices at the fair were favourable, some of the sale money might be diverted into the purchase of new clothes. Clothes-sellers routinely set up stalls on the fair day in order to cater for this demand. It was usual to see quite a few proud schoolboys sporting new, dark brown, corduroy, zipped jackets and knee length trousers following a successful cattle or sheep fair in Claremorris. Girls were more likely to be kitted out by visiting one of the drapery shops in the town. Shiny new boots and shoes would also be in evidence. As the year wore on, the condition of the clothes often deteriorated quite markedly and mending became the norm until replacements could be purchased. Varying levels of expertise in needlework resulted in the appearance of some strange and colourful patches. I cannot recall any instance of a child being teased or bullied because of their clothing but it would be naive of me to claim that it didn't occur.

I don't know whether she acquired her skills from my grandmother or from the nuns who educated her but my mother was very adept at knitting, sewing, or darning. She purchased wool and knitted a constant supply of jumpers, pullovers, cardigans, gloves, socks, and mittens for the family. Early photographs in Murneen show my brothers and sisters kitted out in woollen garments crafted by my mother. Aran wool sweaters and cardigans seemed to roll off her knitting needles at will. As a child, one became accustomed to being singled out by neighbouring women who would handle, stretch, and critically examine a jumper, murmuring approvingly about the quality of the knitting and the intricacy of the pattern. My mother occasionally allowed herself the luxury of purchasing a womens' magazine while doing her weekly shopping and she removed and stored the knitting patterns which were one of the main attractions of such publications. Also, my grandmother collected knitting patterns for my mother from Woman's Own, Woman's Weekly, or Woman's Realm and the patterns were exchanged among neighbouring women.

Having knitted a garment, my mother always retained the leftover wool for later use in darning and repairing. The elbows of jumpers were constantly examined for signs of wear and, before a hole could appear, she would darn and reinforce the garment in a manner which was undetectable. Socks were also constantly being repaired and reinforced in a similar manner.

A rip in a shirt or trousers was a regular occurrence as Mike and I encountered briars and thorny hedges en route to school or to the well. The offending garment was quickly removed by my eagle-eyed mother and she set to work patching or repairing. She had perfected the skill of invisible mending; small tears were repaired so that it would be difficult if not impossible to detect the handiwork unless one carefully examined the reverse of the fabric. More severe damage might necessitate the patching of the garment. Again, she matched the colours and aligned any pattern so that the patch did not attract the eye. The newly repaired clothes were then washed, dried in front of the fire, and ironed so that it felt as if you were wearing a new garment the following morning. As we went to bed, it was not unusual to see her sitting by the fire with two or three garments on her lap as she sewed, patched, and darned so that the clothes would be ready for us in the morning.

Children had to bring their own lunches to school and differences in the quantity and quality of the food were sometimes apparent. Some had cheese, tomato, or ham sandwiches but most were supplied with thick slices of home-made bread lathered with butter and topped with strawberry or raspberry jam. In most cases, the lunch was complemented by milk contained in a screw-capped bottle. Some children seemed to habitually forget to bring their lunch and accepted the offer of shared food from a friend. Occasionally, there were whisperings that some child who claimed to have forgotten his or her lunch hadn't had a breakfast either. I can recall Mr O'Leary, the Master, sometimes calling one particular boy or his brother into the classroom from the playground during lunchtime, indicating that he had an errand which he wanted done. One of the brothers later innocently let slip that the Master needed help because Mrs O'Leary had provided him with a lunch that was much too large. Mr O'Leary gave his surplus sandwiches to the boy who gratefully wolfed them down before returning to the playground. Clearly, this was the Master's strategy of helping a child whom he suspected was being underfed while doing his best to preserve the dignity of the recipient.

Mr O'Leary action reflected the local custom that you acted in a manner which did not cause embarrassment by drawing attention to the poverty or unpreparedness of your neighbour. For example, if you were dropping in unexpectedly for a brief visit to a friend or relative, you might bring a cake or some confectionary items in order to accompany the expected cup of tea. My mother was a strong advocate of such thoughtful pre-planning.

"She walked in with one arm as long as the other" was her quietly disapproving expression when a visitor failed to honour the convention.

Occasional visits to other children's houses while they were eating or when dinner was being prepared led me to realise that we were luckier than most where food was concerned. This was not due to my mother spending more money on food than her contemporaries but was entirely attributable to her exceptional skills as a cook. I'm sure that my grandmother in Cappamore passed on some cooking skills to her daughter but I suspect that my mother's background in catering was the main reason for her versatility in the kitchen. She had experience of working in a hotel and with the railway company where she was tasked with producing tasty and nutritious meals for train travellers during the war years when food supplies were scarce. The cook had to make do with whatever was available; usually farm-produced, seasonal ingredients.

One of the earliest improvements to our new house was the installation of an iron range to replace the open fire. This shining black stove was bought second-hand by my father who saw it being replaced in a railway gate-house by a more modern and fashionable model. The squat range had a grated fire-box with a drawer-like ash pan underneath. The heat circulated through a series of chambers within the range and quickly raised the temperature of the oven until it was ready for roasting or baking. Kettles, saucepans and pots could be heated by placing them side by side on top of the range. The heat under each pan could not be regulated but one could overcome this obstacle by changing its position in relation to the fire-box. A kettle or pan could be boiled more speedily by removing one of the circular cover-plates on the range-top in order to bring the container more directly in contact with the heat. Perhaps the name of the range, Nu-Turf, was intended to signify that it was suitable for burning turf. Nevertheless, coal quickly became our normal fuel, supplemented at times by turf and split blocks of wood.

My mother was delighted with the convenience of the new appliance. Any regret at the absence of the cheerful brightness of the open fire was offset by the effectiveness of the range in heating the living area. The nightly raking of the fire also became obsolete. The range had to be relit each morning by using twisted newspaper and slivers of wood or brittle twigs which we children collected and left to dry in a wooden box under the stove.

The range afforded my mother the opportunity to give full rein to her cooking skills. I now realise that she was economising by using the cheapest cuts of meat but, at the time, we regarded her creations as delicacies which became our firm favourites.

Cuts of mutton were combined with onions, carrots and potatoes to make delicious stews.

Roasted sheeps' hearts, stuffed with breadcrumbs and onion, were mouthwatering for dinner or tasted even better when sliced for school sandwiches the following day.

Boiled bacon with mounds of white cabbage and floury potatoes were a perennial favourite. When white cabbage was not in season, it was replaced with the stronger flavour of curly kale.

Other favourite dishes which were accompanied by cabbage were bacon shanks, *crubeens* (as pigs' trotters were known), and pig's head. Shanks also tasted just as good when sliced and served cold in sandwiches or, during summertime, in salads with lettuce and onions from Gosling Garden.

The garden also provided a steady supply of turnips, carrots, and parsnips which were boiled or sometimes roasted to accompany various dishes.

Oxtails served the double purpose. They producing delicious soup while the slow-cooked meat, falling off the bone, was served with potatoes and vegetables from the garden.

Less expensive cuts of beef, mutton, and lamb were roasted. One of my mother's specialties was her ability to produce, as if by magic, wonderful gravy from the meat dishes. We watched in fascination as she removed the cooked meat from the baking tin, added boiling water to the residual meat juices, added flour, salt and pepper and, tilting the tray precariously from side to side, mixed the thickening liquid with a wooden spoon. The inevitable outcome was delicious thick gravy which was poured or spooned over meat, vegetables and potatoes.

Meat for dinner was purchased at Clarke's butcher shop in

Claremorris or at a small shop in the nearby bacon factory where some cheaper cuts were sold. Over time, the butchers in Clarkes would become aware of the shopping budgets of individual customers and the cuts of meat which they preferred. In my teenage years, I was sometimes delegated by my mother to call to the butchers on my cycle home from school in order to buy some items of meat.

"It's for Mrs Rushe", I said as instructed.

Sometimes, a butcher looked quizzically.

"Your mother or your grandmother?"

"My mother."

"Grand, so".

The cuts of meat which my mother preferred were selected and parcelled. Dignity and privacy were preserved.

Local tradition and custom dictated that the whole village benefitted when a neighbouring farmer killed a pig. Cuts of meat were distributed among friends and neighbours. Black and white pudding was produced by stuffing the entrails of the pig with a mixture of dried blood, oatmeal, and seasoning. After cooking, the puddings were left hanging to cool and dry before being gifted to neighbouring families.

Another annual culinary treat, which was not to everybody's taste, was provided by the availability of lambs' tails. Many local farmers kept a flock of sheep so that a brood of lambs were born each spring. For hygiene purposes, it was considered necessary to dock their tails when the lambs were a few weeks old. We asked the farmer to keep a dozen tails for us even though my mother refused to cook them. We took the tails to Mr Gavin, a neighbour, and watch as he first utilised a hand-held shears to remove as much wool as possible from the tails. He then placed on the hearth some crushed turf from the open fire and positioned the tails briefly on the glowing embers. This had the effect of burning off the remaining wool while slightly toasting the surface of the tails. The tails were then fried in a pan. Eating the delicious tails could only be managed adequately by holding the food in both hands as if one were consuming corn on the cob until all that was left was the bony centre.

Other foods which were available occasionally included mushrooms which we picked in the fields in the early morning and deliciously fried with butter. Duck-eggs, which were larger and more flavoursome than hen-eggs, were a particular favourite of my mother.

In this era before Vatican Two, meat eating was prohibited for Catholics on Fridays so that fish was the obvious alternative. Strangely, herrings seemed to be the only variety of fish which was consumed by the people in our locality at that time. If you had occasion to cycle to town on a Friday, custom dictated that you check with neighbours beforehand in order to see whether they needed herrings. Armed with your order, you visited one of the few shops in town which arranged to have a weekly supply of fish. Having ensured that the herrings were fresh, by checking that the eyes were still red, you purchased the requisite number, had them wrapped in sheets of newspaper and transported them back to Murneen for distribution. Cleaning, gutting, and preparing herrings for the frying pan were skills which children learned at an early stage.

If fresh herrings were not available, the fall-back meal on a Friday was cally, another favourite. Boiled potatoes were mashed with butter and a little milk and sprinkled with chopped spring onions.

On rare occasions, our fish consumption took a more exotic turn. If my father was working at Ballina railway station, he was sometimes offered the opportunity to buy a fresh salmon by one of the fishermen on the River Moy nearby. Occasionally, after much haggling and feigned disinterest he would agree to buy the fish while claiming that he was doing the seller a favour. My mother gratefully received the fish and another memorable meal ensued.

We once benefitted when a neighbour was given a brace of quail as a present. Not knowing how to cook the exotic birds and having no desire to eat such unusual meat, the neighbour passed on the quail to my mother in the knowledge that, if anybody could make them edible, she could.

Although we had poultry scratching about in the garden, we seldom ate chicken. Rather than kill and eat a chicken, it made more economic sense to retain the birds in order to have an ample supply of fresh eggs for the family table. But older hens who were no longer producing eggs, were sometimes killed for the dinner-table. Being unsuitable for roasting, they were slowly boiled. The result was mouth-watering chicken soup as well as meat falling off the bone.

Early potatoes were harvested from July onwards and were eagerly anticipated. The previous years potatoes would be getting tired by then but their age could be disguised by mashing them and adding butter and a little milk.

Strangely, despite my mother's ability to produce food with diverse and delicious flavours, I have no memory of her using spices and herbs apart from an occasional sprig of parsley. She persevered with food which was grown and produced locally. I did not encounter pasta, pizza, or curry dishes until after I left home aged seventeen.

Apples, which were sometimes purchased from neighbours, and rhubarb from our own garden were used to produce baked tarts and pies. My mother also baked copious supplies of soda bread and scones. More occasionally, she baked fruit cakes, currant scones, and, a particular favourite of mine, porter cake, which was flavoured with Guinness. She also produced boiled fruit cakes at Christmas for home use and for distribution among friends and relatives. Pancakes and potato-cakes were seasonal delicacies.

Desserts consisted of apple or rhubarb tart accompanied by smooth custard, jelly, and whipped cream. On special occasions, sherry trifle and cream brought dinner to a memorable conclusion.

Where food was concerned, the quality of the cooking was not my mother's only obsession. She had a conviction that we should have a hot breakfast each morning. The time of year or the weather did not matter; a hot breakfast was mandatory.

A fried breakfast on Monday morning helped to make the beginning of the school week slightly more acceptable. We routinely had a breakfast of fried eggs, bacon rashers, sausages, black and white pudding on Sunday mornings and some of the uncooked leftover food was used on Monday morning when fried bread was added. The fare would vary as the week went on. One regular was porridge, sweetened with sugar and cooled with milk. Over time, cornflakes were added to the breakfast menu but always with boiled milk. Boiled or scrambled eggs were another staple. In the winter, if the hens weren't laying and perhaps because cash was scarce, improvisation was necessary. Fried bread covered with a generous dollop of fried onions made a warm and tasty breakfast. Another alternative was to use some of the thin slices of luncheon roll which was bought for school sandwiches. The slices were lightly fried and eaten with fried bread or perhaps a fried egg.

The quantity, quality, and variety of our food was excellent despite a constrained budget. A close observer at our table might recognise some signs of a lack of disposable income, particularly in the early years. Although soup was a regular staple at dinner times, we did not possess soup dishes. Instead, we used mugs and teacups from which we sipped or spooned our soup. If the soup was hot, it could be cooled by pouring a small amount onto a saucer, from which the liquid could be sipped. This practise was soon outlawed by my mother who considered the slurping unmannerly. Porridge at breakfast was served on dinner plates - by the time we were introduced to corn-flakes, we had already acquired dessert dishes which we could use for cereals. Salt for the table was contained in an egg-cup. For some reason, this practise continued even after we acquired a salt cellar.

CHAPTER TWENTY-ONE

Mystery Train

One of the perks of my father's job as a railway worker was his entitlement to claim a limited number of free family train tickets each year. This benefit enabled us to journey south each summer to Cappamore in order to spend some weeks with my mother's family. My earliest memories of these holidays in Cappamore are from the mid 1950s but family photos reveal that we were regular visitors as toddlers.

Following weeks of excited preparations, my mother piled all four of us and our luggage into a hackney car - another rare treat - and brought us to Claremorris railway station to catch the Sligo to Limerick train. If my father happened to be working at the station, he would be on the platform to wave us off, promising to join us a few weeks later.

As we impatiently craned our necks in an effort to be the first to see the approaching train, my mother issued warnings about the dangers of standing too close to the platform edge. We furtively watched her at the kiosk as she bought a newspaper and also clandestinely purchased some comics and chocolate which she produced later in the journey to combat boredom or to reward good behaviour. We excitedly boarded the train and my mother assigned seats while admonishing us that exemplary behaviour was mandatory. Finally, the doors were slammed shut and the train guard importantly waved the green flag as the station slowly slid away behind us.

We counted down the railway stations as we travelled. Ballindine. Milltown. Tuam. Ballyglunin. Athenry. Craughwell. Ardrahan. Gort. Crusheen. Ennis. Sixmilebridge. Finally we crossed the slow, wide Shannon river and approached Limerick city. A change of trains was necessary here and we were shepherded by my mother onto the local train for the short journey to Drumkeen where we were met by a hackney car which transported us the final three miles to my grandparents' house.

I would hesitate to undertake such a journey now with one small child. Yet, my mother seemed to manage the four of us effortlessly on our annual trips to Limerick. When Sean and Kieran were later added to the group, the older ones were expected to help by tending to the younger children. Nevertheless, the pressure and responsibility on my mother must have been enormous. How did she cope?

For a start, we were well behaved. I do not say this to praise us or to signify that we had better characters than other children. Character and behaviour are often confused nowadays. One regularly hears people self-importantly justify a statement or action which has offended others by saying: "I speak as I feel. That's just the way I am."

No, it isn't the way you are! It's the way you choose to behave, which is quite a different thing.

Each of us makes a choice about how we want to behave. Over time, we may develop a habit of unthinkingly behaving in a certain manner but we still have a choice. Good behaviour in our family was mandatory. It was made clear to us from an early age that there were boundaries which we must not cross and that there were consequences for inappropriate behaviour or "bad manners", to use the usual terminology.

Before each journey, the additional rules to apply were made clear to us. On the train, we were each allocated a seat in which we were expected to remain for the duration of the journey unless my mother allowed us to switch places so that we could take turns in a window-seat. Toilets on trains were for emergency use, we were told. We were expected to use the toilet before we left home and this was expected to be sufficient until we reached Cappamore. If there was a delay before our connecting train in Limerick, we might use the toilet at the station but even this was discouraged. The only exception to this strategy was Mary whom my mother would take for an occasional precautionary visit to the toilet on the train, having first quietly warned us about our behaviour while she was absent and sometimes asked a fellow passenger to keep an eye on us.

Sandwiches, which my mother had prepared beforehand, would be produced during the journey to "keep us going" until we reached Cappamore. In order to minimise the need for toilet visits, there were no drinks. Boredom could also be alleviated and good behaviour rewarded by production of comics or chocolate from my mother's seemingly bottomless bag.

But the behavioural boundaries and occasional rewards and distractions do not tell the full story. Mary required special attention from my mother but otherwise tended to sit quietly and distractedly. The other three of us were healthy, boisterous bundles of energy. We knew that there were rules and indeed consequences but we were not cowed into submission by overbearing parenting. Why were we not making noise, fighting, and racing along the passageway in a manner of childhood behaviour which is acceptable to many parents now?

When my wife and I moved to live in Spain, one of the first major differences we noticed was the behaviour of young Spanish children when compared to children of similar age in the UK and Ireland. Previous experience had taught us to shudder apprehensively when a family group including young children sat at an adjacent table in a restaurant. In Ireland and the UK, seemingly within minutes, the children would be leaving their seats, scampering around between nearby tables, making repeated visits to the toilets, making noise, and generally seeking attention. There might occasionally be half-hearted admonishments from embarrassed parents. More often, the parents would be oblivious to or unconcerned by the impact of the disturbance. Gameboys, iPads, mobile phones, and other devices, invariably played at maximum volume, might be used to provide some temporary if short-lived distraction.

In Spain, or at least in Andalusia, the southern autonomous region where we live, the normal interaction between parent and child is completely different. An hour or two after being seated the child will still be sitting happily in the same chair. I began to observe the manner in which the family interacted and quickly identified the key to the behaviour - communication. Clearly, boundaries are established and understood but the real impact is created by the fact that the child is constantly being spoken to and fussed over by parents, siblings, grandparents, aunts, and uncles. Waiters and waitresses will also casually hug and kiss the children. The child is never bored or ignored.

The Spanish are as wedded to their mobile phones as the rest of us. Yet, children always seen to take priority. I recently watched a young holiday-making, English-speaking mother seated in a Chinese restaurant with her young daughter. The mother was busily tapping on the keyboard of her smartphone while the young girl was eating and making repeated attempts to engage her mother in conversation.

"Can't you see Mummy is busy? Just eat your food and be quiet!"
Some Spanish people watched in astonishment from a nearby table.

The Spanish method of interacting with children is evident on the streets also. Little children are collected from school and can be heard chattering with parents or family members as they walk home. While out walking on one occasion, I slowed my pace, sidled up near a mother and small boy and listened. In spite of my limited knowledge of Spanish and the distinctive local accent, I picked up fragments of conversation as they chatted about school until the child's attention was diverted by some birds. Now they chattered about nests, trees, bird-cages, and bird-song. Suddenly, due to the mention of birdsong, I was transported back half a few decades.

In Murneen many years ago, my brother Mike mischievously placed a cassette tape recorder on the kitchen table as my mother chatted to a woman neighbour. Mike was on a visit to my parents and was accompanied by one of his sons, aged four or five. Mike's intention was to record the two women gossiping and to use it later to poke gentle fun at my mother. He forgot about the tape recorder and went to a bedroom to have a nap. The neighbour left shortly afterwards so that my mother was alone with her young grandson. When Mike listened to the recording later, he heard the soundtrack of our childhood...

With birdsong in the background, my mother went about her housework, constantly talking to her grandchild, engaging him, and eventually encouraging him to respond. Through the open window, the twittering of birds in the nearby trees can be heard together with the clanging of saucepans and pots. Lego pieces click on the tiled floor.

"That's the good boy! You're going playing with the Lego... Wasn't it God that left it?... You can play over there... David left it... Now! Sit down there on the floor. That's the good boy... That's the great ladeen. Aren't you? ...Now. That's the great boy... You're a great boy, aren't you?..

Encouraged, the child eventually responded.

"Look at this."

"Isn't that nice? Weren't you in the luck that they were here, weren't you?"

"Whose are these things?"

"Them are David's."

"It's just like Pat's thing".

"Yea. Isn't it? Is that like Pat's?"

"Pat got Lego."

"Did Pat get Lego?"

"From Santa."

"Santa! Did he?"

"Mmmm."

As the tape concluded, the child is happily playing with his Lego and engaging chattily with his grandmother. If necessary, he will happily remain there on the kitchen floor for an hour or two, playing contentedly and responding to my mother's prompting as she does her housework. As I listen to the tape or to the chattering of the Spanish family, I am transported back to my own early youth in Murneen and the sound of my mother's voice as she praised, encouraged, cajoled, directed, enlightened, and admonished. This constant engagement ensured our good behavior, both inside and outside the home

Although Cappamore is only one hundred miles south, it felt as if we were entering another world. Sights and sounds were different. We had to adjust to new vocabulary and local accents. Sport and games were unlike those to which we were accustomed. It even seemed that we were in a different timezone.

My grandparents' small farm was situated at the edge of the town. Each morning, we awoke to the steady clopping of hooves and the jingling of harness as convoys of horse-drawn carts laden with large, metal, milk-filled containers made their way to the creamery. The local farmland was on the edge of the Golden Vale, the richest milk producing area of Ireland. Each farm delivered its own milk daily to the creamery for conversion into butter.

On Sunday mornings, the sounds were similar but this time the horses were pulling traps and side-cars which ferried families to Mass in Cappamore church nearby. Each of these vehicles had its own traditionally used spot where the horse was tethered during Mass. Some were located inside my grandparents' farmyard and others on the road outside.

Even sport and recreation was different. At home in Mayo, football and occasionally, handball helped to pass a Sunday afternoon or an idle evening. Here, hurling was the popular sport and the breeding and training of greyhounds for coursing and racing was also a local passion.

There was a distinctive local accent but we were familiar with this because my mother still spoke with an east Limerick lilt. Nevertheless, some of the language idiosyncrasies confused or amused us. For example, the word "lads" could refer to either sex and not just to males.

"Are the lads coming home this year?"

This question was raised regularly by friends of the family in Cappamore and we soon discerned that the "lads" were our two aunts, the nuns who were based in England.

The local sights, sounds, and pastimes gave Cappamore an otherworldly feel to us. They did things differently here and this impression was compounded by the attitude and approach to time. At home, the clocks went back or forward an hour in the spring and autumn. In Cappamore, my grandparents had two clocks; one, which never changed, was set to winter time or "old time". The other "new time" clock was put forward by one hour in spring and put back in autumn. The local practise, as far as I could discern it, was to milk the cows and deliver the milk using "old time". The radio was in "new time" as were the trains and Sunday masses. If you enquired about the start time of a hurling match, the answer might be: "Two o'clock. Old time."

The local cinema was another big attraction for us in Cappamore. There was a cinema in Claremorris but I seldom got an opportunity to attend because of the distance from Murneen. But in Cappamore, we went to the "pictures" at least once a week, usually in the company of our Auntie Philomena but sometimes alone. We craved an unending supply of cowboy films.

The exotic cinema… The local accent and linguistics… Waking to the clopping of hooves… The ubiquity of greyhounds and hurling... Being in a constant state of confusion regarding whether to add or deduct an hour in order to convert new time into old time… These things resulted in a feeling of otherworldliness and added to the mystique of Cappamore.

Our disappointment at having to return home after a few weeks was tempered by our excitement at the arrival of my father who had remained at home because of his work. While we were away, he called to my grandparents each evening for his dinner before cycling home to Murneen. He took a weeks holiday in early August and travelled by train to Cappamore to join us. He would try unsuccessfully to keep a straight face as he explained that he had given up hope that we were ever returning home so that he had no option but to travel to Cappamore to drag us back to Murneen. He and my mother would take us to Cappamore Agricultural Show and to the local Mulcair river where we paddled and splashed happily for hours. We were reluctant to leave but at least Daddy would be travelling with us on the return journey. The realisation that we would be home a few days before the Claremorris Agricultural Show, another yearly treat, also lifted our spirits.

As far as I can recall, we were unique among our friends in that we had a lengthy holiday away from our home area. This was possible because we had grandparents who lived in another county. The extended families of other children lived locally so that a visit to relatives did not afford an opportunity to get away from home for a few days or weeks. Of course, it was theoretically possible for families to go to the seaside for a week or two but the cost of such a holiday made it an unrealistic option for families in our locality. Luckily for us, my father's entitlement to free train travel for the family meant that it did not cost any more to go to Cappamore than to remain at home.

CHAPTER TWENTY-TWO
Magic Moments

"Games have always been a serious business for the human species, though their true significance has not always been recognised. In contemporary Western society, shaped by the industrial revolution, they are the vehicles for millions of inarticulate and possibly unattainable dreams."
- Derek Birley.

Games, both indoor and out, were an important feature of our childhood. Football, which in our case meant Gaelic football, was our main sporting passion but was by no means the only outlet for our competitive energy. We played conkers, tig, and hide'n'seek on our way to school. Inspired by films we had seen in Cappamore, we improvised games of cowboys and indians. Indoors, we played card games, draughts, and other board games.

Dusky summer evenings were punctuated by the dull muffled thump of the ball and the shouts, grunts, and groans of a few neighbouring boys as they played a game of football in a nearby field. I escaped from the house as often as possible to participate. If nobody else was available to play, I press-ganged Mike into action or I practised my catching and kicking skills against the side wall of the house.

We were encouraged to participate in games and sport by my parents who used the opportunity to improve our social skills. "Play fair!" and "Don't play rough!" were constant admonishments. My mother chided us if we displayed any sign of being a bad loser. Being a bad winner, by bragging or displaying conceit, was viewed as an equally reprehensible trait.

Passion for sport is, of course, not confined to those who play the games. When Derek Birley wrote the words quoted at the head of this chapter in his book The Willow Wand, he was referring to the inarticulate and possibly unattainable dreams of those whom he referred to as non-participant supporters. These dreams were nigh unattainable if the team being supported had little prospect of winning a major trophy. In Ireland, allegiance to a team or to an individual sportsperson was traditionally determined by geographical location. You supported the team or sportsperson from your town or county, irrespective of their prospects of success. Of course, you craved good results and, ideally, trophies, but failure to achieve success would never result in a switching of allegiance from your local team.

When Birley wrote his book in 1976, he noted the increasing trend of people bestowing their allegiance on teams with which they have no geographical connection. High profile football clubs such as Manchester United and Barcelona have loyal fans throughout the world. Many clubs and teams now focus their marketing strategies on expanding their fan bases both at home and overseas. Football clubs continue to have a core of fans from their local area but, increasingly, supporters are pledging their allegiance based upon factors other than where they live or were born. The criteria used by football fans when selecting a club to support are varied but a craving to be associated with success and glamour appears to be a prime motivator.

In Ireland, Gaelic sport has always bucked this trend and it continues to do so. Support for club and county are dictated solely by geographical factors. You support the county in which you were born unless you relocated at a young age to another county. In that case, it was acceptable to support your new county or a county with a strong familial connection.

All our family were Mayo supporters and continue to be despite the notorious lack of success of the county on the football field. My father was born in County Roscommon but moved to Mayo when he was four years old so that his allegiance was to Mayo. As in many other matters, my mother did not adhere to the orthodox when it came to supporting a county. Coming from hurling obsessed east Limerick, she had no interest in football until she came to Mayo. She pragmatically but passionately supported the Limerick hurling team and the Mayo football team for the rest of her life.

Our childhood support for the Mayo county team and the local Claremorris club were encouraged and abetted by my parents. On summer Sundays, my father regularly took Patricia, Michael and me on train trips to Tuam, Castlebar, Roscommon, and Charlestown to see Mayo playing in the Connacht Championship. With a few of my mother's sandwiches tucked in our pockets we joined the crowds as they approached the playing field and listened to my father's instructions.

"Join hands and don't let go. But if you do, go and wait at that spot over there under the flag. I'll come and find you. If you're frightened, talk to a Guard. You'll see them all around. Mind that flag or you'll poke somebody's eye out. Now, come on. All together."

As we sat on the concrete seating and watched the teams parading behind the brass band, he pointed out notable players, explaining that we should appreciate great footballers from other counties apart from our own. We soon came to admire Willie Casey of Mayo, Packy McGarty of Leitrim, Gerry O'Malley and Aidan Brady of Roscommon, Mickey Kearins of Sligo and Frank Stockwell and Sean Purcell of Galway

"Here's Paddy! Good man, Paddy, ya boy ya!"

We watched as the familiar figure of a rosette-wearing man trotted on to the field and, to the encouraging cheers of the crowd, placed himself in front of the band. As the Mayo team paraded around the ground, he childishly lead the way, beaming innocently and proudly.

"That's Paddy Blewitt, the Mayo mascot. If anybody made fun of him, the crowd wouldn't allow it. And rightly so. Mayo people are basically decent."

We knew that my father wasn't just just speaking about Paddy Blewitt. He was telling us how he expected Mary to be treated and how we had a responsibility to ensure that she was protected. Although Mary was routinely involved in family outings and activities, it would have been unsafe to subject her to the crowds and noise of a match day. My mother later became a regular attender at football matches but, in these early years, she remained at home to look after Mary.

My mother was more actively involved in encouraging and facilitating our other sporting passion. Michael and I developed a keen interest in boxing; not as participants but as avid radio listeners. We scanned the radio listings and the sports pages in the Irish Independent each day for information on upcoming fights. BBC radio commentators such as Harry Carpenter and Eamonn Andrews routinely covered bouts and we soon became familiar with heavyweights Brian London and Henry Cooper, middleweight Terry

Downes and welterweight Wally Swift. We were particularly fascinated by the rivalry between Belfast bantamweights, John Caldwell and Freddie Gilroy, which culminated in an epic battle in The King's Hall in Belfast. My mother insisted that our homework had to be completed before allowing us to listen to these fights on BBC radio.

The fights which generated the greatest excitement for us were the heavyweight bouts for the world title. We were familiar with Floyd Patterson and I recall our surprise when he was defeated by Ingemar Johansson in 1959. We listened as Patterson tussled regularly with Johansson over the following two years, winning back his title in the process. Patterson was our firm favourite so that we were disappointed when he was trampled by Sonny Liston in 1962. Soon, we were marvelling at the glamour, ability, and bravado of the young Cassius Clay who sweet-talked the sport of boxing out of the sweaty gym and triumphantly placed it on the world stage. Suddenly, it seemed that everybody was a boxing fan.

The timing of bouts was the problem for fans such as Mike and me. Most of the world heavyweight title fights were held in New York in the evening and were broadcast world-wide on radio. But, because of the time difference, the live radio broadcast was heard in Ireland in the early hours of the morning. No problem, said my mother. She set her alarm clock for 2 or 3 am and roused us from our beds in time for the fight. Mike and I huddled around the still warm range, sometimes wearing overcoats over our pyjamas, listening to the radio and sipping milk which our mother had heated for us.

As was my habit, I was slow in getting out of bed when my mother called us for the much anticipated Liston - Patterson fight in 1962. When I walked into the kitchen, Michael and my mother told me that the fight was finished. Liston had knocked Patterson out after about two minutes.

My father regaled us with tales of Joe Louis and Jack Dempsey whose fights he had listened to decades earlier. He also had the advantage of seeing highlights of the bouts on the cinema newsreel. Because he had to get up early for work in the morning, my father did not join us as we listened to the early morning radio. He was happy to receive a blow by blow account of the fight from us after he arrived home from work.

My mother had no interest in boxing but she facilitated our enthusiasm and she listened and sat with us before packing us off to bed as soon as the broadcast was finished. While we were probably aware that other parents did not make such efforts on behalf of their children, we did not give my mother's generosity much thought. This was the way our family functioned, we reasoned. The Red Lemonade Syndrome again.

My father had an obsession with promises. He regarded a promise as a binding pact which was made with another person. Failure to keep it was a breach of trust. Promises were not to be made casually and must not be easily cast aside when circumstances changed. He explained to us that we would be judged and measured based upon our steadfastness in keeping our promises. We were discouraged from casually and thoughtlessly giving undertakings which we might not be able to discharge. He led by example.

We were still living in Streamstown when my parents organised a Sunday family outing to Galway in order to spend a day at the seaside in Salthill. Arrangements were made for a hackney car to take us to and from the railway station and my father had pre-booked a family ticket for the train. On the morning of the trip, I had a stomach bug, and was unable to travel. As all arrangements had been made, it was hastily decided that I would be left to recover with my grand-parents while the remainder of the family travelled to Galway. I was in tears with disappointment as I was being dropped off at my grandparents' house. My mother tried to comfort me as she put me to bed.

"Daddy says that he'll make it up to you. He'll bring you to the seaside some other time. Just you and him. Won't that be nice?"

I refused to be consoled as they left without me.

On a Saturday night some weeks later, by which time I had completely forgotten about the disappointment, my mother told me that I needed to be in bed early because Daddy was taking me to Galway the following morning.

"If Daddy says he'll do something, he always does it. You should know that by now."

The following day, I was on the carrier of his bike en route to the railway station for our day-trip to Galway. Memories of the day are sketchy. Eating chocolate on the beach. Watching swimmers racing and splashing into the sea from the diving platform at Salthill. Visiting relatives of my grandfather who lived in the city. And, most precious of all, being alone with my father for the whole day. And learning that promises must be kept...

Another promise resulted in a day-trip in the late 1950s. Unusually, a school outing to Dublin was being organised for children attending Ballyfarna National School. It was planned that the participants would travel by bus, visit the National Museum, and possibly Dublin Zoo. Excitedly, Michael and I brought home news of the proposed outing. Our mother was non-committal but ominously reminded us that, because of the cost, not all children from the school would be able to go on the trip.

A day or two later, our parents explained to us that it did not make sense to pay for a bus trip to Dublin when we could travel on the train free of charge. Instead, Daddy would arrange a family ticket to take us to Dublin and Patricia could come with us. In order to assuage our disappointment at being left out of the school trip, we were promised that we could plan how we would spend the day in Dublin. I suspect that my parents guessed that a trip to the National Museum, however commendable and educational, was not on our list of priorities and they took advantage of this in order to make their proposal more palatable.

One Saturday morning, a few weeks after the official school trip, Patricia, Michael, and I were on a train to Dublin with our father as he explained to us that we must agree on the attraction which we would visit. The National Museum and the National Library were given short shrift and we were soon choosing between the airport and Dublin Zoo. We had already seen elephants, lions, and tigers, at the circus and the prospect of viewing planes taking off and landing was too much to resist. Our father also suggested that, as we would have time to spare, we would also climb Nelson's Pillar in order to view the city.

A wonderful, memorable day ensued. I recall being fascinated and slightly confused when confronted by the diverse array of cutlery when we visited cafés twice during the day and I caused much hilarity when, on both occasions, I dropped spoons on the floor and almost cleared the table of crockery as I scrambled underneath to retrieve the missing items. When we arrived home, the first item of news revealed to my mother about the excursion was "Coleman made a show of himself in two cafés".

CHAPTER TWENTY-THREE

The Last Waltz

The 1950s were about to give way to the 60s. The six, rapidly growing, Rushe children were regularly in need of replacement clothing and footwear. My mother was knitting, sewing, and darning in order to bridge the gap. My father was availing of the limited opportunities to work overtime on the railway and was playing music as often as he could. The experiment with the amplified fiddle had helped to prolong his playing career but, as musical tastes changed, there was little demand for violins in dance bands and work opportunities began to dry up.

My mother tentatively suggested that she might like to try her hand a dressmaking. After all, she was very accomplished at needlework and surely it couldn't be too difficult to master a sewing-machine? She could develop her skills by making a few dresses for herself, Patricia, and Mary. Patricia was thirteen and was about to start at secondary school in September. Mary was a year younger. Maybe, in addition to making some dresses for the girls, my mother could then offer her services publicly and generate some family income. My father shared her enthusiasm for the idea and they began to put some money aside with a view to buying a second-hand sewing machine.

The "for sale" sections of local newspapers were scanned but without success. The Evening Press or Evening Herald, both national newspapers, were a more likely source; sewing machines regularly appeared in the "for sale" section although, inconveniently, almost all of the prospective sellers had Dublin addresses. My father had a solution. He proposed to take a days leave from work and travel by train to Dublin where he would wait at the newspaper office for the first edition of the Evening Press. He could then immediately telephone any prospective seller and, with luck, he might arrive home on the evening train with a sewing-machine.

A few weeks later, my father travelled to Dublin on his quest. Later that day, my mother was at the clothes-line when she saw him coming through the garden to join her. She immediately knew that there was something on his mind. He handed her the evening paper and explained that there was no sewing-machine in the "for sale" column. Never mind, she thought, he could try again. But he went on. He explained that he had spotted something else in the paper - a second-hand electric guitar. And he had bought it.

"He said that he could guarantee me that it would make us more money than a sewing machine. I could have killed him stone dead at the time but, in fairness, he was absolutely right. That guitar helped to put more food on the table than a sewing-machine ever would."

In later life, she often told the story with self-effacing humour while my father grinned sheepishly. But I suspect that her initial reaction must have been a real and heart-felt disappointment. On purely financial terms, an electric guitar may well have been a better investment than a sewing-machine. But dress-making and the challenge of a sewing-machine represented an opportunity for my mother to spread her wings. It would be her personal project which could provide a welcome escape from the routine of daily housework and child-rearing; an opportunity to express herself and to raise her self-esteem.

What did the episode say about my father? Ironically, one of his oft-repeated expressions, which he used in order to describe a stern woman, was: "I wouldn't like to come home to that woman with a new melodeon and half of my weeks wages". When he purchased a guitar with the money which had been painstakingly saved for a sewing-machine, he trusted that my mother would overcome her disappointment, understand the reason for his decision, and forgive him. He was correct in his expectation. She often joked about the episode and never betrayed a hint of regret. Yet, I feel that he should have deferred the purchase, returned home, and talked it over with her. I haven't the slightest doubt that, had their situations been reversed, she would not have acted without first discussing it with him.

This event says a lot about my parents. Having made a pragmatic decision that an electric guitar was a worthwhile investment for the family, my father had the confidence, or the single-mindedness, to go ahead with the purchase without consulting my mother even though he realised that she would be disappointed with his action. Their later agreement that the guitar was a better investment than the sewing machine offers some vindication for his precipitous action. My mother's outward acceptance of the fait accompli and the concealment of any understandable disappointment is the kind of reaction which one came to expect from her. I suspect that she privately made her unhappiness clear to my father; I cannot recall any other such impulsive action on his part during the rest of their lives. But outwardly towards her children, she didn't betray any dissatisfaction. Instead, she generated excitement among us children about "Daddy's lovely new guitar" and its potential.

My father quickly taught himself to play the electric guitar, an instrument which was still relatively rare in the rural west of Ireland. Suddenly, there was no shortage of work in local dance bands for a guitar-playing vocalist. For a while, he doubled on fiddle and guitar but soon he was playing guitar only. The elegant, blonde Hofner Senator was an electric arch top guitar. It was a well regarded and popular model but it had some disadvantages. The absence of a cutaway, made access to the higher frets quite limited. The combination of the relatively deep body and f-holes could result in some feedback unless the instrument was played at low volume. The guitar was suitable for chording as an accompaniment to vocals or other instruments so that, initially, it suited my father's purpose. He soon became interested in embellishing his chording by playing single note runs, however, and he was hindered by the feedback problems. He eventually traded the guitar for a Hofner Club 50. This model, although hallow bodied, had a much slimmer body and lacked f-holes so that it was much less prone to feedback and it suited my father's needs and style.

The acquisition of the guitar coincided with another musical development in my father's life. The rise in popularity of rock and roll was mirrored for a time in the UK and Ireland by a revival of interest in Dixieland jazz. The trad jazz boom suddenly brought back into public focus the New Orleans music which had been popularised by the Original Dixieland Jazz Band and which had caught my father's attention decades before. British musicians such as Chris Barber, Acker Bilk, and Kenny Ball became household names as their bands gained radio airtime and occasionally entered the hit parade.

My father and some friends decided to form a dance band which would focus mainly on trad jazz but would also play some of the pop and rock'n'roll hits of the day. Their commitment to the new project resulted in my father's decision to temporarily set aside one of his oft-quoted principles: his antipathy to borrowing.

"If you can't afford to buy it, do without it until you've saved enough to pay for it".

Nevertheless, the papers which I acquired following his death include a repayment card for a hire purchase loan for "hired goods" which was availed of in December 1959. The loan of just over thirty pounds, which was borrowed in my father's name, was repaid by 18 monthly instalments. This would equate to about 750 euros in todays money and, I surmise, was used to finance some necessary new instruments and a sound system for the band. My father's name on the loan agreement probably reflects the fact that, among the band members, he had the most secure employment.

The six-piece Classic Showband, as the new band was named, comprised guitar, drums, tenor sax, trombone, trumpet and clarinet. They practised in our house in Murneen, and began to play some dates. All the musicians had day jobs so that rehearsals took place in the evenings or at night. Sean and Kieran soon developed the ability to sleep soundly through the noise but the practise sessions were occasions of much excitement for Michael and me. We busily set about helping the musicians to carry instruments and set up amplification. In truth, we were probably more of a hindrance than a help but the musicians went along with the charade and inflated our feeling of self-importance. Pat Nally, the drummer, regularly arrived late after work and, because he left his equipment in our house between sessions, Mike and I soon became expert in setting up a drum kit. Bass drum legs affixed and angled correctly and pedal secured. Check. Hi-hat pedals secured and adjusted. Check. Snare drum and cymbals correctly placed and at the desired height. Check. Stool at appropriate height and in position. Check. Drum sticks and brushes ready. Check.

Abban Hunt was usually first to arrive and instantly became our hero because of his ability to vault over our front gate. Carrying his trumpet case under his left arm, he nonchalantly placed his right hand on top of our five-bar iron gate and, grinning at Mike and me, propelled his body upwards and over the gate without apparent effort, landing upright on the gravel path in front of us and casually handing over his instrument. Brothers Frank and Vincent Gill were proficient on saxophone and trumpet respectively. Willie McGreal was also a saxophonist so that Frank Gill was soon focused on the clarinet, an essential element in trad jazz. The switch was effortless for Frank but his brother Vincent had to cope with a more demanding change. This highly competent trumpeter was encouraged to take up the shiny new trombone, an instrument which was essential for the sound of the band in the absence of a bass player. Vincent was soon effortlessly providing the bass counter melodies as well as occasional solos.

My mother also played her part in helping the new band get organised. She was entrusted with a reel-to-reel tape recorder by one of the musicians. As she went about her housework during the day, she monitored the radio for songs which the musicians requested or music which she thought might suit the band. She recorded the song and, using the playback and pause function, wrote out the lyrics which were eagerly devoured by the band at the next practise session.

My father was happy with the musicianship of the band and particularly pleased with the reaction of dancers to the uptempo jazzier number such as "(Won't you come home) Bill Bailey?", "When the saints go marching in", and "Tiger Rag".

The band arranged to have a professional publicity photograph taken with a view to promotion. In the photo, all six of the band members are wearing Pioneer pins, indicating that they were teetotallers. My father was a non-drinker but I can't speak for all of the other musicians; some of the band members were still quite young and might not yet have been introduced to the attractions of alcohol. Nevertheless, a teetotal band was a rarity then, as now. The band took advantage of their unique selling point by successfully submitting the publicity photograph to the magazine of the Pioneer Total Abstinence Association.

As was the norm at that time, the band did not have a manager but depended for bookings upon their contacts with dance promoters and on word of mouth. I can recall my mother writing on behalf of the band to seek or confirm bookings. The absence of a manager, who would take responsibility for bookings and promotion, resulted in vague discussions about "turning professional" but my father was adamant that he could not risk giving up his day job and I'm sure that his reluctance was shared by some of the older band-members.

The differing levels of ambition within the band were probably a factor in its eventual demise. A perusal of the publicity photo gives an insight into the inevitability of the break-up. A generation gap yawns. The good-looking, fresh-faced Gill brothers and even Abban Hunt and

Pat Nally, who were slightly older, would not be out of place in a present-day boy band. In comparison, my father and Willie McGreal, despite their obvious enthusiasm, seemed like people from a different generation. Imagine Bill Haley photographed side by side with Elvis Presley or Ricky Nelson. Despite his undoubted talent and innovation, Haley could be mistaken for the father of the two younger guns.

The Gill brothers eventually left the Classic Showband to join a new outfit. A professional band, the Royal Blues, was being put together by Andy Creighton, a local man. The decision of the Gill brothers to move on was quite understandable. They could hardly pass up an opportunity to become full-time professional musicians. Their ambition was rewarded when the Royal Blues, under Creighton's management, went on to become one of Ireland's biggest attractions and had a number of chart hits.

The break-up of the Classic Showband was marred by a dispute surrounding the ownership of and entitlement to items of the band equipment. By now, the loan in my father's name had been repaid and it seems reasonable to assume that all the band members contributed to the repayments. After a stand-off, the matter was eventually resolved amicably. My father never revealed to us children any rancour or disappointment about the Gill's decision to leave and was pleased for them a few years later when the Royal Blues hit the top of the Irish charts. He was even more gratified that they achieved this feat with a cover of a Fats Domino recording, "Ole Man Trouble".

During this period, our family were continuing to absorb music from the radio. My father was a avid listener at weekends to BBC music programmes such as Saturday Club and Easy Beat. I can recall him teaching us to do the Twist as we listened to Easy Beat on Sunday mornings before my mother hurried us out and laughingly warned us that we might provoke a visit by the priest if he heard that we were dancing before Mass.

My father reverted to playing with local bands led by Johnny Brady or Matt McDonagh until about 1963 when he decided that, as his fortieth birthday approached, it was time to call a halt to his activities as a musician for hire.

Despite having worked non-stop for the railway company for ten years, he was still regarded as a temporary employee. The opportunity now arose for him to be reclassified as a permanent worker with better job security and pension entitlements. The process involved a medical examination which, in my father's case, revealed a hernia which required surgery. The procedure was successfully carried out and he was recategorised as a permanent employee and soon returned to work. During his recuperation, he decided that he was getting too old for the late nights and long uncomfortable journeys cooped up in an overcrowded car. His career as a paid musician was ended but he continued to play music for his own pleasure and enjoyment for the rest of his life.

CHAPTER TWENTY-FOUR

Beautiful Noise

Following his visit to Ireland in the late 1920s, travel writer H V Morton noted that the island had emerged relatively unscathed from both the Reformation and the Industrial Revolution. It is true that few signs of the Industrial Revolution were in evidence on farms in the west of Ireland in my early youth in the 50s.

Morton wrote: "The curse of industrial nations is the cruel and cynical subjection of man to machines. Ireland may be poor, but at least her flesh and blood are not humiliated by the tyranny of mechanical things which is inseparable from the production of modern wealth." Of course, Morton was referring to the "flesh and blood" which remained in Ireland and did not travel overseas. Ireland's massive emigrant community had to encounter the tyranny of mechanical things at first hand. At home, it was different. There were some rare opportunities for factory work but most people had to work on the land.

On local farms in the Murneen area in the 1950s there was little evidence of mechanisation. Cows were milked by hand each morning and evening. Farmyard manure was collected in manure heaps, loaded with pitch forks onto horse-drawn carts and deposited in small mounds around the fields before being painstakingly spread over the land with hand-forks. The tillage land was broken and levelled by horse-drawn plough, grubber, and harrow. Seed was spread by the farmer who, walking at a steady even pace, reached into the jute bag strapped around his waist and, with a sweeping motion of his arm, released the grain so that it drifted in the breeze and fell evenly over the waiting ground. The level of expertise of the skilled sower only became evident later when the new, evenly distributed crop emerged without bare or thin patches. After sowing, another circuit of the field

158

with the horse-drawn harrow and a roller was sufficient to ensure that the seed was firmly embedded.

Crops of hay and oats were still felled by scythe in many of the small farms in the 1950s. Sometimes, a farmer with a larger land holding could justify the purchase of a horse-drawn mowing machine. Horse and machine could be borrowed or rented for usage on small farms so that, over time, the scythe was confined to less accessible fields or was used to cut the headlands so that the mowing machine could operate more efficiently. Despite the gradual disappearance of the scythe during the 50s, there was ample opportunity to admire the skill and grace of a practised scythe-man. With feet widely planted, the scyther shuffled forward, a half step at a time. Hips, knees, torso, and arms all worked together to ensure that the blade swung at the correct height, angle, and momentum, so that the crop fell neatly into perfectly formed, shining swathes. The only sound was the slow rhythmic rasp and swish of the scythe, punctuated occasionally by a muted curse as the blade encountered a hidden obstacle. The reaper might then examine the blade, cautiously running his thumb along the surface to test the edge. The scythe stone or whetstone were produced and the ritual of sharpening the blade followed. Standing the scythe on its handle with the blade uppermost and pointed away from his body, the mower rubbed the stone along the blade with increasing intensity. The squealing rasp of stone on blade, interrupted by regular tentative tests with the thumb, continued until the blade was sharpened and the mowing could be resumed. The skill of the mower could later be evidenced by the short, even, stubble left behind when the crop was lifted. Tales were told to wide-eyed children about scythers who, in their prime, could fell three, four, or even five acres of grass or corn in a day.

There was no machinery involved in saving the hay or harvesting the oats. The hay was turned with hand-rakes and was spread by hay-fork to expose it to the sun and the drying breeze. It was then gathered into hay-cocks where it remained until taken into the farmyard or hay-shed. Hay-cocks were secured by hay ropes which were hand-wound by mothers and children. Oats was gathered in sheaves which were stood upright and bound together into stooks through which the drying breeze could circulate. Stooks were then assembled into large stakes and left to dry further before being carted to the farmyard and combined into a few massive stacks. I have seen people thresh the oats with flails in order to separate the grain from the straw. Soon, even on small farms, this practise was becoming obsolete and was replaced by the autumnal arrival in the village of the threshing machine. The older steam-powered thresher, which I had seen in Streamstown, had been replaced by a tractor-powered, belt-driven model.

With the exception of the threshing machine, farm practices on local farms had remained unchanged for centuries. Turf for the fire was cut and saved by hand. Rain water was collected in barrels or tanks. Drinking water was carried by bucket from the well. Inside the dwelling houses, the recent arrival of electric power was gradually removing some of the drudgery from housework.

But as the 60s commenced, progress was coming gradually and was reflected in the changing sounds of the countryside. The swish of the scythe was replaced by the high tempo rhythmic rattle of the horse-drawn mowing machine. Other sounds similarly faded into memory. The crunch of a spade or shovel. The grunting and snorting of workhorses. The jingling rattle of chains. The slap of traces. The clicking tongue and mumbling encouragement of the driver. The farmer shouting and whistling encouragement and instructions to a dog as it herded uncooperative sheep and playful lambs. The joyfully singing, soaring lark as it hovered high over a summer hay-field. The raucous, attention-seeking, call of a corncrake in the meadow. The mournful sound of a reclusive cuckoo at dusk. The lazy plod of weary cows as they slowly filed from field to farmyard for evening milking. The scraping of the three-legged milking stool on the uneven stone floor of the cow-house. The singing of a slim stream of milk as it hit the bottom of the bucket and the changing, rising tone as the bucket filled. The muted curse of the milker who had forgotten to position the old bicycle tyre over the haunches of that one malevolent cow and was rewarded by a sharp flick on the face by the animal's swishing tail.

On a summer evening, the mournful sound of the church bell carried for miles because of the relative absence of noise pollution from farm machinery. The tolling of the Angelus bell provided an opportunity to pause in prayer and contemplation as one looked out over the Mayo plain with its distant farmhouses, each overhung by a wispy funnel of smoke. People also paused from their work to look up enquiringly upon hearing the distant call of the evening train, the faint but persistent drone of an airplane, or the purr of a rare motor car, now straining as it changed gear on Day's hill. Women and children chattered as they strolled by on their way to draw water from the well. Closer to home, one might hear the scrape of my mother's fingernails on the inside of an enamel basin as she scooped handfuls of feed and scattered it on the gravel path for the busily circling, scratching, clucking hens.

An early harbinger of change was the village pump. Mayo County Council decided to sink a pump at the crossroads, a hundred yards from our house, so that the locals would no longer need to trek to the wells for drinking water. The drilling process took longer than expected. In order to secure an adequate supply, it was necessary to drill down much deeper that originally calculated. The project was successful and the pump became the new source of water for household use. The transition was not as popular as it should have been. As a result of the low level of the water table, it was necessary to pump the handle strenuously for some time before the water eventually gushed from the nozzle into the waiting buckets. Often, people took turns with the pumping but sometimes more canny neighbours waited while they heard the handle being noisily pumped and they arrived just as the water was flowing. Such opportunism was frowned upon and gradually faded.

The arrival of electricity and the sinking of a water pump in Murneen were early signs that change was happening. But the most profound transformation was brought about by a most unlikely agent of change. Our Janus, our god of change and transition, was Tony Solan, who lived on his parents' farm a few miles away and who, literally and metaphorically, left his mark on local farms and farm-work. Tony, a quiet and unprepossessing man, bought a Massey Ferguson tractor, together with a plough and mowing machine, and he announced his availability for hire as an agricultural contractor. Overnight, horse-drawn machinery and scythes became obsolete. Tony was hired to mow and plough the fields of the parish and all necessary steps were taken to facilitate the new paradigm. Gates and field entrances were widened to accommodate the tractor. Rocks and other obstacles were removed or, at least, exposed to view by cutting around them with a scythe. Tony was chased and harassed by anxious suitors who were anxious to ensure that their meadow was cut in order to benefit from the expected spell of dry weather. Ears were cocked in a effort to discern which field Tony was working in with a view to calculating where his next destination might be and whether he could be diverted. Tony, with unfailing politeness, would explain that a certain field was too soft or wet for his tractor that morning but that he would plough it before night if there was a drying wind in the meantime. His innocent nocturnal habits were also noted and interpreted.

"I heard he was gallivanting in Kiltimagh last night. I'll wager you won't see him before eleven this morning."

People became self-styled experts in tractors.

"I'm told that the new-fangled David Brown tractor is the right boyo. Them Massey Fergusons is on the way out. Like the washboard and the tea dance."

Tony's influence became pervasive. He was ploughing in the spring, cutting meadows in August, mowing oats in September, drawing turf from the bog, and hauling hay and straw from field to haggard. As the 1950s gave way to the 60s, Tony Solan's tractor was noisily hauling Murneen into the twentieth century.

CHAPTER TWENTY-FIVE

Teen Angel

The summer of 1961. "Blue Moon" by the Marcels had just replaced "Wooden Heart" by Elvis Presley at the top of the pop music charts. John F Kennedy and Nikita Khrushchev were locking horns at a summit meeting in Vienna. In the west of Ireland, excitement was mounting because of the imminent arrival from Monaco of Prince Rainier and Princess Grace. The princess was about to visit the Mayo cottage from which her grandfather, John Henry Kelly, had emigrated to America a century earlier.

In Murneen, there was much anticipation among the Rushe children. A baby was on the way and was expected in June. Sean and Kieran were too young to fully understand what all the fuss was about but Patricia, Michael and I were more worldly. We now knew how babies were born; we no longer believed that babies were delivered to our house in the doctor's leather bag. We did not need much heeding from my father to make us aware of our obligation to help our mother and to try to ensure that she rested as much as possible.

Mary, cocooned in her own private and mysterious world, seemed oblivious to the drama unfolding around her. Recently, she had suddenly becoming more demanding. Her behaviour was not as predictable as before and she had quite alarming seizures. On occasion, she would seemed disorientated and on the verge of collapse. My mother reacted quickly, got Mary to lie down on the floor, wiped away the drool from her mouth, and soothed her quietly until she recovered. As far as I can recall, such incidents were quite rare but, realistically, they caused stress and pressure to my mother.

The sense of occasion for us children was intensified by the revelation that Mammy was going to the county hospital in Castlebar to have the baby. The previous three Rushe children had been born at home. Home births were not unusual, especially in rural Ireland. In the early 1950s, one in three Irish births took place in the home. By the mid 1960s, the ratio had dropped to one in ten and, by the end of the century, home births would be extremely rare. The reduction in home births coincided with a sharp decrease in child mortality, which, in 1950, was approximately 50 per 1000 compared to 5 per 1000 in 1999. In Ireland in 1949, one child in 16 did not survive to see his or her fifth birthday.

We did not consider the new arrangement for my mother to be unusual. Her absence from the home would be mitigated by the arrival of her sister. Auntie Philomena, who was now in her mid twenties, travelled from Limerick in order to take over the household duties while my mother was away. It was planned that she would remain to help for a few weeks after the baby and mother were discharged from hospital.

Excitement levels were high as our mother prepared for her departure to hospital to have the baby. She warned us to be on our best behaviour and not to cause any problems for Auntie Philomena. Philomena's arrival necessitated some changes in the sleeping arrangements. She would sleep in the bedroom usually occupied by my parents. My father joined Mike, Sean, and Kieran in the large bedroom while I was moved into the back bedroom with Mary. Because I was having one of my bed-wetting episodes, my mother instructed that I was to share a bed with Mary. As a result, Philomena would have one set of bedsheets to wash and dry each day rather than two. This arrangement had been implemented from time to time by my mother in earlier years.

On a more light-hearted level, my mother encouraged us to give some thought to the name which would be given to the new baby. Michael and I favoured the name Anthony if we were to have a brother. Patricia hoped for a baby sister and preferred to keep her choice of name secret after the baby arrived.

On about the June 1, our mother departed for Castlebar in a hackney car and was admitted to the maternity section of the hospital. Daddy returned home to assure us that she was comfortable and resting and we could expect good news in a day or two.

I'm not sure how the news broke that something was wrong. Perhaps my father went to the Post Office to make a telephone enquiry about her progress or maybe a telegram arrived. What is certain is that we were told by a tearful Philomena that there was bad news. The baby had been born alive but had only survived for one day. Daddy dashed off to the hospital and returned later to reassure us that Mammy was well but would remain in the hospital for a few days to recover before being discharged. Yes, she was upset, he told us, but she was looking forward to getting back home and to seeing us all.

Our disappointment and shock at the news was offset by our relief that Mammy was well and would be home soon. She wanted us to be "good as gold" for Philomena, our father informed us. She also instructed him to say that she would cut the legs off us if we misbehaved. We were relieved. That sounded just like Mammy. She was in good spirits if she was sending such a message.

Any discomfort and concern which I felt about my mother's absence was partly offset by the novelty of having access to my father each morning as he prepared to go to work. While Philomena prepared his breakfast, he quietly entered the room shared by Mary and me and, leaning over the wash-stand in front of the mirror, he washed and shaved. Despite his best efforts not to disturb us, I would wake and, while Mary slept on, we would chatter quietly. Just me and him. A throwback to the time when he teased me about our identical names as we lay in bed on Sunday mornings in Streamstown. These were precious moments. I knew that, as soon as Mammy came home, I would be back to sharing the big bedroom with Michael, Sean, and Kieran.

I awoke as usual when he cracked open the bedroom door on Tuesday morning. As always, I was on the outside of the bed nearest the wash-stand while Mary was inside near the wall.

"Morning", I mumbled as he eased open the door and manoeuvred into the room, holding his steaming mug of shaving water which he watched carefully in order not to spill it. I was in that half-way place between sleep and wakefulness as he positioned the mug safely on the wash-stand and then turned towards me with a half smile. He froze.

"Mary?"

He was staring past me. I turned my head to see what had startled him and he immediately leaned towards me and turned my head and shoulders so that I was facing him again, but not before I had caught a glimpse of Mary's left arm. It was pale and still. It was raised in an unusual angle; as if, as she lay in bed, she had raised her hand to pluck something out of the air and the arm had suddenly remained frozen in that position.

My father's hand was gently but firmly on my shoulder in order to prevent me from turning back towards Mary.

"Philomena! Come here quick."

The tone in his voice brought my aunt dashing into the bedroom. I was fully awake now.

"There's something wrong with Mary. Will you take Coleman into the other room?"

As Philomena looked at Mary, her expression changed just as my father's had.

"Coleman. There's a good boy. Come with me."

As I swung my legs out of the bed, she put her arm around my shoulders, shielding the bed from my view. She quickly walked me out of the room, through the kitchen and hall, and into the big back bedroom where Michael was just waking.

"Michael. Will you keep Coleman and the boys here until I come back? Nobody is to leave the room."

Philomena hurried back out.

"What's going on?" asked Michael. "Did you wet the bed again or what?"

"No… It's Mary."

"What about Mary? What's wrong?"

"I…I think she's dead."

CHAPTER TWENTY-SIX

Everything Is Broken

My recollections of the following days are confused. I cannot recall some things which I should clearly remember. Other memories are vivid.

I have a clear memory of myself and my brothers being sent out to the garden. Standing under the trees, we watched the arrival of the doctor's car and, later, the Garda squad car. Two policeman emerged from the car, donned their hats, and approached the front door where they were greeted by my father. They removed their hats and entered the house. A short time later, they re-emerged, shook my father's hand in sympathy, replaced their hats, returned to their car, removed their hats, and drove away.

A somber Mattie Gilligan slid a small white coffin from his shining black hearse. I had seen coffins before this but all had been made of dark wood. Since Mary's death, I've always felt that there is something unjust, incomplete, unresolved about the sight of a white coffin.

Friends and neighbours arrived at the house as news spread that the Rushes had lost two children in the space of just three days. We were comforted to see Patricia arriving accompanied by Granny and Granda Rushe. There was even a brief mention in a national evening newspaper:

"CHILD FOUND DEAD.

Within a few days after the death of their newly born infant at Castlebar Hospital, a second 12 years old Mary daughter of Mr and Mrs C Rush, Burneen, Claremossis (sic) *was found dead in bed at home."*

My father spoke to us, telling us that Mary was gone to heaven and that he would tell Mammy as soon as the hospital doctors in Castlebar allowed him to do so. If anybody asked us about Mary's death, he said, we should merely say that she died peacefully in her sleep.

Strangely, I have no recollection of Mary being waked in the house or of seeing her body in the coffin. I seem to have blocked this memory. Yet I am sure that she was waked; it makes sense that she would have been. There were as yet no funeral parlours in the area and the local custom was that the dead were placed in an open coffin at home overnight so that friends could call to pay their respects before the remains were removed to the church before burial.

A warm comforting blanket of neighbouring women enveloped the house in support of my father and Philomena. They cooked, cleaned, washed, ironed, and provided an endless supply of sandwiches and drinks to visitors and sympathisers. They talked in hushed tones about the impact that Mary's death would have on "poor Kitty" and, when they saw that we were eavesdropping, they offered us food and then encouraged us to "run off out and play" or to draw some water.

In June sunlight, the pathetic white coffin was carried from the house and placed reverently in the hearse. I suppose that, in accordance with the local custom, neighbours accompanied it on foot to the church at Barnacarroll but again, I have no recollection of this. My next memory is the lowering of the coffin into a grave in Crossboyne cemetery. Mary was laid to rest beside her aunt Patsy, who had died at a young age in 1949, just two months after Mary was born.

Following the burial, my father had to wait until evening to visit my mother; she would not expect him earlier and it was important that the illusion be maintained that he was calling on his way home from work. He had already consulted the doctors who advised him that Mammy was still vulnerable after the loss of the newborn infant and that it would be better to keep the news about Mary from her for a few more days. My father dreaded the dilemma in which he found himself. He did not want to be dishonest when he spoke to my mother but felt an obligation to follow the doctor's advice.

Later, as night fell, we waited in trepidation for his arrival home from Castlebar Hospital. When he walked into the kitchen, we knew from his expression that things had not gone as planned.

"Mammy knew something wasn't right the minute I walked into the ward".

He explained that she brushed aside his repeated assurances that everything was well at home. She knew from his demeanour that he was lying and, sensing that something was wrong, she became more agitated and insistent.

"I took the bull by the horns and told her."

He looked at our silent, questioning faces.

"Ah sure, ye know what Mammy is like. She was more worried about me and all of ye than about herself. She was sitting me down and making sure I was ok."

He had called a nurse who checked my mother, promised to keep a close eye on her and, if necessary, to "give her a little something later on".

And then?

"We just sat there and we cried a bit".

As we sat in the kitchen while Philomena served some dinner to my father, we all quietly cried a bit.

My next vivid memory is of a moment a few days later. I had arrived from school to discover that Mammy was home at last. She must have been in one of the bedrooms when I arrived; I was in the kitchen when she walked in. I thought that her face was paler than usual but she seemed rested. She was wearing a clean fresh apron which signalled that she was back in action. She smiled as she crossed towards the cupboard.

"Ah, there you are, Coleman. How was school?"

"Fine. But how are you?"

She was about to take some mugs from the cupboard but she stopped and turned towards me, recognising that my words were not merely a greeting.

"I'm fine but I'm glad to be home."

She was standing there, watching me carefully now. She went on.

"And what about you? Are you alright?"

"Oh! I'm grand".

"Are you sure?"

"I'm certain. Thanks."

I sensed immediately that she was concerned about the impact on me of Mary's death and the circumstances surrounding the discovery of her body. I hoped that my offhand but quite genuine reassurance that I was "grand" put her mind at ease. But I was touched that, in the midst of her own private trauma, she was finding the grace to be concerned about the possible repercussions for the rest of us. On subsequent days, I sensed that she was observing me carefully. I tried to behave as normally as possible in order to reassure her that she did not have anything to be concerned about.

I have never been conscious that the sudden loss of two siblings and, in particular, the circumstances surrounding Mary's death had any traumatic impact on me although I accept that I might be misguided. With hindsight, I realise that the shock to the family was profound. Sean and Kieran were still very young but must have been bewildered by the escalating sequence of events. It seemed as if the family was being torn apart. A few days earlier, Patricia had been more excited that any of us at the prospect of the arrival of a new baby. Now, in addition to the loss of the infant, she had just lost her only sister. Michael, ever the most sensitive of the Rushe children, had lost his twin sister. Due to his empathetic nature, he was probably more impacted by the tragedy than any of his siblings.

What impact did the catastrophic events have on my parents? In 1967, psychiatrists Thomas Holmes and Richard Rahe conducted a major study on factors which contributed to stress in individuals. They examined the extent to which such stress contributes to illness. As a result of their research, they devised the widely respected Holmes and Rahe Stress Scale which attributes numerical values to life events which caused stress and which occurred over the preceding twelve months. Unsurprisingly, the life event with the highest score is the death of a spouse or child. I've applied the scale to measure the likely impact of the events of 1961 on my parents. The results indicate that each had close to an 80% chance of a major stress-induced health breakdown over the succeeding two years.

Were my parents' generation, the people who lived through World War Two, made of sterner stuff? How did they deal with the impact of the obstacles which were placed in their path? There was no counselling or therapy to help them to cope. Did this lack of support force them to confront and to deal with their traumas? Or did they feel and suffer things just as much as their children and grandchildren did? "Pull yourself together" was the usual advice which was given to people following a setback or disappointment. A short period of grieving or readjustment was expected and considered acceptable. Then the sufferer was urged to "get a grip" on him or herself and to get on with life.

The reality was that, in some cases, people leaned heavily on alcohol in order to cope. As legalised drugs became more readily available, there arose a propensity to rely upon anti-depressant medication. But generally, people seemed to be able to pull themselves together and readjust.

In our small rural locality, our family was not the only one which had to deal with tragedy. A school-boy named Eugene Casserly, one of a large local family, had died in 1954. Margaret Conner, whose sister Ann had been pushed into the dyke by Michael, had died in 1958 at the age of eleven. The families faced the tragedies with dignity and fortitude and, outwardly at least, life seemed to carry on as normal. Perhaps the best example of this stoicism is provided by Tom Walsh, another neighbour.

Tom and his wife Maureen lived nearby on a small farm with their four daughters, with whom we walked to school each day. Tragedy visited the Walsh family when 32 year-old Mrs Walsh died in November 1962 after a short illness. The eldest daughter, May, was about fifteen while the twin sisters, Sal and Nancy were twelve years old. Tina, the youngest, was seven. Tom Walsh was faced with a dilemma. He could have crumbled, sought outside help, kept May away from school to act as a surrogate mother, or sent the girls to live with supportive relatives. Instead, Tom quietly set about bringing up his four young daughters on their small farm while ensuring that they continued their formal education. He raised four bright, humorous, well-adjusted young women and, as the years passed, watched contentedly as they left home, embarked on careers, and started their own families. Tom never remarried and settled into rewarding old age under the watchful eyes of his daughters and grandchildren until his death at the age on ninety-three.

There were numerous examples of this type of stoical resilience. In later life, my father poked fun at the modern tendency to seek professional help in order to deal with difficulties. "I need counselling", he would say when the county lost a football match or after viewing an unsettling tv show. Yet I'm sure that our family tragedy had a profound impact on both my parents even though they hid their pain from their children. Now, as I look back, I try to discern modifications in their behaviour and wonder whether these changes were symptoms of their suffering.

My father began to lose some of his patience and flexibility during the 1960s and he became more demanding of us as children. Chores had to be done promptly and assiduously. Homework had priority and good exam results were expected. He did not lose or abandon his sense of humour and occasional playfulness. But it seemed that he now had less time for frivolity.

It may be unfair to attribute any perceived behavioural change on my father's part to the deaths of two of his children. Patricia was already a teenager and, as is the way with girls her age, was tentatively asserting herself and expecting to be treated as a young woman. Mike and I were about to set sail on the choppy waters of young male adolescence. Perhaps our father decided that, as we were getting older, we needed to learn how to adopt a more responsible approach to living and life.

I became aware as a teenager that my mother was prescribed some type of anti-depressant medication. I hesitate to state definitively that she suffered from depression but this may have been the case. She was not as incapacitated as other sufferers whom I have encountered and who endure dreadful lows. What is certain is that she suffered from occasional bouts of what I would term "melancholia". It was a shock to walk into a room, encounter her unexpectedly, and find her alone, weeping quietly. She would immediately react by smiling embarrassedly and would respond to an anxious enquiry by saying: "Just feeling sorry for myself" or "Sure, wouldn't these dark evenings drive anyone to distraction?"

She may have had a propensity towards melancholia before Mary's death but it certainly intensified during the 60s and continued to impact on her occasionally throughout her life.

Blackie, Mary's constant canine companion, lost his main purpose in life after her passing. Relieved of his self-imposed obligation to perform sentry duty for Mary in the house or garden, he developed an enthusiasm for chasing passing cars and bicycles. Blackie raced after all motor vehicles and sometimes, upon hearing the whirring of a bicycle as it hurtled down Day's hill, dashed from behind the pillar and raced after the startled cyclist, snapping and growling, while we yelled our apologies.

"Get in home, Blackie! Sorry, Sir! Blackie! Give over!"

As a result of writing about the circumstances surrounding the deaths, I have been forced to question my own youthful perspective and to raise questions which had previously been unasked. This has resulted in some clarification and explanation but, in the process, issues arose which were uncomfortable and disturbing, not least for me.

I applied for Mary's death certificate and, as an afterthought, enquired whether the birth and death of the newborn baby had been registered. In response, I received copies of both entries in the official register. The records reveal that both deaths had their origins in the same pregnancy complication. Mary's handicap and the baby's death had identical root causes.

The baby died as a result of a "prolapsed cord". When the umbilical cord slips into the birth canal before the baby does, there is a risk that the cord will become compressed, thereby cutting off the baby's blood and oxygen supply. This can result in brain damage and, if not rectified promptly, will cause death. In such circumstances, an immediate delivery of the baby is essential, by c-section, if necessary. Cord prolapse is estimated to occur in one out of 300 births. The newborn Rushe baby suffered irreparable damage and lived for only one day.

Years later, when I discussed Mary's handicap with my father, he expressed his belief that her problem was caused by oxygen deprivation during delivery. One of the the factors which can increase the risk of prolapse is the delivery of the second of twins. Michael was born first and Mary shortly afterwards. It seems inescapable that Mary's brain damage resulted from a prolapsed cord when she was being delivered in 1949. Now, twelve years later, the same complication which had caused Mary's handicap had struck again and resulted in the death of the infant. In a tragic coincidence, Mary was to die just three days later from causes which are directly and inescapably a result of her own similar birth trauma.

When Mary's death was being explained to family and neighbours, it was said that she died in her sleep from heart failure. This implied that she had died peacefully while sleeping. It was comforting to all of us who were dealing with our feelings about the loss. In later years, I sometimes wondered how a physically strong and healthy pre-teen could suddenly die of heart failure but I had no answer until I received her death certificate.

Mary's death records show that she did indeed die from heart failure but the fuller picture is more unsettling. Her cause of death was "cardiac failure status epilepticus". Status epilepticus is the medical term which describes a lengthy epileptic seizure, or a number of shorter seizures between which the sufferer does not have the opportunity to recover. In the 60s, it was thought that such a seizure or series of seizures would be life-threatening, causing cardiac arrest if enduring for longer than thirty minutes. Nowadays, it is recommended that urgent action should be taken if the seizure exceeds five minutes. Emergency treatment in a hospital setting is required and must start as soon as possible if the sufferer is to survive. Assisted breathing, intravenous fluids, emergency medication, and even an induced coma might be appropriate in order to stop the seizures. People with a history of epilepsy and those with an underlying problem of the brain are most susceptible to status epilepticus.

Mary had suffered a few fits or seizures in the weeks shortly before her death. These were of short duration and my mother responded by laying Mary on the floor and ensuring that she was breathing properly until she recovered. I think that it's highly likely that my mother discussed the seizures with the doctor although I have no proof of this. She was seeing the doctor regularly because of her pregnancy and would not pass up an opportunity to bring Mary with her or at least to discuss her condition with him.

The medical records confirm that Mary died during the night from cardiac failure following a sustained and prolonged epileptic seizure or a series of seizures. Status epilepticus seizures are either convulsive and non convulsive. The convulsive seizures result in a regular pattern of extension and contraction of the arms and legs. The non convulsive category involve no such movement. The stretched and elongated position of Mary's arm, which I witnessed briefly on the morning following her death, now leads me to the unsetting conclusion that she may have endured a prolonged convulsive seizure while I, the titular heavy sleeper of the family, slept peacefully and soundly beside her.

Was there anything I could have done? What if I had been disturbed by her movements? I would immediately have called my father or Philomena. And what then? Our first port of call in medical matters, our neighbour Mrs Gavin, who had nursing skills, might have been alerted and asked for guidance. Even if the true gravity of the situation was grasped and the need for urgent hospitalisation was recognised, nobody in the neighbourhood owned a car. A night-time dash by bicycle to Murneen Post Office to access the nearest telephone would at best have resulted in the arrival of a doctor or ambulance an hour or more later by which time Mary would already be dead. No. I tell myself that I should accept the inescapable reality. There was no hope of saving Mary's life once the seizure commenced. Was it not better that she died as she did? If I had raised the alarm, my father would have been unable to help Mary but would have had to look on helplessly as she died.

And yet I know that Mary deserved any chance of rescue, however remote. It is difficult for me, over fifty years later, to come to terms with this unsettling but unavoidable analysis. How much more traumatic the impact would have been if this information had become revealed to me as a ten year old.

There is a family photo of the Rushes in the summer of 1961. The date inscribed on the reverse confirms that it was taken a few weeks after Mary's death. We are standing on the road outside our house on a sunny day. Joining my parents and the five children is auntie Philomena who had not yet returned home to Cappamore. We children are in short sleeves and are beaming at the camera. The three adults are half-smiling; my mother wears a wistful expression. We seem like a normal, unremarkable family. The only clue that something had changed is that Blackie, a constant presence in previous family photographs, is nowhere to be seen.

What of Mary's short life? She was loved, cared for and, as far as possible, was treated in the same manner as her siblings. She was not placed in an institution or hidden from public gaze as was the case with many of her contemporaries who had learning difficulties. Yet, there is a lingering impression of potential unrealised. One wonders what kind of internal landscape she possessed. She tended not to display an emotional response to any stimulus. On occasions when other children would laugh, smile or display excitement or amusement, Mary's response would be confined to a blank, vaguely interested gaze. She seemed content to sit in her chair in the garden or to stand, swaying from side to side as she tapped out a rhythm with her fingernails and hummed a tune.

There were signs that there was unrealised potential. One wonders what a speech therapist might have achieved if one was available to Mary as a child. The ability to hum a tune suggests some vocal chord activity which might have been developed to facilitate a limited form of speech. The ability to keep rhythm and the coordination displayed by her finger tapping also suggest some skills which could be expanded or built upon. Similarly, Mary's unusual facility to quickly assimilate and memorise songs from the radio might reflect a level of brain activity which could be explored and developed.

As I have written, there were no supports in place for such children and their parents in Ireland while Mary was alive. Society did not value people who were "not right" and was oblivious to their potential. When I talked about Mary to my father towards the end of his life, he expressed great admiration for the manner in which my mother cared for Mary and tried to develop her abilities. He wondered what Mary might have achieved if educational and therapeutic help was available to her. He shared my belief that she had potential but doubted whether she could have become self-reliant. He added that she would have required care from her siblings for the rest of her life. He took it for granted that, had she survived, Mary would have been cared for by her brothers and sisters after the demise of her parents and that she would not have been placed in institutional care. I am sure that his trust was not misplaced.

Let's not dwell on what might have been. Let's consider what actually happened. During her short life, Mary changed and helped to shape our family in her unique way. Her siblings learned how to respect, support, care for, and value people with special needs. We watched our parents lead by example as they accepted Mary's condition unashamedly and afforded her the same status and public exposure as her brothers and sisters. I have no doubt that we are better people because Mary was a part of our family.

CHAPTER TWENTY-SEVEN

I'm A Believer

What role did the twin opiates of the Irish people, alcohol and religion, play in helping my parents to cope during their dark times?

First, a confession…

I don't drink alcohol.

No, I'm not a recovering alcoholic.

And no, I'm not the designated driver.

Yes, I'm Irish.

No, I don't feel miserable as a non-drinker; my social life is fine, thank you for asking…

In truth, I have whiled away many happy hours in pubs and bars. I have no problem with drink or drinkers. I just choose not to drink. I can function socially without alcohol… although I do get frustrated having to explain or even justify my stance. I hide my indignation when people react as if there is something un-Irish about being a non-drinker.

Health data statistics place Ireland in the top five OECD countries for per capita consumption of alcohol. The average person in Ireland consumed 11.6 litres of alcohol per annum in 2011. Germany, at 11.7 litres per person, is broadly similar. But, taken in isolation, these figures are misleading. Nineteen percent of Irish adults do not drink any alcohol. Only four percent of Germans are teetotallers. By adjusting the figures to exclude non-drinkers, we find that average annual consumption of alcohol among Irish drinkers is over fourteen litres compared to just over twelve litres in Germany. That's not all. When binge drinking statistics are measured, we Irish come into our own. According to a World Health Organisation report in 2014, Ireland had the second highest rate of binge drinking in the world.

The statistics indicate that, if we randomly select five Irish people, one of them will be a non-drinker. However, the remaining four are drinking their European counterparts under the table. Yet, despite the prevalence of hard drinking and alcohol abuse, it is easier to be a non-drinker in Ireland than in other European countries. An Irish teetotaller may be a curiosity abroad but at home, the lifestyle choice is relatively common. Yet, non-drinking Irish people do not get any ink. Like happy families, or good parents, they tend not to appear in the Irish written word.

The temperance movement in Ireland was started early in the nineteenth century by a Catholic priest, Theobold Matthew. He cajoled thousands to sign "The Pledge", a promise to abstain from alcohol. Later, when the influence of Father Matthew's movement began to wane, the Pioneer Total Abstinence Association was formed and continued to have an impact during the second half of the twentieth century. Pioneers, as the non drinkers were called, were recruited on the day of their Confirmation. Each child, when being confirmed, was expected to pledge not to drink alcohol until aged eighteen. The wearing of Pioneer pins was a common sight among young and old.

The Pioneer Total Abstinence Association was, of course, a Catholic movement. However, the Protestant churches on the island had similar drives to reduce the dependence upon alcohol. Many of the Protestant Orange Lodges were designated as Temperance Lodges to signify that the members refrained from drinking alcohol.

Although my father was a teetotaller, there was always a bottle of whiskey in the house so that a glass could be offered to visitors. My mother took an occasional drink but only on some social occasion or when a relative dropped by to visit. Her preferred tipple was a small sherry and she rarely took more than one. I can only recall one occasion when drinking had a visible impact on her. Many years ago, a few days before Christmas, I remarked to Patricia that Mam was in good form; she was singing quietly to herself as she went about her housework. It was discreetly pointed out to me that Mam had been making her hugely popular sherry trifle that morning and, while doing so, took an occasional swig of surplus sherry from the bottle.

Alcohol was not an option in helping my parents cope with difficulties and setbacks. What about religion?

Both my parents were practising Catholics. They were regular church-goers for all of their lives and brought up their children as Catholics. We were a Catholic family but so were the vast majority of families and households which we encountered on a daily basis. How did our religion affect us in practise? To what extent was the ethos of our household driven by religion?

From an early age, we were taught how to bless ourselves and were obliged, mainly by my mother, to say a few simple prayers at bedtime. We went to Mass each Sunday and on Holy Days of Obligation. Attendance was non-negotiable, despite Michael's brave attempt to break from the tradition.

On Sunday evenings, we were packed off to Devotions at the local church. I preferred Devotions to Mass. The priest and congregation recited the Rosary and this was followed by Benediction. Soon we were recruited into the choir and were able to sing in Latin the "O Salutaris Hostia" followed by "Tantum Ergo" as the sweet heady aroma of the burning incense wafted up towards us on the church balcony. Our lack of understanding of Latin did not in any way diminish the experience. I loved singing the plainchant hymns and can still recall that surge as the languid "O Satutaris Hostia" is followed, after a momentary pause, by the more urgent tone and changed meter of the "Tantum Ergo".

Attendance at Devotions was optional for Catholics. Not all children returned to church on Sunday evening for Benediction and only a small number of adults were regular participants. My parents did not attend. My mother remained at home to look after Mary. We didn't remark on my father's non attendance. In reality, few men were seen at Devotions which was mainly the preserve of women and children.

At school our teachers, fortified by the occasional visits of the local priest, prepared us for First Holy Communion and later for Confirmation. These ceremonies are eagerly anticipated by youngsters nowadays, not just for their spiritual aspects, but because they are opportunities to collect substantial cash donations from family friends and relatives. This mercenary element was missing in my youth, at least in our family. But there was compensation of a different kind; we were freshly kitted out from head to toe. New clothes and shoes were bought for each of us and, after the ceremony, we were proudly photographed outside the church, usually by a professional photographer.

Another formal manifestation of religion in our lives was the Rosary. Strangely, our participation as a family in this ritual was intermittent. My mother would announce her decision that the family should recite the Rosary together each evening from now on. After dinner, we knelt on the kitchen floor, usually with arms resting on a chair, and made the responses as my mother recited the five decades of the Rosary and added a few prayers for what she referred to as "special intentions".

I have to admit that, for me, the Rosary was an unwelcome chore rather than a spiritual experience. Nevertheless, the Rosary on Friday evenings was rewarding, albeit for the wrong reason. The kitchen floor was scrubbed each Friday and newspapers were then laid down in order to absorb any excess water and to help the drying process. By ensuring that the chair on which I was leaning was facing in the optimum direction, I could kneel and, with my head piously bowed, I could read the newspaper on the floor while the Rosary mumbled on around me. A modicum of positional planning could ensure that I was reading the sports page or the local news rather than the death notices or the small adverts.

Gradually, our family observance of the Rosary fell into neglect. My father might be working a long distance away and would arrive home late. Or he might be hurrying through his dinner in order to work in the Gosling Garden. I would not even notice that our family Rosary had fallen into neglect until Mammy would announce, sometimes after a gap of a few months, that we were going to recommence the ritual. The sequence would start again.

Patricia was envious of our casual attitude towards the Rosary. My Rushe grandparents in Claremorris, with whom Patricia lived during the school week, never failed to say the daily Rosary. Granny Rushe enthusiastically launched into the five decades each evening and anybody who happened to be in the house was obliged to participate. The prayer session featured a seemingly endless series of additional prayers which Granny appended. She prayed individually for deceased family members and also for those who had left home. In addition there were prayers for "special intentions". Granny Rushe had acquired a reputation was a particularly potent sayer of prayers. Some friends and neighbours asked her to pray if they were having some personal difficulty in their lives. If was as if she had God's private number or, as my grandfather mischievously surmised, God was afraid to refuse her requests.

"Your grandmother won't stop nagging so He probably gives in to have a quiet life."

Granda Rushe loved to poke gentle fun at these extra prayers which he referred to as "the trimmings". Years later, when I was about to leave home, he remarked quietly to me that Patricia and Michael had already left and said: "Would a few of ye not think about staying at home and not leaving?"

I knew that he was toying with me because of his sly grin and his sideways glance to ensure that my slightly deaf grandmother was out of earshot

"Why. Do you miss us, granda?"

"Oh God, no. It's not that. But the trimming get longer every time one of ye goes away. I'm on my knees for half the night as it is!"

It might seem that my mother was the driving force in our religious observance. My father was also actively involved, however. Following our move to Murneen, he continued to sing each Sunday in the Claremorris church choir. He eventually abandoned this in favour of attending mass at the local church in Barnacarroll. He got us organised while my mother attended the first mass at nine-thirty. He then shepherded us to eleven-thirty mass and rewarded our good behaviour by handing a few pence to each so that we could buy an ice-cream in Paddy Prendergast's shop which was beside the church.

On one occasion, my father decided that we should walk to Knock to attend Mass at the Marian Shrine. He sold the round trip of about nine miles to us as a mixture of pilgrimage and adventure. Patricia, Michael, and I walked with him to Knock on a sunny Sunday morning. After Mass, when we were about a half-mile from Knock on our journey home, a car unexpectedly pulled up on the road beside us. The driver greeted my father and, stretching across, opened the passenger door and pushed forward the front passenger seat.

"Hop in. I'll drop ye off in Murneen."

Our scramble to board the car was quickly halted by my father.

"Ah, no. Thanks very much but we promised that we'd walk to Knock. You know how it is. It's only right to finish what we started."

The driver looked at my father and then at us crestfallen children.

"Your father is right. You should stick to your promise. And the weather is keeping fine too. Ye'll have great appetites when ye get home."

As he waved and drove off, I muttered to myself that I hadn't made any promise but, at heart, I knew what my father meant. This was just one more example of his demand that we always keep our promises.

"Anyhow, we couldn't take the lift because there's something we have to do."

"What, Daddy?"

"Wait and see. We'll be there shortly."

The disappointment of the missed opportunity was replaced by anticipation. Twenty minutes later, we were excitedly exploring the ruins of Ballyhowley Castle. My father explained that it was built in about the thirteenth century by the Mac Morris family who gave their name to the town of Claremorris and was later the seat of the Browne family, who owned extensive estates in the local area. We children were less interested in historical fact and architectural features than in the possibility that we were treading in the footsteps of medieval knights intent on chivalrous deeds. My father was passing on to us his passion for old buildings while distracting us from the disappointment of the now forgotten missed opportunity to get a lift home.

Other religious activities were less formal but were observed by us without thought or question. As instructed by my parents from an early age, I blessed myself when passing a church or cemetery and said the Angelus when the church bell tolled. As a mark of courtesy and respect, it was customary to salute a passing priest. Michael and I were altar boys at the local church, as were most of our friends.

Attendance at Mass and Devotions, recitation of the Rosary and the other activities which I've mentioned were the rituals - the outward manifestation of our religion. They were observed to varying degrees by everybody with whom we were acquainted. Some people or families were even more observant and, for example, attended Mass daily, joined Sodalities, or participated in Novenas or "The Nine Fridays". But strict adherence to the rituals of a religion can sometimes go hand in hand with an intolerant attitude towards other people who do not "measure up". To what extent did our religion impact or influence the activities and attitudes within our family and in our daily lives?

It is difficult to judge whether the behavioural standards which were inculcated in us by our parents were inspired by their religion or by their sense of moral responsibility. The earliest example which I can think of is our interaction with the travelling community. Families of travellers arrived and set up their roadside camp in a location known as Tinker Hill which was about a half mile west of our house. One became accustomed to seeing the same families arriving at the same time each year. They remained for a few weeks before moving on, to be replaced eventually by another family. The shawl-wrapped women visited the homes in the locality, begging for surplus clothes or a few pence. They sometimes offered prayers and blessings in exchange for a few coins. The older men were skilled tinsmiths and earned money by making or repairing tin cans, jugs, and buckets.

The travellers' tradition of allowing their horses, donkeys, and goats to graze on the "long acre", the grass margin along the roadside, sometimes resulted in tensions with the local farmers. The animals might take advantage of a weak fence in order to break into a field of grass or crops. It was easier to blame the travellers for failing to control their animals than to erect adequate fencing.

Generally, relations between the settled community and travellers were reasonably comfortable, partly because the same families returned year after year and became familiar to the community. This relaxed climate was not universal, however, and some people had dismissive and hostile attitudes towards the visitors. They were untrustworthy and "not like us", some said. It was common for children to speak disparagingly about travellers and to be openly rude to them, secure in the knowledge that there would be no retaliation or complaint to parents.

My mother and father insisted that we treat travellers with respect. We were told that they had their own traditions and codes of conduct which were rigidly adhered to. It was pointed out that, apart from the odd bout of drunkenness among the men on fair days, they were seldom if ever in trouble with the law.

Any traveller woman who called to our house was routinely invited inside by my mother for a cup of tea and a slice of bread and jam. On one such occasion, the visitor settled herself comfortably beside the range, chatting and sipping sparingly of her second cup of tea and, quite understandably, showing no sign of exchanging the warmth of the house for the cold, wet outdoors. My mother hinted that it was time for the visitor to leave.

"I'm afraid I'll have to start getting the dinner ready now. Where did the day go?"

"God bless the work, missus."

No sign of movement.

"Sure, the children will be in shortly looking for their dinner."

"Isn't it great that they have such appetites? God bless them."

Still nothing.

"Look at the time. My husband will be in from the fields shortly. There'll be war if his dinner isn't on the table."

The visitor was startled.

"Cross of Christ about us! Will he beat you, missus?"

My mother laughingly explained to my startled father later that, although she couldn't lie, she didn't want to miss her opportunity to dislodge her guest.

"All I'll say is this. I wouldn't like to test him."

"God between us and all harm. Say no more, missus. I'll be on my way. May God bless you."

While the values of charity and tolerance which were instilled in us may not have been inspired solely by religious belief, my parents had a huge respect for the church and its traditions. Nevertheless, they were quite willing to disagree with the Catholic church when they considered its teaching to be inappropriate or unreasonable. My father's championing of and admiration for Doctor Noel Browne was a subject to which he regularly returned. Following his pivotal role in managing the dramatic reduction in the incidence of tuberculosis in Ireland, Browne, as Minister for Health, introduced the Mother and Child Scheme, a plan which provided universal, free, state-funded healthcare for all mothers and children under 16. The Irish Catholic Church hierarchy, which controlled most of the hospital network, vigorously opposed the measure, claiming that it interfered with parental rights. They were probably more fearful of the prospect of mothers obtaining medical advice which could lead to birth control methods that were contrary to Catholic teachings. The government bowed to the pressure from the Catholic church and abandoned the proposed plan. Browne resigned his ministry in protest.

The subservient reaction of the Government, which reflected the prevailing attitude of many in the country at that time, was best demonstrated by the words of the prime minister, John A. Costello: "I am an Irishman second. I am a Catholic first, and I accept without qualification in all respects the teaching of the hierarchy and the church to which I belong." My father was appalled. He strongly disagreed with the action of the Fine Gael led Government even though he was a supporter of the political party.

This liberal attitude was also apparent in other aspects of my parents' lives. I recall my mother reading "The Dark", a novel by John McGahern, in the mid 1960s. The book was banned in Ireland and earned the strong disapproval of the Catholic church. This did not deter my mother. In earlier years, I can remember my father reading a battered copy of James Joyce's "Ulysses" which he found abandoned in a railway carriage. The book was not banned in Ireland but only because it was not imported or offered for sale. The reason for my recollection is an overheard exchange between by parents. My mothers comment was light-hearted and mischievous as she went about her housework while my father sat near the range, reading the book.

"Pull your feet in. Are you still reading that dirty ould book? Take care would one of the children pick it up."

"Never mind the children. They're in no danger. I can hardly make head nor tail of most of it myself."

What about my personal relationship with religion within the context of our family? Well, I was convinced that I had figured out this whole religion thing when I was about six or seven years old. You might say that I had an epiphany. I had already become aware that there was no Santa Claus; that the whole Father Christmas myth was an invention. I figured that, just as it had gradually been revealed to us that Santa did not exist, we would eventually realise that the Jesus myth was similarly invented. The more I thought about it, the more the similarities became apparent. We had been told by our parents that, if we were good, Santa would reward us. Now, were were being told by parents, teachers, and priests that our goodness would be rewarded in heaven. In both cases, there were sanctions for misbehaviour. Both Santa and Jesus were inextricably linked in my mind with ritual, costume, holiday, and celebration. Both were being used by adults as a method by which children could be kept under control and taught the benefits of goodness, kindness, and generosity. I decided to keep the revelation to myself for the time being. Just as it was taboo to tell a young believer that Santa did not exist, I felt that it would be unfair to undermine somebody's faith in Jesus. I would wait until the scales dropped from the eyes of my less erudite contemporaries.

Over time, my initial certainty about religion as a myth began to fade and I grudgingly accepted that Catholicism was not going to go away. My early wide-eyed innocence was gradually replaced by naiveté of a more insidious kind. When I went to secondary school, I regarded myself as an informed, astute, young teenager despite occasional evidence to the contrary. One example of this self delusion occurred during a school retreat when I was about thirteen. The three day event, which was coordinated by visiting priests, was intended as an opportunity for reflection and spiritual renewal. It comprised prayer sessions for the students and sermons on matters of faith or morality interspersed with designated periods of silence and contemplation.

I was unsurprised when it was announced that one of the sermons would be about sects. I knew about the dangers of sects. I had been reading in the Sunday newspaper about young people being lured away from formal religion and from their families in order to join a religious cult or sect under the malign influence of some Svengali-like figure. I understood immediately why the priests would consider this an appropriate and timely subject.

It was announced that there would be separate session for the senior and junior boys. I did not think that there was anything unusual in the decision of the visiting priest to speak on the subject in general terms with those us us in the junior classes and to have a more detailed discussion in private with the boys in the two senior classes. The senior boys would be more vulnerable and more likely to be targeted by these sects, I figured.

I should have realised that something was amiss when I heard sniggering and I observed knowing looks being exchanged between some of my fellow pupils. The priest was short on specifics as he warned us to avoid sects. I did not quite grasp why we were being discouraged from talking, joking, or even thinking about sects. The fresh outburst of sniggering alerted me that there was something going on here that I did not quite grasp. The priest went on to talk about sects before marriage and sects between a man and a woman... Oh. He's talking about...sex? I quickly joined in the sniggering and the exchange of knowing looks in order to hide my embarrassment. In truth, I was far more knowledgeable about sects than sex but my fellow students didn't need to know that...

Notwithstanding this early mishap, I enjoyed the annual retreats. The sermons gave much food for thought and I benefited from the periods of silence, during which one could wander around the school grounds. The isolation and opportunities for contemplation were soothing and relaxing. Was this how priests felt during their more meditative hours?. Just like most young Catholic boys, I pondered on whether I was destined for the priesthood but, after some thought, I was convinced that the priestly life was not for me. Curiously, a woman from the parish saw me in church and approached my mother.

"That boy will be a priest. I'm sure of it."

I suspect that if my mother considered that my becoming a priest was a possibility, she would have kept the revelation to herself. As it was, she occasionally poked fun at my laissez faire attitude towards religion. She amused herself by pointing out that my sudden bursts of enthusiasm for religion only manifested themselves when I needed something. Nevertheless, she encouraged me to pray and to participate in local religious events. As a result, I attended a few all-night vigils at the Marian shrine in Knock while I was awaiting my Intermediate Certificate results. A similar strategy was adopted with my Leaving Certificate examinations. I climbed Croagh Patrick, the holy mountain, a regular practise for those seeking divine assistance. Such pilgrimages were not acts of cynicism on my part but revealed an ambivalence about their efficacy. I was not convinced that they would result in better exam results but I regarded them as a kind of religious each-way bet. They might help. They definitely wouldn't do any harm. I also had my mother and, more importantly, Granny Rushe praying for my success. With all these irons in the fire, I could hardly go wrong.

I have no doubt that, despite their occasional disagreements with the pronouncements of the hierarchy, my parents found comfort in their religion. Both prayed habitually and my mother was committed to various prayers and novenas. A well thumbed prayer book, her constant accessory, which is now in Patricia's possession, is packed with prayer leaflets and memoriam cards for deceased friends and family members, all of whom were regularly prayed for. I am convinced that my parents' religious faith helped them to cope with the difficulties which they faced.

CHAPTER TWENTY-EIGHT

Harmonica Man

My father did not easily bestow praise. Or perhaps it is fairer to say that he had a complex relationship with the concept of praise. He praised his children when they achieved something noteworthy but seldom articulated his approval directly to them. The achiever knew that Daddy was pleased; his demeanour revealed his delight and pride. Yet he conveyed his praise indirectly. If he was proud of the achievements of one of his children, he told my grandparents, my mother, or the other children. Of course, the achiever was soon made aware of Daddy's praise because my mother or grandparents ensured that it was passed on.

"Your father is delighted with you."

"You're in Daddy's good books."

It seems to me that he feared that praise which was bestowed directly might lead to complacency with the result that the opportunity for further achievement might be missed. On one occasion, while in secondary school, I somehow managed to gain a mark of 98% in a mathematics test. When the results arrived home in the post, my mother proudly showed the scores to my father as I looked on. He nodded in approval.

"That's remarkable."

High praise indeed, I thought. He went on.

"Tell me this. Do you know where you lost the other 2%?"

My mother was furious.

"Why must you take the good out of everything? Is it so hard for you to give credit where it's due? Coleman almost got full marks and you're too miserable to praise him. God give me patience!"

She berated him for his inability to give praise unconditionally. He was taken aback by the passion of her admonishment and tried to defend himself.

"We know that he did great. But what I was trying to say is that he knows 98% of what he was asked so there's nothing more to be gained from concentrating on that. The only other benefit that he can get from the examination is to find out where he went wrong with the other 2%."

He knew from her expression that he was digging a deeper hole for himself. He looked to me in desperation.

"I'm sure Coleman knows what I meant."

She wasn't having it.

"Never mind what Coleman knows or doesn't know! The person who has the most to learn from this isn't Coleman. Wait till I tell Granny and Granda what you said. Taking the good out of the best exam results that ever came into this house... I might as well be talking to the four walls..."

Good school reports were not the only way to win my father's approval. My interest in music had, up to now, been confined to listening avidly to the radio, watching the band practising in our house, and singing with the church choir at Sunday evening devotions. In the summer of 1962, that was to change and music was to provide me and my father with a life-long bond.

At Claremorris Agricultural Show, one of the local social events of the year, I bought a small mouth organ at a novelty stall. The plastic harmonica was little more than a toy and comprised only the eight notes of the scale. Yet, the possibilities of the instrument piqued my interest. At school, Mrs O'Leary had taught us our do-re-mi as she selected and encouraged some of us to sing in the church choir. By experimenting with inhaling and exhaling as I tried to understand the instrument, I soon discovered that I could play the scale. I repeated it incessantly, even displaying my proficiency by faultlessly playing my way up the scale and then, with a flourish, back down again. None of my siblings took a blind bit of notice. Or, if they did, the only response was to advise me to play quietly or, better still, not at all.

"That's not music. Play a proper tune!"

The breakthrough happened when I thought that there was something familiar about the do-re-mi sequence. The penny dropped. It was the first three notes of "Wooden Heart" which had been a hit the previous summer for Elvis Presley. I hadn't liked the song; I much preferred Elvis's more up-tempo, rockier stuff. But it was a "proper tune", so I carried on up the scale. Mi-fa-so was almost the next three notes but wasn't quite right until I discovered the sequence was mi-so-fa. Now I was on a roll. I slowly and painstakingly worked my way through the melody until I could play both verse and chorus. I played haltingly, at first, and then with increasing assurance. I was delighted to discover that the melody utilised only the eight notes which were available to me. I even mastered the introduction which is played on the record with an accordion. This task was made easier because it consists only of the repetition of the same two notes.

Now I had a proper tune. I practised in a secluded corner of the garden, out of earshot of the house. My brother Mike recognised the melody but didn't seem overly impressed at the magnitude of the achievement. Nobody else took any notice... or so it seemed.

One sunny Saturday afternoon soon afterwards, Mike and I had been excused from the dinner table and were playing in the garden while our parents finished their meal. My mother called through the open window.

"Coleman. Come in here and play that tune for Daddy."

Panic.

"What? I don't know it. I'm only learning."

"What tune? Play what?"

I could hear the unmistakeable interest in my father's voice. There was no escape. My mother updated my father as I reluctantly trudged back indoors.

"The mouth organ. He's practising. Just listen."

My mother nodded in encouragement while the rest of the family waited in order to see what was going to happen. Nervously, I stood at the end of the kitchen table and took the harmonica from my pocket, being careful to clap it on my palm to shake free any breadcrumbs or other debris which might impede the reeds. Trying hard to maintain an even tempo, which I knew my father would notice, I played the obligatory two verses, the chorus and the final verse. I had forgotten to start with the introduction but I added it at the end to give a final flourish.

It seemed to me that my father was looking at me as if he hadn't really noticed me before.

"How long did it take you to learn that?"

"Not long. I practised a bit."

Mike grinned in approval at the response to my playing.

"He never shuts up. He's at it morning, noon and night."

My mother beamed at my father.

"Didn't I tell you?"

"Show me here".

My father reached out and I handed the harmonica to him. He turned it over in his palm as he scrutinised it.

"You'll have to learn some more tunes."

"It's hard to find the right ones. A lot of tunes need more notes than...."

I wasn't sure how to explain.

He nodded. He understood.

"Keep working on it. I'm sure you'll find more where that tune came from."

I was walking on air as I returned to the garden. I hadn't even realised that my mother had heard my tentative efforts to play. Now my father had listened, liked what he heard, and encouraged me to persevere. But it wasn't the positive response alone which raise my spirits. Now, I realised, I had something of my own. A personal thing which differentiated me from my brothers and sisters. Like Mike and his Meccano.

From an early age, Mike had shown an aptitude for working with his hands and he developed an abiding interest in mechanics and carpentry. Whereas I was content to watch Granda at his woodworking in his small work-shed in his back garden, Mike wanted to be involved - to get his hands dirty. He bombarded Granda with questions and was fascinated when shown some new technique. A child's carpentry set was one of his early Christmas presents. He also displayed a tendency to take toys apart in order to understand how they worked. When he was about ten or eleven, his interest in mechanics was recognised by the receipt of a Meccano set as a Christmas present. He utilised the model construction kit to assemble miniature cranes, machines, and vehicles. Soon, he had outgrown the assembly instructions on the box and he was inventing and building his own models, to the approval of my father and grandfather.

Now, the mouth organ had enabled me to discover my own "thing". As I look back now, I recognise that I needed to strike out on my own. I had many of the characteristics which are now associated with Middle Child Syndrome. With all the unreasonableness of a self-absorbed preteen, I resented that Patricia could "swan in" from Granny and Granda's for the weekend and boss the rest of us younger children. I was regularly becoming involved in petulant arguments with her. I did not resent Michael but I recognised that he was much more popular and likeable than me. The two younger boys, Sean and Kieran, were still at the stage when anything they did or said was regarded as adorable by all and sundry.

"A pair of dotes!"

Now I had stumbled upon something which allowed me to differentiate myself from my siblings. Playing music resulted in an increase in my self-esteem and a closer bond with my father.

The change had come about because my mother had drawn my father's attention to my ability. One of the outcomes of writing this book has been the opportunity to reevaluate my mother's seemingly low-key but ultimately pivotal role in various family events. Did she recognise that I needed to establish my own identity within the family? Did she study and subvert? Did she identify and capitalise on an opportunity to create a bond between my father and myself?

A few weeks later, she was centrally involved again. She was making a rare solo journey by train to visit her father in Cappamore. When she arrived back home, she handed me a package.

"Daddy asked me to get that for you."

I fumbled excitedly with the wrapping and the cardboard box inside to reveal a gleaming Hohner harmonica. It was beautifully curved and was bulkier than the old plastic toy. I immediately discovered that, apart from the eight notes of the C scale, it had a further half octave above and below.

"Now I can learn any tune I want!" I explained to my father, after I had thanked him when he came in from work. He examined the instrument, asked me to play something and marvelled at the tone. It had a lovely sweet, mellow timbre on the upper register and a fuller warm sound on the lower notes.

My mother, quietly pleased at my father's approval of her choice, explained that she had visited a music shop in Limerick city and explained to the "nice man" that she knew nothing about harmonicas. He questioned her about the age of the musician and the type of music which I played. He then recommended the model which she should buy. My father was impressed and, as usual, his praise was carefully couched.

"I never thought that you could get a mouth-organ with a tone like that without paying out a small fortune".

Although he didn't play the harmonica, my father gave me a few pointers on how to read music. He taught me the rudiments of the treble and bass clefs and the time signatures. Many great musicians can not read music, he explained, but it helps to have even a basic knowledge of "what's going on". He explained that certain combinations of notes, when played together, sounded pleasing to the ear. The harmonica has limited scope for playing such chords but he encouraged me to find them. He also explained how to "vamp" as accompaniment to a singer and showed me how to cup my palms and flutter my fingers in order to mute or add tremolo to the notes.

Thus started the musical bond between us which evolved over time, shaped our relationship, and continued right up to the end of his life.

CHAPTER TWENTY-NINE

Tougher Than The Rest

Following the family upheaval caused by Mary's death during the summer, the prospect of returning to the routine of the schoolroom in September 1961 was an attractive and comforting one. But storms were brewing. Winds of change were about to blow, sometimes literally. On 16 September, Hurricane Debbie wreaked havoc in the locality. Houses were damaged and trees uprooted. Our school building in Ballyfarna was unscathed but the handball alley on the school grounds was flattened. The local church bore the brunt of the storm because of its exposed location on the hill at Barnacarroll. Although the church had been extensively rebuilt and re-roofed during the summer, the hurricane ripped off the new roof and flung it into the middle of the old graveyard, flattening or damaging several gravestones.

Having gladly escaped from the clutches of Mrs O'Leary two years earlier, I was about to start fifth class. I was now being taught by Mr O'Leary, the school principal. A gentle man, Mr O'Leary rarely used corporal punishment and had a reputation as a good teacher. Most of his pupils were destined for emigration but others had gone on to become teachers, civil servants, nurses, and occasionally, nuns or priests. But, in truth, Mr O'Leary was losing his enthusiasm for teaching. He had been in Ballyfarna school since 1924 and was now approaching his 65th birthday.

Looking back, it seems to me that Mr O'Leary's attention, in his final years as a teacher, focussed on a few pupils whom he considered to have potential. These tended to be children whose parents he had taught in the past. He knew that the families had the financial means and the motivation to send the children to secondary school. His strategy was understandable. A large percentage of pupils did not continue with formal education when they left primary school.

At the end of September, Mr and Mrs O'Leary both retired from their teaching posts at Ballyfarna school. Mr O'Leary was replaced by Tom Morley, a young energetic teacher who quickly made it clear he was the harbinger of fundamental changes in our schooling. He was not a native of the parish so that he did not have a history with the parents and therefore had no favourites among the pupils. When he questioned us in order to take an inventory of our progress in various subjects, he seemed satisfied with our reading and writing in English and Irish, less so with our mathematics, and aghast at our lack of knowledge of history and geography. We assured him that Mr O'Leary taught us history and, as evidence, explained that stories were read to us about Finn McCumhaill, Oisin, and the Red Branch Knights. Mr Morley explained to us that these stories were defined as mythology and folklore, not history. He was soon teaching us about the earliest peoples who arrived in Ireland, the advent of christianity, the arrival and ultimate defeat of the Danes or Vikings, and the arrival of the Normans. We were also memorising the names and locations of Irish mountains, lakes, and rivers as well as the principal towns in each county.

Another innovation was "mentals", which was the name given to mental arithmetic. We were expected to be able to make basic mathematical calculations without recourse to pen and paper.

The raised standards and curriculum changes were exactly what we needed and, not least in my case, were beneficial. It all sounds idyllic, and should have been, but for one overshadowing issue. Mr Morley, in order to usher us into this new era, used corporal punishment to a degree which now seems grossly disproportionate and which, at least as far as I was concerned, introduced an atmosphere of fear and intimidation into the school.

The practice of caning children in schools has a long history and was in common usage in Ireland until the 1980s. Teachers saw themselves as acting *in loco parentis* and it was quite understandable that the methods which were utilised to impose discipline in the home were replicated in the schoolroom. The teachers could be forgiven for believing that corporal punishment was necessary or even essential on order to punish misbehaviour or disruption in the classroom. But beatings in school were not confined to the management of behaviour. Children were caned for making mistakes in spelling or mathematics or even for failing to understand some concept which was grasped by the majority of their peers. For example, "mentals" became a nightmare for some children who struggled to carry out the calculations. Mathematics was one of my better subjects and I found that I could quickly work out the correct answer. Nevertheless, the near panic caused by the schoolmaster as he stood over me impatiently flexing his bamboo cane, almost caused me to miscalculate on occasions. Some children, either because they didn't grasp the concept or because they struggled with figures, received canings virtually every time the subject was called. Failure to remember important dates in history or to correctly identify specific rivers or mountains on the map would also result in the dreaded swish of the cane.

Teachers from that era might argue that many errors in class or homework are due to indiscipline rather than to a lack of ability, and were thereby deserving of corporal punishment. But when the same children are being punished daily for the same errors, it should become clear that the approach is not working and that a different strategy is needed.

Because we were accustomed to the benign regime of Mr O'Leary, the changes seemed more traumatic to us children. On the rare occasions when Mr O'Leary had considered corporal punishment to be necessary, he might reluctantly have administered one or two slaps on the palm with a light ruler. Such punishment was administered for misbehaviour, never for mistakes or errors in classwork. I had not seen a cane until Mr Morley produced one from inside his overcoat one morning and proceeded to administer slaps on the palms to anybody who made a mistake or answered a question incorrectly.

I was warned. Upon the arrival of the new teacher in Ballyfarna, my mother cautioned me about my behaviour.

"Don't get on the wrong side of him. Don't be showing off or making any smart alecky comments. You don't want him getting his knife into you from the beginning."

She didn't have to warn Michael. She trusted that he would behave well as always and his cheerfulness and likability would see him through. Her concerns about my relationship with the new teacher were well founded. I cannot recall any misbehaviour or "smart alecky comments" on my part. But, for some reason, I was one of the children who got off on the wrong foot with Mr Morley. He seemed to single us out for attention. In my case, he quickly made it clear that he thought that I was underachieving. I realise now that he was correct in his diagnosis. I had sailed through Mr O'Leary's classes without any problem. His laissez-faire regime had suited my relatively casual approach. Mr Morley was more demanding and I ultimately benefitted from the change of teacher but yet I retain much resentment about the methods used.

In my case, I received canings on almost a daily basis over my remaining two years at Ballyfarna school. At first, I responded by raising my standards. The quality of my homework improved as did my attention and concentration in class. Perhaps, having seen the efficacy of his methods, Mr Morley decided to persevere. It soon became apparent to me that, no matter how hard I tried to improve, I would not avoid further punishment and the teacher's insistence that I push myself even harder. My perception was that Mr Morley would persist in asking questions and devising new problems for solution until I inevitably made a mistake and caning would follow. My main memory of this period of schooling is one of complete helplessness. I became convinced that there was nothing I could do in order to avoid further canings. This feeling of impotence blighted by final years at Ballyfarna.

I was not alone as a recipient of regular punishment. There were a few others in the class who received similar treatment. My brother Mike remembers this period with particular anger also. Although he was not caned with anything like the regularity which I experienced, he resented the treatment which I was receiving and which sometimes reduced him to tears.

I recently discussed my memories of school with another contemporary pupil and he had a slightly different perspective. He agreed that a few children, including myself, suffered excessive corporal punishment but he was convinced that we were singled out because we were perceived to have academic potential and that, ultimately, our achievements might enhance the reputation of the school and the teacher. Conversely, he was convinced that the remainder of the class were effectively written off by the teacher who concentrated his efforts on the chosen few.

The situation became even more bizarre in our final year. All pupils completed a state examination upon finishing primary school and, if successful, were awarded a Primary Certificate. In addition, Mr Morley decided to prepare some pupils for an optional examination which was organised by the local county council. A student who achieved an acceptable standard in the county council examination was awarded grant aid in order to help fund the cost of secondary education. I was one of four or five pupils whom the teacher singled out for this extra tuition. He made it clear that he was undecided whether to forward all or any of us to sit the examination but he would make a decision based upon his judgement of our progress. Now I was in the baffling situation of having been designated as one of the students with potential while simultaneously receiving more regular and severe canings than many of the pupils who were not selected for advancement.

Mike was not selected to prepare for the council examinations despite being at least as bright as I was, as he has clearly demonstrated by the achievements in his later working life. He was not disappointed but was concerned that our parents might be. We pledged not to mention the situation at home. We would have to explain the situation to our parents if I was to eventually sit the examination but, for the moment, we decided to keep our secret.

There was another underlying reason for our reticence. Our parents had made it clear that they expected both of us to go to secondary school as Patricia had done. It was intended that we would attend together at Saint Colman's College for five years following which we would sit for our Leaving Certificate examination. We would then enter the workforce with a level of education which had been denied to my parents because of lack of opportunity and financial constraints.

Mike had his own ideas. His interest in mechanics and carpentry had intensified as he got older. Even at his relatively young age, he was averse to the prospect of a life behind a desk. The thought of spending five years studying Latin, Irish, and English had no attraction for him. He secretly wanted to go to the Tech.

Claremorris Technical and Vocational School, known colloquially as The Tech, had recently opened. Students prepared for the Group Certificate over a three year period. As well as the standard subjects such as languages, mathematics, and science, there were classes in wood-work, metal-work, and mechanical drawing. Part of the school's mandate was to prepare young people for careers in such areas as engineering, plumbing, electricity, carpentry, and mechanics.

Mike was interested in exploring subjects offered by the Tech. He was horrified by the prospect of having his head stuck in a book for the rest of his life. But he was not ready to broach the subject at home. I was similarly reluctant to reveal my difficulties with corporal punishment. Our mother gradually sensed from my demeanour that something was amiss. She realised that I was under pressure and questioned me about it. Her initial suspicion was that, despite her warnings, I was misbehaving and thereby incurring the wrath of Mr Morley. She warned me to behave and trusted that I would gradually "get on the right side" of the teacher. When she saw that there was no improvement, she questioned us about school but we gave little away. Not to be outdone, she made discreet enquiries through neighbouring parents of fellow pupils. She was relieved and pleased to discover that I was receiving extra tuition and, naturally, she attributed the pressure associated with this to the change in my demeanour.

Why did I not tell my parents about my problems in school? I could have. Mike would have backed me up and confirmed his belief that I was being victimised. But I had made him promise not to say anything. I did not want to cause problems for my parents who would have had to confront the teacher. In truth, I was not convinced that they would do so. This was the early 1960s. Teachers, like priests, were figures of authority and were inviolable. My fear of inaction by my parents against a teacher was completely unjustified as will be proved later. I very much regret that I did not confide in my mother and father at the time.

Despite having "beaten me into shape" for the Council examination, it seems that Mr Morley was unconvinced. When the time came to sit the examination, he decided that he would not send my name forward. My recollection is that he allowed three pupils to sit the exam and held back two of us. He never offered any explanation but it seems reasonable to assume that he adjudged that we were unlikely to do as well as he had hoped. I was ambivalent about the decision. The financial help with my secondary education would have been a welcome boost to my parents. I was relieved that the pressure was taken away from me but regretted the opportunity to get a good result and show Mr Morley that he was incorrect in his decision to exclude me.

Unexpected but welcome vindication was forthcoming when the Primary Certificate results were released and they revealed that I had received better results than some of the pupils who had sat for the Council examinations.

A postscript to the events at Ballyfarna school occurred many years later. The occasion was my mother's funeral. I was standing in the funeral home in Claremorris with family members, accepting the sympathetic handshakes and condolences of neighbours and friends who were paying their respects to my father and our family. Having lived away from Murneen for thirty years, I struggled to remember some names and faces. Between handshakes and murmurs of sympathy, something made me glance across the crowded room to where Mike was standing. He was staring at me with a look of horror and apprehension. He began to make his way towards me. I shook a few more hands and, as there was a brief gap in the row of sympathisers, I stepped forward to meet him. His look had changed to one of relieved anxiety.

"I was sure you were going to hit him!"

"What? Who?"

"Tom Morley. I didn't see him until he was standing in front of you. I was afraid you were going to hit him."

"I didn't even recognise the man.

"That explains it. I figured you wouldn't be able to hold yourself back. Nobody could blame you."

I was taken aback at the vehemence of Mike's reaction. I explained to him that I had long ago put any resentment about Mr Morley behind me. I firmly believe that the teacher was convinced that he was doing the right thing and that he perceived, from my gradual improvement, that his methods were working. I had not complained to my parents about the impact on me and he had no way of knowing that he was causing me such distress. But I was startled too by Mike's reaction. He is the most kind-hearted man and abhors violence. For the first time, I appreciated the impact that the events had on him. Because of his sensitivity and empathy, he had suffered from the corporal punishment at least as much as I did.

What of the role of my parents while all this was going on? I didn't tell them and was determined to hide my discomfort. If I had spoken to anybody, it would have been to my mother. Instead, I persisted with the omertà which Mike and I had devised. I didn't want to add to my mother's own pressures by letting her know that I was having problems and, at some level, I thought that, being a non-confrontational person, she would not be in a position to do anything about it. I was wrong.

A year or two after I finished school, my younger sister, Kay was attending the local national school. Her friend and classmate was Eugene, a grandson of next-door neighbour Mrs Glynn. When he got home from school one day, Eugene innocently mentioned that the female teacher had hit Kay, causing her to have a nosebleed. The word was quickly passed to my mother who immediately questioned Kay.

Eugene had told the truth but the story was not nearly as serious as it appeared. Kay sheepishly confirmed that she was daydreaming and the teacher gave her a mild slap on the arm to make her pay attention. The unexpected jolt gave Kay such a shock that, much to her embarrassment, it triggered one of her occasional nosebleeds. Kay was quite happy to allow matters rest but, to her surprise, our mother was not to be mollified. The following morning, she was waiting at the school when the teacher arrived and the two women had a lengthy private discussion. From then onwards, Kay was treated with kid gloves by the teacher. When I heard about the incident, I regretted that I had misjudged my mother and that I had not confided in her many years earlier.

CHAPTER THIRTY

Summertime Blues

In 1963, the long summer beckoned as Mike and I gladly said farewell to Ballyfarna school. In former years, the family would have headed for Cappamore but this year, all was to change. There were two reasons.

The first was joyous. My mother was expecting a baby again. There are reasons to believe that the birth was not planned. The deaths of Mary and the baby two years earlier might have led my parents to decide that the family was large enough. In later years, my mother would joke to Kay, her youngest daughter:

"As for you. You weren't on the agenda at all. You shouldn't even be here."

Another clue about my parents' intentions was the disposal of the pram which had been used by all of us earlier children. It was passed on to a friend who had recently had a first baby.

I recall being excited at the prospect of the arrival of a new family member. Despite the problems associated with the death of her previous child, I have no recollection of being worried for my mother but I'm sure my parents had huge concerns. I remember being hopeful that it would be a girl so that Patricia would again have a sister and, anyway, I figured that I already had more than enough brothers.

My parents had shielded us from the impact of the double tragedy in 1961 and had tried to ensure that family life continued as normal. Patricia, Mike, and I were now teenagers, however, and could sense the significance of things which, in our earlier years, we would have missed or ignored. For example, we gradually came to realise that the family financial situation was finely balanced; my parents struggled to make ends meet. The physical growth of the children was reflected in a gradual increase in the food bill and the extra income from my father's activity as a musician was no longer available. From September onwards, there were to be three of us in secondary education and school fees had to be paid. Mike and I required bicycles in order to travel to school and there would be a long list of school-books to purchase.

From a financial viewpoint, it was far from the ideal time for an addition to the family. Yet the safe arrival in mid July of a baby sister, who was named Kay, gave a great lift to the family and other issues seemed to fade into relative insignificance. Patricia, who was 15 when her sister arrived, was overjoyed and, when she arrived home from our grandparents each weekend, fussed over the baby and lifted her from her cot at every opportunity. The four brothers were enthused about having a baby sister to protect and care for. Under our mother's supervision, Mike and I quickly became experts in changing nappies, feeding, and "winding" the baby.

Sean and Kieran were no longer treated as the babies of the family by their bigger brothers. They also benefitted from the readjustments in the sleeping arrangements necessitated by the arrival of a baby girl. It was decided that Kay should sleep in the smallest bedroom which had previously been used by my parents. Patricia would share the bedroom with her at weekends. My parents would move to the room behind the kitchen which had been Mary's room so that the four boys would share the largest bedroom. There was space in this room for two double beds, one of which was shared by me and Mike. In sharing the other bed, Sean and Kieran were pleased to be treated on an even footing with us.

The real beneficiaries of Kay's arrival were my parents. My father always had a special father-daughter bond with Patricia. She was now entering young womanhood and naturally their relationship was evolving and changing. They would always be close - although he tried to be even-handed, I think he had a closer affinity with Patricia than with any of the rest of us - but she was no longer his "little girl". Now he had Kay as the recipient of his affections. She beamed up at him from her cot and he loved every second of it.

My mother was sparkling again; she had a new focus and purpose in her life. Kay's arrival was perfectly timed. It was exactly what the family and particularly my mother needed. She and Kay went on to form a close and mutually supportive bond which would sustain for the rest of my mother's life. Kay's arrival reinvigorated the family which was slowly emerging from the shadow of the deaths of the two children two years previously.

Unlike the pram, the baby cot had not been disposed of. I suspect this was because it was built by my grandfather in his carpentry workshop and my parents would not part with it to somebody outside the family. But a pram was needed and new prams were costly. My father came up with a solution. He had seen used prams listed in the "for sale" section of the evening newspapers. The majority of the sellers had Dublin addresses but this did not deter him. One Saturday, his free day from work, he arranged his free train ticket and travelled to Dublin. As he had done some years previously when he made his abortive attempt to purchase a sewing machine, he waited outside the newspaper office until the first edition of the Evening Press became available in the early afternoon. Having scanned the adverts and made some calls from a nearby phone box, he caught a bus to visit a house in the Dublin suburbs where he examined, bargained for, and purchased a pram. The seller correctly warned him that he would not be allowed to take the pram onto a bus. Undeterred, he walked and pushed the pram from the Dublin suburbs into Pearse Street railway station from where he travelled back home to Claremorris with the pram stored safely in the guard's van.

Apart from the expected arrival of the new baby, there was a second reason why our usual trip to Cappamore did not take place that summer. Mike and I had summer jobs. The trend had been started by Patricia who got a job working as a waitress in Knock on summer weekends when the village was inundated by pilgrims visiting the Marian shrine.

Mike was first off the mark and bagged the prime target. He got a job working on Tommy Keane's farm. Tommy, owner of Gosling Garden, raconteur, amateur veterinarian, and gentleman, lived with his mother on their large farm and he employed Mike to help with milking, feeding calves, haymaking, and general farm chores. I was at a loss to know where I might find work to emulate Mike. Many of the other holdings in the area were family farms where there were already children available to help with farm chores. Other farms were operated by siblings and there was barely enough work to keep them occupied.

My mother made a suggestion. She pointed out to me that Bill Melia was farming on his own and might need a helper for the summer. I knew Bill by sight but had never spoken to him. He was a tall and imposing man who, I learned, had spent many years working on the building sites in England. Possibly as a result of the manual labour, he had developed some muscular problem which made it difficult for him to bend one leg so that he walked with a slight limp. Following his return from England, Bill had built a house on his small farm but he continued to live with his married brother and family in Mace, a few miles away. He cycled to his farm each day and returned to Mace each night.

I called to his farm at milking time one evening and enquired whether he needed a helper on the farm for the summer. I stood at the door, blinking into the gloom of the darkened cow-house. After a preliminary glance in my direction, he turned back to his milking, his forehead pressed against the flank of the cow as he directed the squirts of milk into the galvanised bucket.

"What work can you do?"

"Ah.. anything you want."

"Can you milk?"

"Ah... no... I mean I know how it's done... and I could learn."

"You mightn't be much use to me. I wasn't looking for anyone."

"Thanks anyway. I thought there was no harm in asking. I'll be off so..."

As I turned to leave, I was disappointed that I hadn't got a job but also relieved, having been put off by his gruff manner.

"Who are you anyway."

I turned back.

"I'm one of the Rushes...... my father works on ...."

"Is he the railway man?"

"That's right."

I waited. The only sound was coming from the spurts of milk which were flowing more freely now. Then he went on.

"Your mother is a decent woman. Show up here at nine in the morning and we'll see if you're worth keeping on."

"Right so. Thanks. I'll see you then."

He carried on with his milking, his forehead embedded in the cow's flank. I hesitated.

"Ah... will I bring a sandwich for my lunch or will I have time to go home?"

"Mother of God! You're already thinking about your belly before you've done a stroke of work. Don't worry about sandwiches."

My apprehensions when I turned up for work the next morning were unfounded. The work in the hay field was light and undemanding and Bill chatted away for most of the day. I suspect that, having spent many bleak winter days alone on the land, he was glad of the company and the willing ear.

At lunchtime, we went back from the fields to Bill's house. It was clear that it had never been lived in. There was not much furniture: a table, a chair for Bill, and a wooden stool on which I sat. Bill's bicycle was resting against one of the smoothly plastered but unpainted walls of the kitchen. A few old newspapers were stacked in the corner. I later discovered that Bill read them on wet days while waiting for the rain to clear.

Having boiled the electric kettle and brewed some tea, he unfastened a bag from the carrier of his bike. He produced two packets wrapped in newspaper and handed one to me. It contained two sandwiches which, he explained, were prepared by his brother's wife. Slices of thickly-cut, fresh, home-made bread were generously packed with cold, lean, boiled bacon. He watched carefully as I wolfed down the sandwiches and accepted a second cup of tea.

The following day, there were three generous sandwiches in the package which he handed to me. I was brought up to believe that good manners dictated that you ate everything on your plate. To do otherwise was to imply that you did not like the food. Two sandwiches would have been enough but I managed to eat all three while endeavouring to show the same level of enthusiasm as on the previous day.

Yes. On day three, there were four sandwiches. This could not go on. I would have to say something. Before I could say anything, Bill spoke:

"I told her four was too much. Just eat what you want. Leave the rest."

"They're lovely sandwiches. But two.... or maybe three is more than enough..."

"I told her. The lad thinks it's bad manners to leave anything behind, I said. But, did she listen? Did she hell! He's a growing lad, she said."

"Please tell her I said thanks very much and they're lovely sandwiches but there's no need for four."

"That's grand. I'll pass on the word."

The quantity of sandwiches stabilised at three and the quality was maintained for the summer. The only variable was the type of sliced meat. I suspect that extra meat was cooked for the family dinner and the surplus used for our sandwiches. The aroma of freshly baked bread and sliced meat was a cherished highlight of a twelve-year-old's summer.

Bill was a kind and entertaining workmate. He regaled me with stories about his experiences on the building sites of England. As a younger man, being over six feet tall and strongly built, he was regularly challenged to fist-fights by others who resented him and fancied their chances. His method of avoiding fist-fights was to turn the tables on his aggressor by challenging him to partake in a feat of strength or even a foot-race to be supervised and, as an added incentive, wagered upon by the workers. In his prime, he was confident that he could win such contests and, more importantly, his opponent's aggression was soon overtaken by exhaustion.

Bill's only fault was that he had a terrible tongue when he got angry. His bursts of anger were solely directed at his donkey whose persistently stubborn streak occasionally annoyed Bill to the extent that he railed and shouted at the unfortunate animal using the most profane and graphic language. I suspect that these occasional flashes of bad temper were a result of muscular or joint pain in Bill's leg aggravated by unfavourable weather conditions.

Being unaccustomed to profane language, I was initially shocked but I soon became immune to the occasional outbursts. As the summer neared its end, however, a neighbouring farmer heard one such tirade and mentioned to my father that it might be unwise to be exposing an innocent and sheltered boy to such profanity. My father suggested that we might look further afield when choosing a summer job for me the following year.

There were a number of reasons for obliging us to get summer jobs. The extra money, although quite modest, was a welcome addition to the household budget. We handed over all we earned, safe in the knowledge that pocket money would be available if we wanted to go to a football match or, in our mid-teens, to go dancing or to the cinema. Another benefit was that a summer job kept us occupied during the three month holiday break which was the norm for secondary schools in Ireland. Unless shortened by state examinations, holidays lasted from the first week in June until the first week in September. Summer work also provided us with another benefit. We were gaining experience in working for and with other people.

My father was a union man. He strongly believed in the effectiveness of trade unions and the advisability of worker involvement in trade unionism. He often spoke about trade union solidarity and the necessity to keep pressure on the employer to treat the workers fairly. But he was equally vocal about the obligations of workers to their employers and was a firm believer in the concept of "minding your job". By being punctual, obedient, and doing "a decent day's work", you were giving your employer value for money and convincing him that he had made the correct decision in creating the job and in entrusting it to you. In a sense, you were striving to make yourself indispensable. You had an obligation to mind your job; to ensure that the job opportunity continued to exist after you left. If the job was seasonal, you should be trying to ensure that the opportunity would be available for you or somebody else the following year.

During the six summers surrounding my five years in secondary school, I had a variety of summer jobs. In 1964, my grandfather arranged for me to get employment as a shop assistant in a hardware store in Claremorris. My father was pleased when I was eagerly taken back by the same employer the following summer. Towards the end of the summer of 65, I was occasionally directed to assist the lorry driver with deliveries and quite enjoyed the diversion. A builder friend told my father that he had seen me toting bags of cement which we were delivering to his building site. My father was unhappy that, at the age of fourteen, I was being asked to do such heavy work and the result was a change of job for the following summer. My grandfather, who had now retired from the railway, was working part-time as a carpenter with a building firm which was erecting an extension at the local Convent of Mercy. He spoke to his employers and got me a job working in the site office. In 67 and 68, I replaced Mike as a summer helper on Tommy Keane's farm.

When the time came for me to apply for post educational full-time work, I had the advantage of being able to point out at interviews that I had experience in manual, office, and retail work. More importantly, I had demonstrated that I could take and carry out instructions, work satisfactorily with colleagues, deal with cash in a trustworthy manner, and "mind my job". I didn't consider it appropriate during job interviews to add that I had also acquired other life skills. It would not have been helpful to add that I could kill, pluck, and clean a chicken, drop slits, make a hay rope, swing and sharpen a scythe, scuffle, tackle an ass, foot turf, spread manure, spray potatoes, and fry lamb's tails…

CHAPTER THIRTY-ONE

What Do You Want?

"One of my regrets is that I left all the educational decisions to Mammy. It wasn't fair to put that load on her shoulders. I should have helped out a lot more."

I was puzzled when my father made this observation shortly after my mother's death. I had always assumed that they had a discussion about any such matters but was convinced that he had the final say. That was very much the impression that my mother gave when conveying any decision about our education to us. But I realise now that this was her way of managing the situation.

My father was vocal on the subject of education. We knew from an early age that he was determined that we should understand the crucial impact which it could make in our lives. Education would provide us with choices.

"You can spend your life pushing either a pen or a shovel. It's up to you and your schoolwork."

He never denigrated manual work. But he regularly pointed out that having what he termed a "sitting down job" was far preferable to being "up to your knees in water, digging ditches in the middle of winter". He wanted his children to have an easier life than he had and he saw education as the obvious pathway to achieving this goal.

While my father issued policy statements about the importance of education, my mother was operating quietly at a much more practical and effective level. She was less vocal but, in her way, was even more persuasive and insistent that we perform to our potential at school. She was constantly reminding us to do our homework and, when we attended secondary school, ensuring that we spent sufficient hours at study and that we were undisturbed while doing so. She occasionally checked our copy books to read essays or exercises and to view the teachers' comments and the marks awarded.

The level of commitment to education varied widely from home to home in the rural west of Ireland. I have no doubt that the ambition of all parents in our locality was to improve their children's lot; to enable the next generation to have better lives than their parents. But, for many people, emigration rather than education was seen as the means by which this could be achieved.

One of the problems faced by parents was that post primary schooling had to be paid for and many families could not afford this outlay. Some others, who were slightly better off, had to prioritise. The child or children whom the parents considered the brightest were sent to secondary school while the siblings were earmarked for emigration.

Another inhibiting factor was the perception that one needed to have influence, known colloquially as "pull", in order to secure a job, particularly in the public sector. A quiet word with a local politician might be necessary when applying for a job in the police force or the civil service. Seeking employment in a bank was regarded by many as a waste of time because priority seemed to be given to the family members of existing bankers or the sons and daughters of valued bank customers. The teaching profession was a more realistic option but even this was not without potential problems. Even after graduating from teacher training college, influence with a parish priest could dictate whether or not you were appointed to a teaching job.

Some wealthier parents avoided the local secondary schools and sent their children further afield to boarding schools. There was a perception that attendance at some of these more prestigious schools gave access to an influential network which would open doors in the future and eventually facilitate entry into the financial, legal, and medical professions.

My parents were not oblivious to the reality of patronage in the job market in Ireland but they were adamant that education provided the best pathway for us. They had no aversion to emigration. Both of them had siblings in England who had made good lives for themselves. My father loved London during his sojourn there and often articulated his opinion on the benefit to be gained from leaving your own country, at least temporarily.

"You see things from a different perspective when you've been out of the country for a while."

Nevertheless, he had an ambition, shared by my mother, that none of us children would be forced to emigrate. If we emigrated, it should be by choice, not through necessity. We should be given every opportunity to make our lives in Ireland and, to facilitate this, we were going to receive secondary education, the best level of schooling which my parents could afford. After successfully completing the five years at secondary school, we should be in a position to secure reasonable and secure employment in "sitting down" jobs.

University education was never an option, at least for Patricia, Mike, and me. The level of college fees and the attendant costs for accommodation and living expenses were far outside my parents' means. In truth, I never harboured an ambition to go to university. It just never entered my mind as an option. To the best of my knowledge, I had never met anybody who had been to university. A select few locals had attended teacher training college and this was the only third level education with which I was familiar. It could be argued that my parents had "ideas above their station" in their determination to send all three of us to secondary school.

As the summer of 1963 drew to a close, plans were well underway for Mike and I to enrol in Saint Colman's College in September. Second hand bicycles had been sourced by my father and grandfather so that we could cycle the round trip of 6 miles each day.

There was only one problem. Mike didn't want to go.

He had found out more about the curriculum in the Tech and, as a result, was even more convinced that this was where his future lay. He was worried that our parents would be disappointed by his choice and he felt guilty that I would have to attend the college alone; we had been classmates for eight years. I tentatively suggested that he might test the water by going to the college for a year and then, if he wasn't happy, he could switch to the Tech. My brother was made of sterner stuff.

Mike finally bit the bullet and spoke to our mother. She listened carefully as he explained his preference for the Vocational School and its curriculum. He had no desire to spend five years studying subjects such as Latin and French. He suggested that he might struggle with the academic demands of the college and that he was best suited to the more practical work in the Tech. In truth, I felt that Mike was being a little disingenuous about his ability to cope in school. I don't think there was any difference between us in terms of academic ability. He didn't read as voraciously as I did and he disliked studying. Or, more accurately, he disliked studying subjects which didn't particularly interest him. Yet, if something caught his imagination, he became absorbed by it. He would later devour textbooks about mechanics and technology and could assimilate and understand complex diagrams and plans.

"We'll see what Daddy says."

My mother's non-committal response wasn't unexpected. I thought then that she would make the case for Mike and then Dad would decide. I'm sure that they discussed it but I now realise that she made the final decision. My father was not indecisive. He could be quite firm and dogmatic even when he knew that he risked making himself unpopular with his children. I now believe that he left the decisions about educational matters to my mother because he completely trusted her judgement and he also knew that she had the ability to deliver a decision in a far more diplomatic manner than he could. But this responsibility must have weighed heavily on my mother at times and my father's realisation of this is evidenced by the regret which he expressed later.

This episode illustrated another facet of my parents' attitude towards their children which was apparent on a number of occasions in subsequent years. When we were faced with crucial decisions, they advised and guided us and, if appropriate, strove to influence us. When we were younger, they refused permission when they felt that a refusal was warranted. But in our teenage years, when we expressed contrary views on matters such as education or career choices, they listened carefully to what we had to say. They used persuasion to try to bring us around to their way of thinking. But, if we were still convinced that we were taking the right course, they did not withhold permission and so we were allowed to choose our own destiny.

Mike was reprieved. His courage in broaching the subject and my mother's willingness to listen resulted in one of the pivotal decisions in Mike's life. Because he had his wishes acceded to, Mike was determined to show that the correct decision had been made. He immersed himself in his studies and the practical work in the Tech and did well in his final examinations when the three year term was completed. He joined the Irish Air Corps as a fitter/technician and, after amassing a wealth of training and experience, left to work in the private sector. A combination of job changes, promotions, and personal development eventually resulted in a successful career in management roles in multi-national companies.

When Mike and I started secondary school, Patricia was already receiving secondary education as a day pupil in the Convent of Mercy in Claremorris. She continued to live with our grandparents during the week, arrived home each Friday evening, and departed on Monday mornings. Mike and I were about to embark on our daily bike rides to our respective schools. But, despite the longer absences from the house of the three eldest children, my mother continued to have her hands full. Sean was now eight years old and already combining a promising talent for pencil sketching with an antipathy to formal study. Kieran was two years younger, highly intelligent and studious, and stubborn as a mule. And, of course, Kay had recently arrived to bring a smile to everybody's face.

Despite his more passive role in the decision-making on educational matters, my father constantly urged us to give attention to our school-work and took great pleasure in any academic success. Nevertheless, his true quality was revealed in adversity. Many years later, my sister Kay telephoned home to tearfully explain to my parents that she had not achieved the necessary marks and would have to repeat her nursing exams. Sensing her acute disappointment and her fear that she had let herself and the family down, our father immediately sat down and wrote a letter which is now one of Kay's treasured possessions. She quoted to me her favourite line which our father had written in the supportive and reassuring letter: "Love cannot be measured by examination results".

Kay passed the repeated examination in flying colours.

CHAPTER THIRTY-TWO

School Days

In 1963, change was in the air. I was finally breaking out and entering the world of adulthood. I was about to start secondary school and, for the first time, I was embarking on a new adventure without Mike by my side. In reality, I would be cycling the six mile round trip to the College but it felt as if I was unshackling myself from my childhood. There would be new experiences, new teachers, new school books, and new friends.

The sense of a paradigm shift was reflected in and underscored by radical change in the music scene, my window into the outside world. In 1962, pop music on the radio was, with a few exceptions, bland and uninteresting. Burl Ives, Frank Ifield, Bobby Vee, and Pat Boone dominated the Irish radio airwaves with songs such as "Johnny Will", "Speedy Gonzales" and "Little Bitty Tear". There were occasional rays of sunshine breaking through the murky clouds of mediocrity. Ray Charles, whom I had already heard on BBC radio performing r'n'b, had explored his country music roots and achieved international stardom with "I Can't Stop Loving You" and he went on to become a great favourite of my father and me. Another record for which we had a shared admiration was "Stranger On The Shore" by Mr Acker Bilk.

Elvis Presley, who had been releasing a seemingly unbroken series of hit singles since 1956, was still capable of mixing the bland and uninspiring with records which could make your neck-hairs stand on end. Although it is relatively unheralded and sometimes dismissed, "Good Luck Charm" became and remains one of my favourite Elvis records. The song, the guitar sound, the backing vocals of the Jordanaires, and the singing of Elvis somehow caught my imagination and I was glued to the radio each time the record was played. Unlike most other pop songs from this era, it still sounds as fresh and vibrant today as when I first heard it. I was not to know that the record would mark a turning point in Elvis's career. It remained for five weeks at Number 1, a feat which Elvis would not repeat until "The Wonder Of You" in 1970.

The massive upheaval in the music industry in 1963 was caused by the arrival of the beat groups. Suddenly, the charts were dominated by the Beatles, Searchers, Dave Clark Five, Brian Poole and the Tremeloes, Freddie and the Dreamers, Gerry and the Pacemakers, and Billy J Kramer and the Dakotas. Older people, who were formerly opponents of rock and roll, now complained about the eclipse of Pat Boone, Burl Ives, and even Elvis Presley. They loathed the sound and appearance of these interlopers, and their disapproval made the groups even more attractive to us teenagers. There were other casualties too. Fats Domino, Little Richard, Jerry Lee Lewis, Chuck Berry and Sam Cooke were all eased out of the music charts by the arrival of the groups. Only Roy Orbison seemed able to stand toe to toe and slug it out with the groups.

Not all parents were alienated by the new music. My father demonstrated a capacity to adapt to new trends and he retained this openness to musical innovation for the rest of his life. He did not jump on the latest bandwagon. Instead, he listened carefully and openly before deciding on the merits of the new music or performer. A good, expressive singing voice always caught his attention but he would also enthuse about the arrangement and the musicianship. His only reservation about some of the groups was a well-founded suspicion that many did not play on their records. He had no objection to the use of studio musicians but took exception to performers who masqueraded as players of musical instruments.

With "She Loves You" and "Sweets For My Sweet" ringing in my ears, I cycled to the College on my recently acquired refurbished bike in the first week of September to start my secondary education.

Only four boys from my class in Ballyfarna school had gone on to attend the College and two of those did not complete the five year course. This was not unusual; the dropout rate was high in Irish secondary schools. Some pupils left at the age of fourteen - as early as the law permitted. Others waited to complete the Intermediate Certificates at the end of their third year. A few remained for the full five years until they achieved their Leaving Certificate. In Ireland in 1950, 10,200 pupils sat for their Intermediate Certificate examinations but only 4,500 of them stayed on to gain their Leaving Certificate. Even in 1970, following a massive increase in secondary school attendance as a result of the abolition of fees, the corresponding figures were 35,900 and 19,000.

On my first day in the college, I joined a class of 45 boys. Such a first-year class size was not unusual. Over the previous five years, the average number of pupils who enrolled in the college each September exceeded forty. If they all remained in the school for the allotted term of five years, the pupil numbers would exceed two hundred. But the school only had the physical capacity and the teacher numbers to deal capably with a little over one hundred pupils. It was therefore necessary that over half the pupils who enrolled would drop out of the school. Fewer than half of the 45 boys who enrolled with me in 1963 remained to complete their Leaving Certificate examination in 1968.

There were a number of reasons for this attrition rate. As I mentioned earlier, some families lacked a commitment to education. Other families struggled to pay the school fees. I also believe that the regime of corporal punishment in the school was a significant contributory factor in the drop out rate.

The school teaching staff, with one exception, was comprised of priests. Not all of them used corporal punishment. Most of those who considered it necessary utilised it in moderation and in a manner which could be regarded as acceptable given the ethos of the time. Nevertheless, there were appalling instances of excessive caning, mainly perpetrated by one individual teacher. My perception was and continues to be that such excesses were mainly directed at boys from a poorer background rather than the sons of people whom the perpetrator was likely to encounter on the golf course or on social occasions. Students from families who had the financial resources to send them to university or to other third level institutions were not singled out for such excessive punishment. Pupils whose older brothers had demonstrated the family commitment to education by satisfactorily completing their five year term were similarly spared. Others were not so fortunate.

One of the four boys from my class in Ballyfarna school who enrolled in the College was Frank Kelly, who would become a close friend. Frank was the eldest child of a couple who returned from England to their small Mayo farm in order to raise their family at home in Ireland. He was bright and boisterous and, like me, was slightly apprehensive about the unfamiliar surroundings of the college. As a past-pupil of Mr Morley in Ballyfarna, he was not unaccustomed to corporal punishment. But, as he often confided to me in later life, he was convinced that he was singled out for particularly harsh punishment in secondary school. Although he conceded that I was sometimes caned excessively, he was sure that he and a few others suffered much more. After enduring regular and sustained punishment for a number of months, Frank dropped out of the school. In later life, he was unshakeable in his view that he was driven from the school because of the perceived social standing of his family. I also witnessed other cases where boys suffered particularly excessive punishment and did not return to school.

Notwithstanding Frank's view, I am not convinced that there was a deliberate policy in the school to identify and drive out certain pupils. But it is undeniable that the school could not have functioned if all pupils had remained and there was acceptance that student numbers would reduce and classes would become more manageable as boys dropped out. It should also have been obvious to the management of the school that the level of corporal punishment was a major contributory factor to the attrition rate among pupils.

Corporal punishment was not new to me because of my experience at national school. But this was different, or at least more impactful. Only one priest out of a total of eight teachers considered it necessary to constantly cane a select number of us pupils. I made an effort to pay special attention to classwork and homework relating to the subjects which he taught but it soon became apparent that this made no difference. He would find fault with our work and, it seemed to me, continue to ask us questions and pose problems until he caught us out.

Was this perceived victimisation a reality or merely the fanciful opinion of a naive teenager? It is true that I am writing about my personal perception of what happened. Yet, there is evidence to suggest that the special attention which I was getting was undeserved. At the beginning of the second year, nine of us from the class were selected to join the third year class, leaving the remainder of our classmates to form the second year class. As a result, we were allowed to sit the Intermediate Certificate examination after two years rather than the usual three. I mention this to show that I was considered to be in the higher 20% of the class in terms of schoolwork and potential. Yet, I continued to be one of the minority among my peers who were suffering at the hands of this teacher. When I joined the higher class, he regularly made it clear to me that, in his opinion, I had been unjustifiably promoted and that I would be unable to cope with the challenge.

My abiding impression from this period was a feeling of powerlessness. No matter what I did, I convinced myself, he would find fault with it and punishment would follow. The situation persisted for at least three years before it noticeably improved. My results in the Intermediate Certificate examinations were good, although this alone would not have been sufficient to rehabilitate me in the eyes of my nemesis. What made the crucial difference was my emergence as a football goalkeeper. I had been a distinctly average outfield player and decided to try my luck in goal. I quickly developed a liking for the role and found that I possessed the quick reflexes which enabled me to make saves and the physical courage which was necessary in an era when goalkeepers could be physically manhandled and bundled into the net. I broke into the school teams and it seemed that, as a result, my foe saw me in a new light. This change of attitude by him caused me to loath him even more than previously and, despite some conciliatory gestures on his part, our relationship continued to be adversarial during my remaining schooldays.

When my brother Mike feared that I would punch Mr Morley at my mother's funeral, I put his mind at ease that I retained no ill-will against the teacher. The same does not hold true for the priest in secondary school. Although I believe that I have sufficient self-control to behave correctly if I met my nemesis in later life, I admit that it would not take much provocation for me to punch him. He certainly deserved it during my schooldays and it was only the certainty of expulsion that stopped me from retaliating.

What emotional or psychological impact did this regime have on the later lives of my contemporaries? They were subjected to cruel and unnecessary corporal punishment at a time when, in James Joyce's phrase, "they were yung and easily freudened". I can only speak with authority about the impact on me. One unwelcome outcome was that occasionally, years after I had left school, I emerged into wakefulness in the morning with a feeling of panic, believing that I was about to face my tormentor and convinced that I was unprepared and was about to be punished again. As my confused drowsiness abated, the dread was replaced by a combination of relief that the danger was not real and a resentment that my school experience could still have this impact on me decades later.

Is there any point in revisiting this stuff? The writer Colm Toibin, while being interviewed on Imagine, a BBC arts programme, said: "I don't think writing is a form of therapy or self-help, because it isn't really helpful. It isn't really good for you because you're not only mulling over things but you're actually solidifying them in a strange sort of way. So I don't think it helps you as a good….. healthy human being to actually work....churning material that belongs so closely to yourself…"

In 1975, I was contacted and asked to write a piece for a magazine which was being published to mark the 50th anniversary of the founding of the College. After much thought, I decided to write a piece about the excessive use of corporal punishment during my years as a student. I soon realised that, in the interests of fairness, I needed to give a balanced picture of my five years at the school. This forced me to think about, and record, the many things which I had liked about the College and the benefits which I received as a result of my education there. Apart from the academic work, I itemised the many extracurricular and voluntary activities which the teachers organised and encouraged. An active interest in sport was fostered which enabled me to represent my school, my local club, and later my county. Stage experience in musicals and plays gave me confidence and a facility in public speaking which was helpful in my later career. Although we attended an all male school, functions and even dancing lessons were organised so that we could gain the confidence to socialise, in a controlled environment, with girls from the local convent school. Art and music appreciation, while not on the school curriculum, were also encouraged and facilitated by some teachers.

As I wrote, I acknowledged all the positives but went on to discuss the unfavourable impact which corporal punishment had on the school. I set out the statistical analysis which I alluded to earlier and attributed the drop-out rate of well over 50% to excessive use of corporal punishment.

I expected that the article would be unpublished or severely edited but I was determined to get the matter off my chest and I pulled no punches. When the booklet was published some months later, I was gratified to discover that the item had been included. Some minor editing had taken place but not nearly as much as I expected and it did not detract from the thrust of the article.

I did not get any response or reaction to the piece. I do not live in the catchment area of the College and was not in contact with any of my contemporaries. But the article did have an impact, albeit in a completely unexpected manner. A few months later, when talking about the piece to Frank Kelly, who hadn't read it, I suddenly realised that I had not experienced my morning "panic attack" for some time. I wondered whether there would be a resumption and waited. Eventually, I realised that my unwelcome intruder had ceased his occasional visits after I wrote the piece. In the twenty years since then, I have not experienced a recurrence. I attribute this to the cathartic impact of thinking about, researching, reconsidering, and ultimately committing my thoughts to paper. Colm Toibin was mistaken. Writing can be a form of self-help.

And what of Frank Kelly, the other player in this tale? In 1970, when an industrial dispute temporarily closed the bank in which I worked, I went to England where Frank was now working on a building site. We worked together for the summer and he introduced me to a young woman who was later to become my wife. Frank talked regularly about his intention to return to Ireland. I sceptically pointed out to him that most of the other Irish men and boys on the site harboured the same aspiration and we both knew that few if any would achieve their ambition.

"You'll see", said Frank.

In the mid seventies, Frank bucked the trend and returned to Ireland. He successfully sat the examinations for the police force and became a Garda. He married and settled again in Mayo where he and his wife raised a family. He became godfather to my son and we remained close friends until his early and untimely death in 2003.

CHAPTER THIRTY-THREE

Teach Your Children

"Are you off out again with that football? Have you your lessons done? And your jobs? Good! Don't take your jumper off and catch a chill, there's a good boy!"

In the summer evenings, there was plenty of time for playing football or other games, either among ourselves or with neighbourhood children. But there were rules, as my mother reminded us. Priority had to be given to "lessons", as homework was known. We were also obliged to do our "jobs". Some of these chores varied depending on the season but others were constant. Water had to be drawn from the pump, potatoes had to be washed and sometimes collected from the potato pit. Heads of cabbage, carrots, and onions had to be unearthed from the garden or brought in from the shed, depending on the time of year. The table had to be set for meals and the dishes washed afterwards. One might be asked to feed the baby which was far preferable to changing nappies but this duty too was delegated from time to time. Another important chore was ensuring that the hens were safely secured in the hen-house overnight.

Another unwelcome duty was dealing with "the pots". The daily emptying of the chamber pots required some logistical enterprise if potential embarrassment was to be avoided. As our house did not have a back door, there was the distinct possibility that a bearer could emerge from the front door, carefully toting the chamber pot like some votive offering, and unexpectedly come face to face with a neighbour who was walking or cycling by. The problem was solved and dignity was preserved by opening a window and placing the receptacle on the window sill for retrieval and disposal into the chemical toilet. Two of the bedrooms had windows at or near the rear of the house. The pot from the front bedroom had to be carried through the house and placed on the rear windowsill. At nightfall, after being rinsed and disinfected, the pots were relocated in the bedrooms via the same clandestine route.

Some chores were delegated at random by my mother but responsibility for a few others was given to individuals whom she trusted to perform them properly. For example, when she arrived from Granny Rushe's house for the weekend, Patricia was entrusted with the delicate job of cleaning Daddy's spectacles. During the working week, he accumulated spots of paint or other small markings on his glasses. Patricia was trusted to clean them delicately, being vigilant not to scratch or damage the lens, before proudly returned the glistening spectacles to him.

My particular chore was polishing all the shoes in the house each Saturday night. I quite enjoyed the job and became adept at cleaning, polishing, and shining the shoes, which I then placed in a row beneath the kitchen table. I can still see the glint of the firelight reflecting on the array of shoes as they peeked out from the semidarkness.

In my later years at secondary school, after Patricia and Mike had left home and the younger children had already departed for school in the morning, I was last to leave the house. In order to help my mother, I fell into the habit of washing all the breakfast crockery. She often picked up a tea towel and kept me company by drying the dishes. I handed the shining, dripping items to her and she brusquely dried them and stacked them on the table. Often, we worked side by side in silence. Sometimes, we engaged in small-talk. Many years later, when I read Seamus Heaney's poem "Clearances", I was struck by his description of being alone with his mother as they peeled potatoes. The close, comfortable, intimate, fleeting moment between my mother and myself was evoked perfectly in the poem. Just as in Heaney's case, my mother and I were "never closer the whole rest of our lives".

I was also forming a closer bond with my father during this period. As usual, with us, music was the catalyst. I was by now a reasonably accomplished harmonica player but, as an impressionable young teenager, I was becoming aware that the instrument wasn't a particularly fashionable one. I had studied and copied the harmonica breaks on "Hey! Baby" by Bruce Chanel and, latterly, on "Love Me Do" and "Please Please Me" by the Beatles. But I'd never heard of anybody who aspired to be a harmonica player. As for a guitar... that was different. My father's guitar on its stand in his bedroom became more and more attractive to me.

"It's remarkable that you're a musician and yet none of your children can play the guitar or the fiddle. "

My father was piqued by what he regarded as a provocative comment from a visiting cousin.

"The guitar and the fiddle are sitting there if any of them want to learn to play."

"But would you not think that you have an obligation to give them lessons?"

My mother glanced anxiously at my father. She knew that he was sometimes rattled by what he perceived to be condescending comments from some of his cousins. Unlike him, they had a secondary education, having attended one of the expensive boarding schools. My father's sensitivity may have sprung, at least in part, from his own relative lack of formal education. He saucered his tea-cup carefully before speaking.

"Well, the way I see it is this. I'm not a fan of music lessons. I see too many children being packed off to violin or piano lessons and hating every minute of it. Some of them end up not even touching an instrument for the rest of their lives and most of the rest cannot play a tune unless they have the written music in front of them.

There aren't many rules in this house but there are some things that the kids have to do. They have to do their lessons and their jobs around the house. But music should never be something that children have to do. It should be something that they want to do. Of course, if any of the kids pick up an instrument, I'll help them and point them in the right direction."

The visitor was unconvinced.

"But if they show the inclination, they'll still need to be taught. Will you give them lessons if they make a start?".

Another pause.

"I'm not so sure that you can teach music. It's a bit like riding a bicycle. You have to learn to do it rather than be taught. But if any of the kids show an interest in playing music, I'll help them to learn."

Encounters such as this summed up my father's attitude towards music education. His thinking may have been the result of his own experience in learning to play the fiddle. His neighbour, Johnny Brennan, showed him the basics of bow technique and fingering but my father considered that he had taught himself by constant practise and by trial and error. He trusted his ear and only taught himself to read music afterwards when he required this skill in order to play in a band.

Emboldened by my father's attitude and attracted by the attention-seeking opportunities available to guitarists, I tentatively picked up the guitar and began to doodle and experiment. I did this surreptitiously while my parents were out of earshot. Just as I had done with the harmonica, I hoped to master a tune or two before revealing my new found ability to my parents. It soon became apparent, however, that the guitar presented a more formidable obstacle than the humble mouth organ.

I examined some instruction booklets which belonged to my father. I quickly realised that these tutors were intended for competent guitarists who could read music; there was much mention of modulations and chord substitutions. I needed something more basic but there was no music shop in Claremorris where I could hope to buy a more appropriate instruction booklet. I send a note to my sister, Patricia, who had just moved to Dublin, and, by return of post, received a "guitar for beginners" tutor. I was on my way.

The booklet incorporated chord diagrams and note tablature rather than written music. By carefully and painstakingly following the diagrams, I taught myself to play a basic arrangement of "Loch Lomond" which incorporated single notes and chords. After a time, I became more emboldened and began to practise more openly. I was sitting on the bed, playing tentatively when my father walked in.

"Mammy tells me you can play a tune."

I should have realised that, despite our best efforts, my mother knew everything that went on in the house. She merely chose when to notice things or when to turn a blind eye.

"I'm only learning. I'm working on this one."

I played it well, I thought, but somehow it didn't sound nearly as impressive as when I'd previously played it on my own. In fact, I had previously been bemused by the fact that, while I'd been practising, the piece of music sounded much better on some days than others. I suspected that it might be something to do with the tuning but, according to the tutor, one ideally needed a piano in order to tune the guitar. I knew that my father used pitch-pipes to tune the fiddle.

"That's very good. And you're killing two birds with one stone by learning notes and chords at the same time. But you need to tune the guitar every time you pick it up. Here, I'll do it for you."

He took the guitar, adjusted the tuning pegs, ran his thumb across the strings, and handed it back to me.

"Try it again now."

The difference was startling. The notes rang out clear as a bell and the chords sounded ...well ... right.

He encouraged me to learn other tunes from the book and explained that I could tune the guitar by using my harmonica. All I needed was to tune my top string to the "E" note on the harmonica and I could then use this string as a guide in order to tune the remaining strings.

It took me a while to become adept at tuning the guitar but my father made a practise of fine-tuning it for me. He also set about helping me to learn to play the instrument. His interventions were not always welcome, even if they were necessary.

"You have that one mastered now. It's time to put that tune aside and move on to the next one."

He had recently cultivated a small vegetable patch behind the house. His voice carried in through the open bedroom window to where I sat and strummed. When I was able to play a tune well, I tended to play it incessantly, especially if I knew that he could hear it through the open window as he worked in the vegetable patch in the evening. Instead of enthusing about my latest masterpiece, he urged me to move on and learn something new. He realised that this was not what I wanted to hear but he persevered with his strategy and, as a result, I soon realised that I was learning something new with each different tune and was expanding my repertoire.

Another musical breakthrough occurred on 1965 and, this time, my father had nothing to do with it. He could only look on in bemusement at first and later with admiration. As we did not have TV, my only visual reference for music and musicians was the odd photograph in a newspaper or an occasional visit to the cinema to see an Elvis Presley film. I saw a magazine photograph of Donovan who had just had a hit with "Catch The Wind", a song featuring a harmonica break. I was fascinated that he was photographed wearing around his neck a contraption which held his harmonica in place. I had previously heard Bob Dylan on the radio but assumed that somebody else played the harmonica. I did not realise that he also used a harmonica harness.

Using pieces from Mike's Meccano Set and a length of strong but pliable wire, I built a harmonica harness. I affixed the mouth organ to it and, as I expected, I could immediately play hands free. I was soon able to play folk songs using guitar and harmonica. When, the following year, Johnny McEvoy had a major Irish hit with "Mursheen

Durkin", I was able to replicate the vocal, guitar, and harmonica arrangement effortlessly, to the admiration of those who did not realise that I could only play it in one key and was using only three basic chords. My father admired my innovation but later shook his head ruefully and gently pointed out that there were various other keys and a myriad of chords yet to be mastered.

While helping me to learn, my father also showed me techniques which I could use to make the guitar accompaniment more interesting. He explained about chord progressions and, later, modulations which could make the chords flow together. As an alternative to bashing out chords, he showed me how to add variety by alternating the chords with single notes on the bass strings. Although he always played with a plectrum, he was interested and supportive when I began to experiment with finger-style playing and he encouraged me to develop this technique.

On at least one occasion, I expressed doubts about the value of being able to play in all scales and in diverse styles.

"Most people don't know the difference', I said. "They couldn't care less whether the musicians are good or bad so long as they're having a good time. No wonder many musicians look as if they're bored out of their tree when they're playing."

My father wasn't having it.

"You have to set a standard for yourself, even if many people don't notice it. You have to play for the fellow in the corner."

"Who? What fellow in the corner?"

"There's one thing I've found to be true in all my years of playing. If you're a good musician and you're thinking about what you're playing, there's always that one fellow in the corner. It doesn't matter where you're performing or who you're playing for. If you look around, you'll spot him. He's never in front of the stage. He's over to one side, often in the shadows, and he's watching you and listening to every note you're playing. He might be a musician himself but not always. He might nod to you when you're playing or even sometimes, he might stop to talk to you afterwards. But he knows. That's the fellow you play for. If you do, you'll never get bored. You have to set your own standard."

I was sceptical but when I later began to play regularly in public, I found his observation to be true. Sometimes it was only one rapt, attentive and discerning listener and at other times, there were a few. By playing for the fan in the shadows, I was kept on my toes and driven to improve as a musician.

CHAPTER THIRTY-FOUR

Making Ends Meet

The Red Lemonade Syndrome had insulated me from the impact of some of the difficulties which my parents were enduring. But, now that I was a growing older, this began to change gradually. I became vaguely conscious that running the household was becoming more expensive and this became particularly evident in our family from 1963 until about 1966. Now that three of us were attending secondary school, our family was encountering the type of financial pressure that most parents have to endure from time to time when family income is uninterrupted or expenditure is suddenly increased.

As teenagers, Patricia, Mike, and I were frequently outgrowing our clothes and shoes. Financial constraints necessitated some improvisation and remedial action. My parents had habitually purchased quite a number of Sunday newspapers. Apart from the Sunday Independent, Sunday Press, and Sunday Review, they also bought a few British newspapers such as the Sunday People, News of the World, and Sunday Express. Both of my parents read the newspapers assiduously. Now they announced that they were no longer going to buy the British papers. The rationale offered was that some of the content was unsuitable for children. I now realise that the move was motivated by financial factors. Because the Sunday Review ceased to be published around this time, we were suddenly reduced to two Irish Sunday newspapers.

My parents social life did not provide an opportunity for them to economise. They rarely went out. In the 50s, the opportunities for married people such as my parents to have a social life were limited. Of course, some wealthier married couples joined golf or tennis clubs, went regularly for a few drinks to the pub, had dinner parties, or attended functions organised by trading bodies such as a local Chamber of Commerce. My parents did not have the financial means, or indeed the inclination, to become involved in such activities. The only exception which I can recall was their occasional attendance at the annual CIE dance, a function which was arranged during the Christmas season for employees of the railway company. Even then, my mother was a somewhat reluctant attendee, being of the opinion that preparation for the event was "more trouble than it was worth". She fretted over what she should wear but, with Patricia's help and encouragement, overcame her reservations and surprised herself by thoroughly enjoying the occasion.

The above might evoke a picture of my mother, seated at a laden dressing table, reluctantly applying make-up in preparation for a night on the town. To me, such an image is unthinkable. My mother didn't wear make-up. Her only concession was to possess a small compact of face powder. Sometimes, before going to town, she would stand in front of the wall-mirror, brush her hair, faintly pat her cheeks with a powderpuff, and briefly gaze inquiringly at herself. I do not recall her wearing lipstick and she had no use for eye-shadow or mascara. I am reluctant to characterise her antipathy to make-up as an effort to economise or as a conscious decision to prioritise child-care over her own appearance. As a young woman, she had clear skin and her twinkling, enquiring eyes did not need any enhancement. As she grew older, she was obviously satisfied with her facial appearance.

As we children grew bigger and stronger, our increasing need for clothes was partly catered for by parcels sent from aunts in England. My mother's two sisters, the nuns, regularly sent clothes for the children. These included shirts and t-shirts as well as coats, jackets, and trousers which were taken to the tailor to be adjusted. A measure of the prevailing economic climate in towns such as Claremorris was the number of tailors, dressmakers, and shoemakers who were available at low cost to carry out modifications and repairs so that garments and shoes could be handed down.

As small children, our father regularly brought Mike and me to town for a haircut at Tully's barbershop. Now, it was decided that we would have our hair cut by Mike Fallon who provided this service locally. This was the same Mike Fallon whose donkey could walk home from town through unlighted roads in the early hours while Mike lay asleep in the cart. We disliked our visits to Fallons' house for an occasional haircut. Mike had a manual hair clipper which was prone to pinch the scalp if not used carefully. In fairness to Mike, it was difficult for him to control a twitchy younger while trying to apply his rudimentary barbering skills. The resultant haircuts left a lot to be desired and were not much cheaper than the superior service provided in Tully's. My father was not to be outdone. To our trepidation, he purchased a manual hair clipper and began to tentatively practise on us. He was gentler and more patient than Mike Fallon but there were occasional pinches and yells. In order to hide his lack of skill in shaping and styling hair, he decided that my brother and I should have "Mountjoy haircuts". The name of this crew-cut reflected the fact that the style was associated with inmates of Mountjoy Prison in Dublin.

I sported a crew-cut for the first year or two in secondary school until the longer hairstyle popularised by the Beatles belatedly began to appear locally. By then, my father's barbering skills had much improved and I was happy to allow him to cut my hair until I left home in 1968.

In secondary school, I was conscious that some boys were dressed better than me but I cannot recall feeling any embarrassment or sense of deprivation. This was attributable to the self esteem which my parents had instilled into me. I was never teased by classmates about my dress or appearance. In fact, I rather revelled in my occasional displays of originality, particularly in my "army jacket". I don't know where the jacket came from and I suspect that it was part of the US Airforce uniform. The short, pale green, belted jacket sported a military collar and buttoned breast pockets. All insignia had been removed. It was warm, hard wearing and, importantly to me, distinctive. I wore it constantly, in the classroom and outside. In summer, I wore it opened with a shirt or t-shirt inside. In colder weather, I could wear a jumper underneath but the jacket was ever-present throughout the year.

During my first year or two of secondary school, my look must have seemed incongruous: a Mountjoy haircut, military jacket, denim jeans, and wellington boots. My distinctive look extended to the sports field. I wore black football shorts during my first year in contrast to everybody else who wore white. Mine had arrived in a parcel of clothes from the nuns. Black shorts were unknown in Gaelic football at that time and were the preserve of rugby or soccer teams.

My perception at that time was that many other boys were dressed with similar abandon and variety so that I did not stand out from the crowd. I am not so sure that this was true. An edition of the Saint

Colman's College magazine contains an early photograph of me as part of a football team. Each year, a football league took place in the school and all boys who wanted to play, irrespective of talent, were selected on a team. I was a member of the team captained by T.J. Farragher which participated in the school league in 1964. I had not yet discovered my potential as a goalkeeper and was a poor if enthusiastic outfield player who can take no credit for our teams' success in winning the league. A close inspection of the photograph of our winning team is revealing. The players are attired in their own football gear and, without exception, the other boys are wearing regulation long-sleeved football jerseys of various colours and have regular short back and sides haircuts. I stand in the back row, a crew-cut figure wearing a short-sleeved t-shirt which is a few sizes too large for me. I'm wearing white shorts and the toe of one of my massive football boots is visible.

My father had spotted the boots on a shelf while painting a railway house. Knowing that the last son in the family had recently emigrated, he enquired whether the boots were for sale. When the homeowner heard that the boots were to be shared by two brothers, she would not accept payment for them. Instead, she gifted them to my father. They were old style, heavy, leather, high sided boots into which the studs had to be inserted by means of a hammer and last. They were much too large for me so that, in an effort to compensate, I had to wear a few pairs of thick woollen socks.

The team photo indicates that, rather than blending in with my team-mates, my individuality made me conspicuous. Yet, I was not conscious of this at the time.

Perhaps my appearance may help to explain an encounter which I had with Father Colleran, the President of the school. His tall imposing appearance was emphasised by his black, floor-length, soutane with its short cloak which flapped behind his shoulders as he walked. He tended to stroll stern-facedly around the school grounds at lunchtime in the knowledge that his presence would ensure that the students behaved correctly. I was walking with two classmates from the science hall towards the main school building when we encountered Father Colleran.

"Master Colman!"

All three of us froze. Had we done something wrong to attract his attention? He beckoned to me to step forward. He half-turned to look enquiringly at my two friends who were waiting nearby, startled by the sudden intervention. They took the hint and walked quickly away, occasionally glancing back over their shoulders. Although Father Colleran was my mathematics teacher as well as being the school president, this was our first encounter on a one-to-one basis. The possibilities flashed through my mind. Had somebody complained about my behaviour? Perhaps he thought that my first year school fees were overdue? Had he forgotten that I had paid them a few weeks earlier?

He glared sternly at a few other boys who had sidled closer, hoping to hear what was going on. As they scattered, he moved closer to me and spoke quietly, now gazing intensely at me.

"Master Colman. Does you father work on the railway?"

"He does, Father."

What was going on?

"What kind of work does he do?"

"He's a labourer, Father."

He nodded, as if satisfying himself that his information was correct.

"And do you have a sister attending Mount Saint Michaels?"

"The convent? I do, Father."

"And a brother in the Vocational school?"

"Yes, Father."

He had been gazed down on me but now glanced around to ensure that we were not being closely observed. He withdrew his hand from the pocket of his soutane and slipped a small packet to me.

"Put that carefully in your pocket and bring it home to your mother."

He turned, joined his hands behind his back in his customary fashion, and strolled across the schoolyard.

When I got an opportunity to secretly examine the package, my suspicions were confirmed. Father Colleran had returned the school fees in full.

That evening, my mother interrogated me. What exactly did Father Colleran say? Where did it happen? Did he hand money back to anybody else? I explained that he ensured that nobody saw him give me the money and that I had no way of knowing whether he made similar refunds to other pupils.

"We'll see what Daddy has to say when he gets home."

Later, while doing my homework in the bedroom, I heard snatches of a lengthy murmured conversation between my parents. I was then summoned to the kitchen to repeat to my father my description of the sequence of events. As my parents listened silently, I understood their dilemma. They were reluctant to accept charity but also knew that a refusal ran the risk of offending Father Colleran by gracelessly rejecting his thoughtful and discreet gesture. Fearing that I might be asked to reopen the matter with Father Colleran, I offered the opinion that the only polite and realistic response was to accept the refund as intended. My mother agreed and I knew then that my father would eventually acquiesce.

I have no idea how Father Colleran gathered information about our family circumstances or how he discovered that my parents were paying school fees for three children. Was it solely a practise undertaken in the college or did Father Colleran routinely compare notes with the principals in the other two secondary schools? Perhaps, in their own schools, the other head teachers also made similar gestures to deserving families and decided which school should make the refund. Patricia and Michael continued to pay fees at their schools.

Clandestine refunds of fees were also made to me in the following two years. Then, under the leadership of Donough O'Malley, Minister for Education, free secondary schooling was made available to everybody. Some boarding schools opted to continue on a fee paying basis but, from 1966 onward, any Irish student could avail of secondary education free of charge. This boon for our family coincided with the departure from home of Patricia and Michael, both of whom had now completed their secondary school education. Both were now self-supporting and there were no longer any school fees to be paid which was of considerable help to our family budget. In the September following the abolition of school fees, I returned to school with my first pair of brand new football boots.

CHAPTER THIRTY-FIVE

Hit The Road, Jack

Across the road from our house in Murneen, behind the eye-catching, copper beech tree, lived the Conroys. Peter Conroy and his wife Celia, the lady who had shown me how to get rid of my warts, were now in their seventies. They resided with their unmarried daughter. Monica, a kind-hearted but somewhat naive woman in her forties, had lived a relatively sheltered life, seldom leaving the parish. She cared for her ageing parents and, apart from cycling to town to do the weekly shopping, her social life was confined to crossing the road to visit my mother or Mrs Glynn for a chat and a cup of tea.

Suddenly, all changed. Monica had a gentleman caller. He was not from the locality but he had a car, which immediately gave him a certain cachet. Cars had become more common in our area in the mid sixties but the news that a car owner was reported to be interested romantically in someone like Monica was enough to raise eyebrows. Any suspicions about his motives were mitigated when he chose not to furtively arrange to meet Monica. Instead, he was calling to the door and was being invited in to meet her parents. Monica's father, who occasionally visited our home at night, confided to my parents that he was hopeful that the courtship would end in marriage. He did not yet know much about the suitor but was reassured that he was obviously relatively wealthy and seemed to be a salesman or commercial traveller. It was clear that Monica was completely smitten and overwhelmed by the admirer.

My father was carrying out maintenance and repainting work at a railway station in a mid-Mayo town and, each afternoon, walked up the main street to buy the early edition of the evening newspaper. On one such venture, he recognised a familiar parked car; he had seen it regularly outside Conroys. Then he saw Monica's suitor walking along the street with a woman by his side. The newsagent responded to my father's seemingly casual enquiry by revealing that the couple were man and wife. He added that they lived in the town and that their children attended the local school.

When my parents discussed the situation that evening, they were in agreement that something had to be done but were unsure about the best course of action. They had no doubt that Monica was unaware of the marital status of her gentleman caller. My father thought about speaking to Monica but worried that she would disbelieve him or that she would console herself that there was an innocent explanation and, more crucially, she would believe what she was told by her suitor. An alternative option was to speak to Monica's parents. They might believe my father but, as proud and dignified people, they would be hugely embarrassed by my father's discovery and would worry about the local gossip which might ensue.

A third course of action was decided upon. My father waited in the winter evening darkness and listened for the sound of the approaching vehicle. The familiar car slowed to a halt in its usual parking spot in the gateway under the copper beech tree and just out of sight of the Conroy's front door. As he was getting out of his car, the startled driver was confronted by my father. In the course of a brief, quiet, but terse conversation, the visitor was told that he was rumbled and that, if he ever showed his face in the locality again, my father would be visiting his wife and family at their named address. The miscreant quickly climbed back into his car and drove out of Monica's life.

We were sworn to secrecy about my father's discovery and subsequent intervention. Mr and Mrs Conroy were at first mystified and disappointed at the sudden loss of interest by Monica's erstwhile admirer but could console themselves that, if she remained unmarried, at least she would still be around to care from them in their declining years. Outwardly, Monica seemed quite sanguine and philosophical about the unexplained disappearance. She shrugged her shoulders and got on with life as if she accepted that such a good thing was not destined to last.

Monica's mother Celia died in 1967 and her father followed in 1971. Monica had cared for her parents in their last years and was now living alone. She was occasionally assisted by a nephew in the running of her small farm. Although she was now in her 50s, Monica's new status as a farm owner attracted attention. Mike Fallon, local farmer, occasional barber, and possessor of the donkey with night-vision and navigation skills, decided that a single woman in possession of a farm must be in want of a husband. He began to pay court to Monica. After dark, he would arrive unsteadily on her doorstep having been fortified by a few pints of porter or a shot or two of whiskey.

Monica made it clear that his advances were unwelcome and, after a few visits, she refused to answer the door to him. The ardent suitor was not to be thwarted. He decided to charm her into amenability by standing in the darkness under the copper beech tree and calling drunkenly.

"Come on out, Monnie! I know you're listening. I have a wee drop of whiskey here. Come on out and we can have a chat and a drink. Sure, where's the harm in that? Monnie? Are you in there? It's a lovely night. Come on out."

Mike wasn't aggressive; merely drunkenly philosophical. He seemed to have deluded himself that his advances were not unwelcome and that Monica's resistance would break down. In fact, she confided to my mother that she was quite uncomfortable and not a little embarrassed by Mike's increasingly regular visits. She knew that his nocturnal serenades could be heard by the near neighbours and she sought advice from my mother who decided that my father's previously displayed propensity for interventions should be put to good use. When Mike's night-time, plaintive, mating call was next heard, my father was dispatched to do his duty while we listened carefully through our open front door.

"Mike. Go home like a good man. There's no sense in making this racket."

"Ah sure, Coleman, it's only a bit of harmless carry-on. Monnie doesn't mind."

"Go home, Mike. If she wanted to talk to you, she'd be out here. Now, off you go, Mike"

"Monnie! Can you hear me? You don't mind me, do you!"

"Stop the racket, Mike! I have a houseful of kids in there. They shouldn't have to listen to this carry-on. I'll have to call the guards if don't go home."

"Ah Coleman! You're a man yourself. You know how..."

"Beat it, Mike!"

"What? Where? Beat what...?"

"Clear off, Mike! And don't let me see you here again or I'll go for the guards and you'll end up in Mountjoy."

Disgruntled but chastened, Mike retreated, wandering off into the darkness, muttering to himself.

My mother ribbed my father unmercifully.

"Beat it?! Merciful hour! Where did that come from? You sounded like someone out of a gangster film. The poor man didn't know what you were on about. Beat it, is it? Lord between us and all harm! I hope none of the neighbours could hear you. You could have the priest down on top of us for abusing the poor old devil."

The strategy was successful. Mike Fallon abandoned his midnight rambling. My father also abandoned his interventions.

CHAPTER THIRTY-SIX

The Times They Are A Changin'

When our family relocated in 1955, the Murneen house had been in need of redecorating and improvement. Apart from the minimal shelter provided by a few scrawny trees along the roadside, the site was bleak and exposed.

My father immediately set about painting the doors and windows as well as applying a protective coating of white masonry paint to the exterior walls. This had the added benefit of giving the house a bright and cheerful appearance. Another early development was the planting of trees all around the boundary of our one acre site. Over time, the trees matured to provide shelter for the house and also to give it more character.

My mother's contribution to improving the outward appearance of the home was to dig flower beds on either side of the pathway leading to the front door. Soon, a variety of seasonal flowers were gently swaying in the summer breeze and scenting the garden. The grass in the small area surrounding the flower beds was gradually brought under control by regular usage of a lawn-mower. Grass was allowed to grow on the remainder of the site and was cut each summer; the hay was saved and sold to local farmers.

Inside the house, change was gradual but inexorable. The concrete floor was relaid and then covered with floor tiles. The solid wooden front door was removed and the replacement door had opaque glass panels which allowed much needed light into the interior. Later the wooden sash-windows were superseded by hardwood windows.

As already explained, the arrival of a TV set was delayed because of my father's concerns but eventually his resistance was overcome as a result of my mother's technique of study and subversion. Like many people in Claremorris, my first view of TV was in the window of the ESB shop in Mount Street. It became quite common for people to buy a TV set on an instalment basis from the Electricity Supply Board. In order to attract sales, a TV set was placed in the ESB shop window and it was normal to see a cluster of people standing outside the window at night, bathed in ghostly blue light, gazing at the soundless, flickering TV images.

Other changes were also taking place and none occasioned more discussion and concern than the new practices in the Catholic church following Vatican Two. People took time to become adjusted to the replacement of Latin by English and the physical changes in the church building which resulted in the priest facing the congregation. The innovations were welcomed by some. Others felt that something dependable and comforting had been lost.

Previously, women were obliged to wear headscarves or veils when in church and there was also a rigidly observed segregation of the sexes. Women were confined to the right hand side of the church. Although most men sat on the left hand aisle, it was acceptable for them to sit on either side. Even though such practises ceased to be mandatory, they were still extant during the 70s, 80s, and later. The attempted relegation of women to a lower status than men was not confined to churches. Women were unwelcome in many pubs and, even when granted admission, were segregated into a "snug" while the menfolk drank publicly in the main bar.

Change was impacting on my father's life also. His mode of transport to work involved a combination of bicycle and train. He could sometimes be delegated to work at railway stations some of which were located as far as 40 miles from Claremorris. If he was lucky, he could cycle to the local station and catch a goods or passenger train to his destination and a return train in the evening. More often than not, the train timetable did not facilitate this strategy. Even if the morning train to Athenry enabled him to arrive at work on time, there might not be a return train that evening. His solution was to bring his bike in the guard's van of the train and to cycle home after work; a journey of 35 miles. Some locations necessitated both morning and evening journeys by bicycle. Collooney, where my father worked on occasion, was 42 miles away.

My childhood recollection is that the train schedules were generally helpful in getting him to work but, more often than not, he was obliged to cycle home in the evening. I can recall him arriving home jauntily on summer evenings, jacket over the handlebars, shirt sleeves rolled. But some such journeys were undertaken on dark winter evenings, in driving rain and wind or on icy roads. As children, we were conscious of the difficulties which our father endured depending upon his work location. Yet, he never complained or sought sympathy when he finally reached home, tired, cold and drenched to the skin. On the contrary, I recall such arrivals as occasions of mirth. The first warning of his pending arrival was be a sudden burst of activity from Blackie, who ran to the closed door and impatiently sniffed and growled. About ten minutes would elapse before the sound of the opening front gate confirmed my father's arrival. We surmised that Blackie's hearing enabled him to recognise the sound of the bicycle but we were bemused by the ability of the dog to signal the pending arrival against a background of driving rain, blaring radio, and noisy children. Having parked his bicycle behind the house, my father walked into the kitchen, dripping with rainwater, red-faced from the exertions of his journey, to be greeted loudly by the children.

"Who's talking to me? Where am I. I think I've gone blind!"

As a result of his entry into the heat of the kitchen from the cold, wet conditions outside, a thick layer of condensation clouded his spectacles and he waved his arms and pretend to stumble around in a disorientated fashion. The older children smilingly cast their eyes towards the ceiling in mock exasperation while the younger ones excitedly shouted advice and encouragement.

"You're alright, daddy. It's only your glasses. Ha! Ha! They're all fogged up."

As he stood in a pool of rainwater, my mother helped him to remove his cap, sodden overcoat, boots, and waterproof leggings. On a rainy night, a complete change of clothes would be waiting so that he could change before sitting down to his dinner. I can recall him experimenting with rubberised overshoes and a poncho in an effort to minimise the discomfort from rain as he cycled. Yet, when I try to remember his rain sodden arrivals and to appreciate his uncomplaining attitude, my first reaction is a smile at the memory of a father mugging and feigning confusion in order to amuse and distract his children.

In 1963, the passenger train service from Claremorris to Sligo was discontinued as part of a major restructuring of the railway network. The line between Claremorris and Ballinrobe had already closed in 1959. Goods trains continued to operate on the Sligo line but there was less rail traffic so that my father had to use his bicycle much more often to get to work in outlying railway stations. He adjusted to the new circumstances and avoided unwelcome long cycle journeys by hitchhiking. "Thumbing" for lifts was becoming more feasible because of the increasing numbers of cars and lorries on the roads. My father became adept at getting lifts and had devised a strategy which he found to be effective. He observed that drivers were much more likely to pull over and give a lift to a worker on his way to or from his job. His strategy was to keep his tin lunchbox in plain view of oncoming drivers, thereby establishing his status as a working man. Rather than walk along with his back to the driver, sticking out a hopeful thumb, he considered it essential to turn and look the oncoming driver in the eye. His success rate was such that he set off each morning in full confidence that he would get a lift and he was arriving home earlier than previously and eager to spend some time in the vegetable garden.

After a few years of uninterrupted usage, the Gosling Garden needed a break from constant tillage. In the meantime, my father had been using cart loads of farmyard manure supplied by Tommy Keane to fertilise and improve the soil in our back garden. This garden was not big enough to cater for our potato needs and Tommy offered a strip of ground in one of his big tillage fields. We sowed potatoes in Tommy's field and grew vegetables at the rear of our house. My father finally gave up sowing potatoes in the late 1960s. By then, three of us had left home and potatoes could be purchased in the shops for the remainder of the family.

Since our arrival in Murneen, we had been buying milk from Gavins' farm and, if our hens weren't laying, we purchased fresh eggs from Conroys across the road. There were no concerns about families consuming milk which was not pasteurised; we trusted the farmer to provide us with milk from a cow that was free from tuberculosis. Farmers usually had a favourite cow whose milk was preferred by the family and the surplus was available for sale to neighbours. One of our chores was calling to Gavins with a tin can for four pints of milk. Mrs Gavin used her measuring jug to carefully and accurately dole out the required amount. Then she generously added an extra half jug of milk while explaining that it was "a drop for the cat".

My mother's weekly routine also changed gradually. She avoided cycling to town unless absolutely necessary. Instead, she sent me or Mike with a list to Kean's grocery store. The bulging cardboard box of groceries was then delivered to our home each weekend.

CHAPTER THIRTY-SEVEN
Don't Be Cruel

Writing this book has obliged me to study the manner in which my parents related to their children. Their relationship with one another also merits examination. I've already touched upon how they interacted with each other when I examined their decision making processes. The relatively benign manipulation which arose from my mother's strategy of study and subversion was forgivable. Perhaps less so was my father's abdication of responsibility in respect of educational matters although his later expression of regret is to his credit. But there is a real danger that my admiration for my parents will result in an unbalanced and hagiographical account of their lives. It therefore seems appropriate for me to enter the uncomfortable area of describing their daily interaction.

For the vast majority of the time, they were affectionately mutually supportive and were relaxed and casual in each others company. In the evenings, while he was eating his dinner, my father detailed for my mother the happenings of his day at work and they chatted easily. As was his way, my father was less likely to praise my mother to her face but was constantly telling us as children that we were lucky to have such a wonderful person as our mother and he urged us to avoid doing anything which might cause her difficulty. Equally, she regularly reiterated how hard he worked uncomplainingly in order to provide for the family and she obliged us to meet the standards which he expected from us. They displayed a mutual respect and affection... usually.

It would be unrealistic to expect that tension would not arise between them from time to time. The management of such tensions are a feature of all marriages. In my parents' case, I suspect that the difficulties, obstacles, and tragedies which they endured and which I have described, placed an additional strain on them from time to time so that occasional arguments were the inevitable consequence.

My memory of their altercations is fixed in terms of timing, development, and conclusion. I associate their rows with Sunday afternoons after dinner although they must have had arguments at other times. There would be an uncomfortable sense of foreboding. Perhaps my father would be uncharacteristically quiet, brooding, and unresponsive; all indicators that he was in bad form. If my mother was annoyed about something or with him, she would not hesitate to articulate it and would become antagonised either by his response or by his lack of engagement. Soon, they would be arguing loudly.

These arguments took place within earshot of the children and it did not seem to occur to my parents that this would make us uncomfortable. Over time, we developed the practice of drifting out of the house and embarking on some activity to distract ourselves until things calmed down. The subjects of the arguments are long forgotten and are unimportant because the focus of each row soon shifted to the relative merits of their respective families, the Rushes and the Ryans. An accusation that the Rushes were constantly "looking down" on the Ryans might be countered by a comment that the Rushes thought that the Ryans had ideas "above their station" because they owned a few acres of land. During these exchanges, it seemed to me that my mother's sharper intellect enabled her to marshal her attack more efficiently so that her ripostes could be more cutting and effective than those of my father. His resultant frustration almost inevitably resulted in him finally launching the decisive verbal blow. Inexcusably, he would make some hurtful comment about her weight. The combination of ageing, childbearing, and medication caused my mother's weight to fluctuate. She was constantly changing diets and making attempts to reduce her weight with mixed success and she was understandably sensitive about it. As a result of his devastating comment, my mother would cry and tearfully defend herself. As if deflated and embarrassed by the progress of events, he would vaguely accuse her of resorting to tears when she was losing the argument and he would lapse into silence while she sobbed quietly. After the passage of an hour or two, it would be as if nothing had happened; we would all be sitting around the table having our Sunday evening tea.

I hated the rows. Especially the inevitability of their progress and conclusion. My father's cruel comment about my mother's weight appalled me but I was also annoyed at her because I felt that she persisted in goading him despite knowing the inevitable conclusion. I thought that she could have gained the higher ground by stating that she refused to argue any more because she knew that it was futile. But perhaps this was naive. The argument would probably have resumed or, if not, the unresolved tension might have caused deeper problems. Perhaps they just needed to let off steam occasionally.

The rows did not take place every Sunday but were still prone to recur from time to time.

Then Mike stepped in.

One Sunday afternoon in the mid 60s, Mike and I were in the bedrooms doing our homework when the early shots of another confrontation were fired in the kitchen. The 16 year old Mike suddenly snapped. He charged into the kitchen. I hesitated, then followed. Mike was already in full flow.

"How the hell do you expect us to do our homework with this racket going on. Both of ye are going on and on all the time about education and how important it is for us to do our homework. How can we do a thing when we can't even hear ourselves thinking?"

He pointed to the open-mouthed Sean, Kieran, and Kay.

"And what's more, I know you're frightening the daylights out of these children because these rows used to frighten the daylights out of us when we were their age. Isn't that right, Coleman?"

"Eh... Well...Yes! It is."

Our parents were dumbstruck and embarrassed. Before they had a chance to muster a response, Mike turned on his heel and returned to the bedroom. The three wide-eyed youngsters switched their bewildered gaze to me.

"Run off out and play".

As they scampered off, I followed in Mike's footsteps. There was a stunned silence from the kitchen.

I cannot recall any Sunday altercations following Mike's intervention. I'm sure that they had arguments but the vindictiveness and inevitability of the previous ritual was ended.

There was an earlier occasion when tension between my parents resulted in a learning experience. My father occasionally recounted a self-deprecating anecdote about an argument between my parents which took place during the early years of their marriage. As a result of a row with my mother, he became annoyed, stormed out of the house, grabbed his bike, and cycled to my grandparents' house in

Claremorris. He intended to visit for an hour or two and then return home to Streamstown by which time the situation would have cooled down. My grandmother spotted him approaching and, probably recognising from his demeanour that something was amiss, met him at the front gate as he was dismounting from his bike.

"Where are you going at this hour of the day?"

"Ah... I just had a bit of a row with Kitty."

"Go off home. This is no place for you."

"I think it might better for everyone if I stayed out of the firing line for a while."

His attempted justification cut no ice with his mother.

"And where can Kitty go when you have a row? She has no family around here to go running to so you can't be coming here. Off home with you and sort it out."

He turned and cycled immediately back to Streamstown and told my mother what had transpired. They both laughed about the event many times over the years. But my grandmother had sent a clear message to each of them. My father was made aware that he could not go seeking comfort from his mother if he had a disagreement with his wife. My mother learned that her mother-in-law appreciated that she was at a disadvantage because her family lived a few hundred miles away. She now knew that her mother-in-law would not automatically take her son's side but would support her if she needed it. The two women were to remain close and mutually supportive as the years passed.

CHAPTER THIRTY-EIGHT

I Walk The Line

It was in the early 1960s. A few days before Christmas. In the small hours of Monday morning, a station wagon was wending its way along the dark, country road towards Claremorris. My father was dozing to the comforting sound of the motor engine, cosily crammed between two other musicians in the back seat. The band members were returning from a dance and were just a few miles from home. Suddenly, the wagon swung off the road into a laneway and the driver brought the vehicle to a stop alongside a darkened wood.

"This is it, lads. Come on."

"I'm grand. I'll wait here."

My father assumed that this was another toilet break. The regularity of these "relief" stops was in direct proportion to the amount of alcohol consumed by some of the band-members earlier in the evening.

The driver brandished a saw which he had just removed from under his seat and pointed towards the trees.

"Wake up, Coleman! Did you not hear us saying? We're grabbing a few Christmas trees. Sure nobody will be any the wiser. Come on."

As my father told us later when recounting the cautionary tale, he should have refused to become involved. But, as he explained, it's always easier to go along with the crowd that to take a principled stand. He watched guiltily as the young pine trees were cut and he helped to secure them on the roof-rack.

Over breakfast, he told my mother what he had done. She already knew that he was vehemently opposed to theft, almost to the point of paranoia. One of his duties at work was painting the railway houses which guarded level crossings. Often, there were partly empty cans of paint left over when a job was completed. It was common practise for the railway men to take some of these cans in order to carry our some decorating at home. Similarly, leftover lengths of wood might sometimes be salvaged and brought home for use as firewood. My father did not condone such action, even when it was explained to him that the paint or wood were destined to be dumped or would deteriorate and disintegrate in a darkened corner of the station warehouse. On one occasion, my father enquired from his foreman whether he could pay a nominal amount for the goods but was told that there was no process in place for this. Taking the items could not be officially sanctioned but, he was assured, a blind eye would be turned. This did not satisfy my father. He regularly spoke to us disapprovingly about people in the workplace who pilfered tools or even pens and pencils. Even seemingly trivial acts were dishonest, he cautioned, and he pointed out that hardened thieves started out by stealing pencils or paperclips. If you can justify taking even a small item, he explained, you will gradually convince yourself that the taking of increasingly large items is acceptable.

He was in a quandary about the Christmas tree which was now stashed behind the house.

"I should give it back."

My mother was more practical.

"What good is it to the man now that it's cut? I'll tell you what you'll do. You're going to confessions this evening. See what the priest says."

My mother expected that the priest would tell my father to say a few Hail Marys as penance. She hoped that this would serve to ease his conscience and enable him to put the matter behind him. The priest had other ideas. He told my father that, as penance, he should make restitution by offering compensation to the owner of the trees.

The following evening, my father cycled to the scene of the crime, located the owner of the wood, explained what had happened, and asked him to name a price for the tree. The farmer was dismissive.

"Go home and have sense, ya ould eejit."

When he arrived back home, my father explained that the farmer was trying to be kind but he admitted that he was far more embarrassed by the response than if he had been allowed to pay for the tree.

"At least he didn't ask me for my name. Hopefully, he won't know who I was."

My parents, and in particular my father, had strong feelings about reputation and behaviour. Theft or other forms of dishonesty were morally wrong but this was not the only factor to be taken into account. We were also told regularly that such acts could damage the "good name of the family". My father echoed a view which was also expressed regularly by his own mother to us, her grandchildren. Families were judged based upon behaviour. One "bad egg" or bad deed could damage the family name. It was impressed upon us that children from families with bad reputations found it doubly difficult to get jobs or to make their way in the world. Similarly, if one of us achieved something noteworthy, the standing of the family in the community was enhanced, to the benefit of all.

At times, I felt that my father was oversensitive to the opinions of others. On one occasion, during my awkward early teenage years, I was walking along a lane which led from Claremorris railway station towards Mount Street. I was in the company of another boy and three girls and we were chatting gaily. We were approaching a stile-type metal gate which was designed to allow through one person at a time while preventing animals from escaping. I suddenly spotted my father approaching in the distance and was momentarily flustered that he would see me with the girls. I quickly overcame my embarrassment and we filed through the gate and noisily went on our way.

When my father arrived home from work that evening, he immediately took me to task. He explained to my mother:

"I was never so embarrassed in all my life. To think that one of your own would show you up like that. I can only hope that too many people didn't see it. What will they think?"

I was confused. I thought at first that he was upset because I was talking to and laughing with girls but, on reflection, I considered this unlikely.

"I couldn't believe what I was seeing. Instead of standing back and letting the girls through the gate first, he walked straight through before anybody else had a chance and the poor girls had to trail after him."

I cast my mind back. He was correct. I knew that there were two factors which influenced my action. First of all, I was momentarily flustered that my father had rumbled me as I chatted with girls. Secondly, while I did go through the gate first, I then held it and swung it back and forth each time to allow the others come through. But I knew that such excuses wouldn't wash. I could just as easily have waited, held and swung the gate to allow the others to go through and then followed. The truth was that it did not occur to me to allow the girls go through first and it should have. But I was reasonably sure that the girls didn't notice or, if they did, didn't think badly of me as a result.

I didn't argue with him but I was contemptuous of my father's attitude. I felt that he was not angry because of what people might think of me. He was angry because they might say: "Isn't that one of the Rushe lads. You'd think their father would have raised them better."

This desire to protect and promote the reputation of the family could have embarrassing consequences when my grandmother entered the fray. She was on friendly terms with a stringer for the local newspapers and she alerted him from time to time when one of us achieved something which she considered to be deserving of publicity. When I was lucky enough to have job offers following my Leaving Certificate, I was embarrassed to read the details in a congratulatory note in the local newspaper. During the subsequent years, any promotion or accomplishment, however modest, which was achieved by myself or any of my brothers and sisters was again detailed in the "Claremorris Notes" section of the paper. It would not be unreasonable to suggest that such anxiety for public recognition betrays a hint of desperation on the part of my grandmother and, to a lesser extent, my father.

"Behave with integrity" and "Do things right" were phrases often uttered by my father. We were expected to do the right thing and, just as importantly, to instinctively know what was the right thing to do. The phrase "Do the right thing" implies that there is one correct way to act and that you must follow that path only. "Do things right" has a slightly different meaning . There may be more than one "right way" or sometimes there might be no "right way" at all. But you must deal with each situation with integrity and honesty and you must act as your conscience tells you so that people will recognise that you acted with probity.

Many years later, my father was clipping the hedge in front of the house when Mike Conroy was passing by. The neighbour stopped and engaged my father in conversation. This was unusual because Mr Conroy was not a man who normally indulged in small talk. My father admired the Conroys. Mike and "Mrs Mike" had raised and educated their children, all of whom had now left home and had embarked upon professional careers. When we were growing up, my parents constantly pointed to the achievements of the Conroy children as the standard to which we should aspire.

As he leaned on his bike, Mr Conroy enquired individually about each of the Rushe children, all of whom had left home by this stage. The two men went on to talk about each others families and then the conversation drifted towards local issues. Finally, Mr Conroy turned to leave. After taking a few steps, he turned back.

"Coleman. I just stopped to say that I admire what you and Mrs Rushe have done in raising your family. I don't know of any other couple who could have started with so little and achieved so much."

My father was deeply touched by the compliment. The reputation of his family had been acknowledged by somebody whom he admired and respected.

My mother was conscious of what other people thought about the family but she was not quite so precious about it as my father or my grandmother. She poked fun at any pretentiousness which she observed. On one occasion, when my father and a few of us sons were pontificating at length about some subject, she interjected.

"Will ye listen to yerselves? It's no wonder some of the neighbours think the Rushe men are a bit above themselves!"

She laughingly refused to elaborate on who, if anybody, thought that we had a superior attitude. But she had made her point. "Don't be getting above yourself" was one of her frequently used admonitions.

My father's crisis of conscience regarding the Christmas tree contrasts with the more cavalier attitude displayed by my mother many years later. She and my father were visiting our home in a leafy suburb on the east coast of Ireland. After dinner, my mother went for a sunshine stroll along the road which was bordered by elegant homes fronted by lush spacious gardens. She arrived back from her walk with an armful of short stems from various plants. These cuttings, which she refereed to as "slips", could later be sowed in potting compost and replanted in her garden in Murneen. She explained that, as she walked and viewed the shrubs and flower beds, she occasionally leant over garden walls and broke off small stems from plants which caught her fancy. As she displayed her armful of slips, she was amused when I diplomatically pointed out that her actions could be classed as theft and vandalism.

"Nonsense! You're too long living up here among big shots! Down at home, it's a great compliment if somebody takes some slips from your garden. It shows that they admire your shrubs and it doesn't cause any damage if you know what you're doing. Sure, how else would you think people get all those new shrubs for their gardens?"

"People go to garden centre's and buy them", I suggested.

"Garden centres! Far from garden centres you were reared! People had lovely gardens long before garden centres were ever heard of. A few slips here and there and you soon have a garden full of flowers and shrubs without throwing your money away in garden centres."

She turned to my wife who was amused by my mother's actions and also by my response. Both women were enjoying my discomfort.

"Look at him! He's worried about what his big shot neighbours might be saying. The bank manager's mother is up from the country and is vandalising and stealing from people's gardens! Lord between us and all harm! He'll be the talk of the town when this gets around!"

CHAPTER THIRTY-NINE

I'm Into Something Good

My father tended to leave the day to day management of the children to my mother. As time went on, however, he became more actively involved in other areas of our lives. In a sense, it could be argued that he became more comfortable with us as we left our childhood years behind.

I've already alluded to my father's encouragement of my interest in music. Apart from helping me to learn, he constantly talked to me about music and musicians. As we discussed the relative merits of various groups and recordings, he showed an interest in the music to which I was attracted. Although some of this music didn't appeal to him, he never denigrated it. This acceptance that my musical preferences were just as valid as his only served to strengthen the bond between us.

My father's encouragement was not confined to music or to me. When any of the family showed an interest in or talent for some extracurricular activity, he immediately demonstrated his support. Mike's interest in carpentry and mechanics continued to develop following his enrolment at the Tech. Soon he could repair engines and carry out electrical work. This resulted in a special rapport with my father whose respect for Mike's ability continued to grow over the years. Mike was the first port of call when help or advice was needed with any kind of maintenance or repair work around the house.

Sean's early obsession with drawing and sketching was encouraged and soon developed into a passion and talent for visual art. My parents, and particularly my father, urged him to develop his drawing skills and would eagerly take down from the mantelpiece Sean's latest drawing of a horse to show to a slightly bemused visitor.

Although he was bright, intelligent, and able, Sean was not enamoured by school and homework. He would gaze out the classroom window, studying how the sunlight was casting the shadow of a tree onto a nearby wall. At that time, there were no art classes in either primary or secondary schools in our area. After spending some time in secondary school, Sean became increasingly frustrated with formal study and the non-availability of art classes. He wanted out.

Sean decided that a move to Dublin represented his best opportunity of achieving his goal. His intention was to find a job which would enable him to support himself and to attend art classes in his spare time. Patricia was now married and her husband, John, worked in the bar trade. John reassured Sean that he possessed the interpersonal skills which would enable him to find employment as a barman.

Sean broached the proposal with our parents and, after much discussion, he was allowed to follow his dream. Patricia arranged accommodation for him and, because I was working in Dublin at that time, I was asked by my father to accompany Sean to a few job interviews. My father felt that my position in banking might lend some gravitas and credibility to Sean's work application.

I met the gangly teenager, fresh off the train from Mayo, and I secretly fretted about how I would "sell him" to prospective employers. As soon as we introduced ourselves to our first prospect, any apprehension which I harboured about the success of our venture was dispelled. Sean immediately struck up a rapport with the bar owner who was clearly impressed with his easy manner and air of efficiency. Having been briefed by John, Sean was fully conversant with the nature of the work and the expectations of the prospective employer. A few hours later, Sean had a choice of jobs and was on his way to building a successful life in Dublin.

As Sean developed his skills as an artist, my father was his constant ally and encourager. Ironically, the man who admitted in his interview with Decca Records that he knew nothing about art now became interested in painting and painters. When he visited Dublin, he and Sean invariably visited the art galleries and discussed the various works. I anticipated that my father would like paintings in the classical styles, and he did, but I was surprised when he developed a passion for the expressionist paintings of Jack B Yeats. The artist's intense, experimental works in thickly applied paint which depict real and imagined scenes from rural Irish life, are not immediately accessible but reward study and contemplation. My father was soon talking knowledgeably about the Yeats collection in the National Gallery and discussing the relative merits of various works.

My father was later awestruck when he saw the newly discovered "The Taking of Christ" by Caravaggio. The magnificent painting had hung unrecognised and unattributed in the dining room of the Jesuit order in Dublin before being rediscovered, cleaned, and displayed in the National Gallery in Dublin. My father enthusiastically urged me to go and view the masterpiece. His interest in and passion for art and paintings was awakened as a result of his bond with Sean.

When Kieran became involved in theatre a few years later, the familiar cycle was repeated. As Kieran acted in school productions, in amateur dramatics, and later on the professional stage, my father and my mother attended most of his plays but my father was most infected by Kieran's enthusiasm. He deepened his own interest in contemporary actors and acting. He had always professed admiration for actors such as Spencer Tracy, Robert Mitchum, Humphrey Bogart, and George Raft. Now, energised by Kieran's enthusiasm, he was extolling the virtues of Robert De Nero, Gene Hackman, Al Pacino, Robert Duvall, and Dustin Hoffman as well as the modern playwrights in whose work Kieran was making appearances.

My fathers encouragement and involvement was mainly directed at the four boys in the family. Patricia had spent most of her school going years living with our grandparents who urged her to read and brought her for occasional visits to the cinema. There was less opportunity to become involved in her extra curricular activities although I recall the whole family attending a school musical in which she was participating.

While Kay, the youngest, was attending primary school, she took up Irish dancing. Dance competitions, or feiseanna, were held regularly during the summer. On many occasions, my parents huddled in the car while Kay and her friends displayed their dancing skills on a flat lorry trailer in the middle of a windswept field.

Football provided another opportunity for my father to bond with his children. As soon as we were old enough, he brought us by train or bus to watch the Mayo county team and sometimes the local Claremorris club team. When I played football in secondary school, he took an interest in my progress. At first, he was slightly nonplussed when I opted to become a goalkeeper.

"When an outfield player makes a few mistakes, he is usually switched to another position on the field. When a goalie makes a blunder, there's only one option. The sideline!"

When I was selected as goalkeeper to represent Saint Colmans College and later the local club at underage level, he overcame his reservations but was unable to attend my matches which took place during school hours while he was working. Nevertheless, new football boots were provided for me despite the family's financial constraints. When I progressed from the school teams to play for the county minor team and the club senior side, my father was a regular attender.

I had just turned eighteen when I was selected to play senior football with Claremorris. My elevation at a relatively young age was due to the unavailability of the usual goalkeeper and my recent involvement with the county minor team. Although goalkeepers were much less protected than nowadays and could be legitimately bundled to the net by opponents, I do not recall being apprehensive about testing my ability against older, toughened and experienced opponents. Unknown to me, my father was quite concerned about my safety.

One of my earliest matches at senior level was against Castlebar Mitchels in our home pitch in Claremorris. Any nervous tension I might have felt were allayed by our full-back, Cathal Cawley, a Claremorris based Garda who was an experienced and highly regarded member of the County Sligo senior team. He spoke to me as we left the dressing room.

"Don't worry out there. I'll look after you. Just get rid of the ball as fast as you can and boot it down the field."

Early in the game, the ball broke loose in the penalty area directly in front of my goal, a few yards from the goal-line. I instinctively threw myself on the ball in order to deprive the opposition of possession. I looked up and, towering menacingly over me was Mick Ruane, a burly full forward who was a mainstay on the Mayo senior team during the 60s. My immediate thought was that, if I got up, Mick would deposit me and the football in the back of the net. When I failed to move as I waited for reinforcements to arrive, Mick was obliged to take action. Later partisan accounts of the incident suggested that Mick Ruane had kicked the daylights out of me as I lay defenceless on the ground. In fact, Mick was a model of restraint. Like a man encountering a curled hedgehog lying in the road, Mike tentatively and enquiringly poked me with his toe and waited for a reaction. All hell broke loose. Cathal Cawley, arrived on the scene, bellowed at Mick Ruane to desist, and punched him in the jaw. Ruane, more surprised than hurt, found himself sitting on the grass beside me, protesting to the referee.

"What was I supposed to do? The lad was just lying there on top of the ball. It should be a penalty."

Rather than take any action which might result in the suspension of two respected and valuable senior county players, the referee wisely decided to ignore the fisticuffs and awarded a free kick to me.

At home later that evening, as I was washing myself in the adjoining room, I overheard my father quietly describing the incident to my mother. It transpired that he had spoken to Cathal Cawley before the game and, from his muted tone, I realised that he did not want me to know about his intervention. I don't know whether my father approached Cathal or whether the full-back recognised the fatherly concern and initiated the conversation.

"Guard Cawley told me not to worry. I'll look after him, he said. And he was true to his word."

At home, the children were all urged to read but our parents did not impose any quality control restrictions on our reading material. It did not matter whether we were reading comics or literature; it was enough that we were reading. My parents reasoned that, sooner or later, we would seek out more demanding material. In my case, having progressed from comics to graphic novel versions of "Under Two Flags" and "A Tale of Two Cities", I was soon reading the original versions of "The Three Musketeers", "The Count of Monte Christo" and "The Man in the Iron Mask." Mike and I were urged to join the local lending library and to borrow and read whatever books took our fancy. There was also a natural graduation from cowboy comic stories to western novels. Before long, I was refining my tastes and seeking out the works of Zane Grey and Louis L'Amour.

The encouragement to read was not universal in Ireland at this time. Reading for pleasure was often frowned upon, even by some teachers and priests. The writer John Mc Gahern stated that, while he was in secondary school, reading a book was considered "dissolute, a waste of time" unless it was helping the reader to pass an examination with a view to getting a job.

This attitude towards reading was illustrated when a neighbouring woman was visiting my mother. As they had a fireside chat over a cup of tea, I sat by the front window reading a book.

"Merciful hour, Mrs Rushe! Will you look at the time! Coleman. Did my husband pass down the road on his way home from the bog?"

"I'm sorry. I didn't take any notice. He might have."

The visitor looked at me with distain and shook her head in weary exasperation as she put down her teacup and rose to leave.

"Mrs Rushe. You have your work cut out with that fellow. That lad will never make anything of himself. He always has his head stuck in a book!"

CHAPTER FORTY

Carry That Weight

As we have seen, my father had firm views on a diverse range of subjects. Most were shared by my mother, if not with the same sense of certainty. Some of my father's convictions bordered on the bizarre. For example, he was perplexed by women who painted their toe-nails, regarding the activity as a sign of dissolute idleness and unhealthy self-absorption.

"And who looks at or notices painted toe-nails anyway?"

This retort failed to take into account the reality he himself has just spotted the offending pedal extremities, thereby undermining his point. To his credit, he laughed at himself when I pointed this out.

"I still think it's a bad sign in a woman, though."

A more sustainable conviction, which my parents shared, was the importance of the role of the eldest child. My father, as was his wont, was the more vocal on the subject.

In the Ireland of my parents' youth, the eldest child was normally the first to leave home, usually on the emigrant ship. It was expected that this child would become established overseas and should then send money back home so that the next child could follow. The eldest would also seek out accommodation and employment for the new arrival. Younger siblings would later benefit from the groundwork laid down by the first-born.

My father had a firm conviction that the success of the eldest child was critical to the subsequent achievements of a family. He pointed to instances of eldest children who left home and were unsuccessful or who failed to keep in contact with their families. The younger children, in the absence of a good role model, struggled to establish themselves and drifted away from each other. My father believed that a resilient and resourceful eldest child was the constant factor in all families which had achieved success after leaving home. As if embarking on a military campaign, the first-born must advance, establish a bulwark in hostile territory, and light a beacon so that the next division could follow.

This expectation and obligation must have placed unwanted pressure on Patricia from time to time but she never gave any visible sign of it, at least to parents or siblings. She passed her Leaving Certificate examination in 1966 and successfully applied for a job in the Civil Service in Dublin. The initial euphoria about the first of the family to get a "sitting-down" job was soon tempered by the need to arrange suitable accommodation for her in Dublin. Patricia had been living part-time with her grandparents in Claremorris and it was probably my grandfather's idea to write to his sister Ellen, who lived in Dublin. Since the dispersal of the Rushe family in Claddagh, Galway many decades earlier, my grandfather had kept intermittent contact with his siblings. He was closest to his brother John, who also lived in Dublin, and especially his sister Ellen. I later discovered that Ellen, as a young girl, had played a pivotal role in ensuring that her younger brothers kept in touch with the family or each other. This partly explains the high esteem in which she was held by my grandfather and my father.

Ellen McGrath, formerly Rushe, and her husband were raising a young family in Dublin and the last thing they needed was the arrival on her doorstep of another waif from the country. Nevertheless, they warmly welcomed my father when he arrived with Patricia in tow. Aunt Ellen, as she was reverently known in our family, agreed to look after Patricia's welfare until she "found her feet" in the capital. Patricia's plan was to move into a flat with work colleagues or some of her school-friends from Claremorris, who expected to move to Dublin soon afterwards.

Patricia stayed with Ellen and her family for one night. The following day, the resourceful hostess took Patricia on the bus across the city to Tallaght where her nephew Tom and his wife Daire lived with their young family. It was quickly agreed that Patricia would stay with Tom and Daire and would help with child-minding when needed. A short time later, Patricia did indeed make arrangements to move into a flat with some other girls but Tom and Daire prevailed upon her to remain with them. Having formed a close bond with the family and especially the children, Patricia was happy to stay and continued to live with them until her marriage, seven years later. Then she and husband, John, bought a house nearby.

Patricia became the beacon for each of her siblings when we eventually left home. She met the train in Dublin, arranged accommodation, and provided whatever ongoing support was needed. Her help was not confined to the family. When my mother became aware of friends and neighbours who had to go to Dublin for job interviews or medical appointments, and who were unfamiliar with the city, she alerted Patricia who would meet and help them, ensuring that they caught the appropriate trains and buses and she even sometimes accompanied them to their destination.

After Patricia left home, Mike was to be the next of the Rushe children to stretch his wings. He had completed his education at the Tech and successfully applied for a job as a maintenance fitter with the Irish Air Corps. He was located at Baldonnell Airdrome near Dublin and was poised to obtain the best possible grounding for the type of role which he craved. But there was another tempting opportunity.

My grandfather was just about to retire from his job on the railway. Although he was sixty-five, he wanted to continue his carpentry work and hoped that Mike would go into business with him. His plan was to extend the workshop behind his house where he and Mike would jointly operate a carpentry business, specialising in the manufacture and installation of furniture. Apart from Mike's carpentry ability, which our grandfather rated highly, his electrical and plumbing skills would also be invaluable.

Granda mooted the proposal with Dad and also with Mike. Although he was excited about his opportunity with the Air Corps, Mike was also attracted by the prospect of going into business with his grandfather and would probably have gone along with the proposal if Dad had approved. No such approval was forthcoming.

Dad felt strongly - another firmly-held conviction - that it was important for any young person to get away from home and family, at least for a period, and to experience the world outside. Horizons should be broadened and perspectives changed by viewing ones home from afar. Later, if an opportunity arose to return to the home place, an informed and rational decision could be made, rather than an emotional one.

It is not clear to me why my father held such a strong view. Did he regret that he did not leave home as his two sisters and my mother had done? Or did his belated and enforced temporary sojourn in London have such an impact on his world view that he decided such opportunities should not be passed up?

Granda was disappointed but, when Michael did not disagree with Dad, he let the matter drop. Instead, he got a part-time job as a carpenter with a building company which was extending the local Convent of Mercy and he arranged a summer job for me in the site office. Working in close proximity to my grandfather enabled me and him to get to know one another better and, I like to think, went a little way towards mitigating his disappointment at Mike's departure.

CHAPTER FORTY-ONE
Mama Tried

While my father took on the responsibility of supporter and encourager of our extra curricular activities and talents, my mother quietly developed a different but no less effective role both inside and outside the home.

In addition to organising the household, she focused on ensuring that school work was completed satisfactorily. When we were coming to the end of our schooling, she switched her attention to our vocational needs. Each evening, as I emerged from the bedroom after a few hours studying for my final exams, hoping to spend an hour in front of the recently acquired TV, she handed me the newspaper. Encircled in pencil in the Irish Independent were advertisements for jobs which she deemed suitable for me and for which she wanted me to apply in writing. The jobs varied widely. On one occasion, she was urging me to reply to two adverts. One was for a job as a helper in a warehouse in Dublin. The other offered employment as a trainee chartered accountant. I tried to explain to my mother that the meagre weekly wage associated with the warehouse job demonstrated that the advert was targeted at someone who lived at home in Dublin and who did not have to pay for accommodation. I was unsure of what exactly a chartered accountant was. I suggested that it made more sense to delay my job search until my Leaving Certificate results came out. Then I could know which jobs I was qualified to apply for. My mother was unimpressed by my proposed strategy.

"Apply for all the jobs you might be qualified for. If you're offered more than one, then you can afford to be picky."

I did respond to some job advertisements, though not all she earmarked for me. When I was called for interview for positions as a chartered accountant and later as a laboratory technician, I was embarrassed when my lack of knowledge about the roles was uncovered by the interviewers. I became determined to be properly prepared for future interviews, so the experience was not wasted.

There was another supportive gesture which I attributed solely to my father although I now see my mother's fingerprints all over the deed. When I was attending job interviews, I did not yet have a wrist-watch. On the day of each interview, my father passed on his watch to me so that I would attend on time. When Mike heard about this, he promised to buy a wristwatch for me when I finally got a job.

It was about this time that I changed my name. I was given the name Coleman after my father. I was becoming increasingly agitated, however, because of occasional confusion which resulted from our identical names. Replies to my job applications or other occasional items of mail which were intended for me were being handed to and opened by my father. I decided that I would spell my name "Colman" when submitting job applications and gradually adopted that version of my name. I felt justified because the patron saint of the parish, after whom the College was named, was Saint Colman. The change was partly driven by pragmatism but, I now recognise, was also a subconscious bid to assert my independence.

My mother's qualities were also having an impact outside the home. She possessed a natural empathy and approachability which encouraged people to trust her and to confide in her. My father would laughingly point out that she could meet somebody for the first time and, five minutes later, they would be telling her their life story and pouring out their most intimate secrets. These confidants were exclusively women but could be any age or from any background. They instinctively trusted her judgement and valued her advice. More crucially, they sensed correctly that their revelations would be handled in the strictest confidence.

As well as being a good listener and a provider of practical advice and support, she often undertook to pray for people or, better yet, to get Granny Rushe to do so.

Because of the confidential nature of her relationships and interactions, one rarely became aware of her impact. A letter which my father received following my mother's death gives an indication of her effectiveness in dealing with the troubled teenage daughter of a friend. The former teenager, who was a successful woman in her thirties at the time of writing, fondly described my mother's intervention when the relationship between teenager and parents was undergoing stress. She was "a kind, loving and joyous woman who was always ready to offer a helping hand and words of encouragement or comfort. She was the woman who arranged for me to go to my first disco before I even knew I wanted to go and she was there when I couldn't decide what to do at university and my own family had thrown in the towel... That's what I will always remember, her constant presence, wishing you well, congratulating you when you reached some goal and giving you hope and encouragement when things weren't going according to plan."

When my mother had spells in hospital, necessitated by complications associated with hip replacements, the area around her bed inevitably became a "confessional zone" for women of all ages. They dropped by for a chat or, more often than not, to tell her about some family or lifestyle problem and to seek her advice. Following her discharge from hospital, there followed an inevitable stream of correspondence as new found friends wrote to her with updates on their progress.

In the days and months after her death, I became aware of many such interventions which, due to their sensitive nature, I am unable to describe here. To detail them would risk recognition, speculation, or identification.

The Irish tradition of making Saint Brigid's crosses goes back many centuries. Each year in January, rushes are cut, interlaced in a traditional manner, and weaved into a cross which is brought to church to receive a blessing on Saint Brigid's Day, February 1. The cross is then hung in the home until replaced by a fresh cross a year later. Sometime in the early 1960s, my mother began to produce these crosses. She started with one cross for her own kitchen. Soon, she obliged neighbours who asked her to make a cross for them and she also produced a few extra. When she took the crosses to church to be blessed, they were immediately snapped up by parishioners. My mother's journal reveals that the demand for her crosses increased each spring and soon she was crafting over forty crosses to be blessed and left at the church to be taken away by neighbours. By then, there must have been one of Kitty Rushe's crosses hanging in most houses in the parish and others were sent by post to family members who had left the area.

One of my favourite photographs of my mother was taken by my brother Sean. She is seated on a chair in the middle of the living room, wearing the ever-present apron. She is ankle deep in rush cuttings, smiling broadly at the camera as she holds aloft a half-completed Saint Brigid's Cross.

CHAPTER FORTY-TWO

Welcome To The Working Week

Since Mike left home, I had become more independent. Although we had been inseparable since childhood, I cannot recall being regretful at his departure. Because we attended different secondary schools, we had each become accustomed to functioning without the others constant support. We had also developed our own divergent interests and each had made new friends.

A more practical but welcome result of Mike's departure was that, for the first time in my life, I had a bed to myself. I still shared the bedroom with Sean and Kieran but having my own bed seemed like a luxury.

Another benefit was that I inherited Mike's summer job with Tommy Keane. I loved the outdoor work and especially Tommy's non-stop chat but my favourite memories do not involve farm work. I fondly recall the days when the rain prevented us from going out into the fields. We sat in silence in the kitchen, reading from Tommy's massive hoard of Western paperback novels and listening to the soothing patter of the rain on the tin roof of the lean-to.

Working for Tommy during the summer had its responsibilities. My father was regularly urging me to "mind my job" and reminding me that my primary obligation was to give a good days work to Tommy Keane. As a result of my selection on the school teams, I had been approached to play under-age football for Claremorris, our local club. Usually, one of the selectors collected me by car after I arrived home from work in the evening and dropped me back home after the match. One one occasion, we had a fixture quite a distance away in the north of the county and I was told that I would be collected at five o'clock. I usually finished work at six but I agreed to the earlier time; I trusted that Tommy had no objection to my early departure. My confidence was justified when I mentioned it to him. He assured me that I could leave early on any such occasion.

To my dismay, when my father heard about the arrangement, he refused permission for me to leave work before the normal finishing time. I pleaded that Tommy Keane had no objection to my request for an early departure. My father wasn't having it.

"What could the man say? He's too nice to refuse but all the more reason why you shouldn't take advantage of his good nature. It wasn't fair to put him in that position."

"But footballers regularly are allowed time off work to play matches and even for training."

"That's different. Sometimes, a firm will employ a well known footballer because he'll bring in extra business. In that case, it's in the employer's interest to give him time off to play or for training. But Tommy Keane has nothing to gain by giving you time off. Instead he's losing an hours labour that he's paying you for."

My pleas and arguments went unheeded. Over-dramatically, I claimed that my father was forcing me to give up football. He dismissed my argument.

"In life, you'll sometimes have to make choices. But remember always that your first obligation is to the person who's paying your wages. But, if you use your imagination, you can work your way around most problems. You can often pass the problem back to the other fellow."

"You mean to Tommy Keane? But he..."

"No. I mean the football people. They want to collect you at five. Either they don't know that you're working or they don't think it's important. If you tell than that you can't be picked up until after work, then they have a choice to make. If they want you badly enough, they'll find a way. I'm sure they have to deal with problems like this all the time."

At my mother's urging, I got in touch with the football club and explained my problem. Problem? What problem? No problem! The other players could go ahead while a second car could pick me up from work at six provided I had my football gear with me. If I togged out during the car journey, we should be there in time for the throw-in. If not, another player would "stand in goal" until I arrived. No problem. Why didn't you ask?

On the appointed evening, Tommy looked at his watch.

"Why aren't you away? It's gone five o'clock."

He watched me carefully as I vaguely explained that I was being collected an hour later. I avoided giving the reason but Tommy didn't need to be told. He smiled.

"Your father put his spoke in, did he?"

I shrugged.

"My father can be as odd as two left shoes."

He grinned.

"He's a quare hawk, your father. You won't go far wrong in life if you pay heed to that man."

My mother's insistence that I apply for various jobs as I waited for my Leaving Certificate results had the desired outcome. I sat an examination for a clerical job with the Post Office, did an aptitude test for a job in a bank, and was interviewed and rigourously medically examined for potential acceptance into the Irish Army Cadet School. When my Leaving Certificate results arrived, they were acceptable and confirmed my academic qualification for the jobs for which I had applied.

My mother's oft repeated maxim that I would have a choice if I applied for more than one job was prescient. I was offered jobs in the Post Office and in a bank and I was accepted into the Cadet School. A bank job seemed to offer more potential that the role with the Post Office but I had to decide whether to accept the "sitting down" job or the more active one in the army. I discussed the options with my parents. They offered opinions but made it clear that the choice was mine to make. My mother leaned more towards the army career. She figured that the active lifestyle would suit me and she also comforted herself that, while in the Cadet School, food and accommodation would be provided. My father favoured the bank job as did my grandmother who was elated at the prospect of one her grandchildren working in a bank, an unprecedented boost for the reputation of the family, in her view.

There was no career guidance facility in the school. I did not know anybody who worked in a bank. In fact, I had only set foot in a bank office on one occasion when I was dispatched to collect some coin for the hardware shop in which I had a summer job. My initial impression was negative. The dark hardwood counters and glinting brass fittings gave a church-like ambience to the grim, austere, bank office. The teller, possibly sensing my discomfort in the strange surroundings, was chatty and cheerful as he handed over the bag of coin, joking that it was hardly worth my while absconding with the cash. Now I wondered what life would be like as a bank clerk or whether I might be better advised to embark on an army career. One or two of the older boys in the College had joined the Cadet School but I did not know them well enough to seek candid career information from them.

My mother sensed my dilemma in choosing the job and my desire not to displease anybody by my choice.

"Hop on your bike and go and talk to Father Colleran. Ask him what he thinks would suit you best. He knows you better than most people after you've spent five years in his school."

I was sceptical about how well Father Colleran knew me but I agreed to the suggestion and I cycled to the College to seek him out. We walked side by side along the gravel drive, his hands clasped behind his back as he listened carefully while I explained my dilemma. There was a long pause after I'd finished.

" Well, master Colman. Let us think this through."

I smiled at his quirk of always referring to his pupils as "master".

"The Army Cadet school is a great opportunity and, I'm told, a character-building experience. The drawback, as I see it, is that you'll be run off your feet for the first two or three years. You'll spend every available minute studying, drilling, and doing physical exercise. After that, you could be sitting on your backside for the rest of your life waiting for something to happen. Now, sitting on your backside would be no problem for you but I'm not sure that you would relish the harsh discipline which you would have to endure during the earlier years."

He came to a halt and then turned to me.

"I understand that you don't take a drink. Is that correct?"

I was startled. Where did that come from? And how did he know?

He was still looking at me.

"Uh. No, Father. Not so far, anyway."

He turned away and we resumed our stroll. The only sound was the gravel crunch of our footsteps. After a contemplative pause, he resumed.

"The Post Office and the bank can be good jobs but the bank has better promotion prospects. As with most things in life, however, there's a drawback. You see, most of the small bank branches are situated in quiet country towns. The work is done and the bankers are out the door and sitting in the pub by four o'clock in the afternoon because there's nothing else to do. As a result, a lot of country bankers become alcoholics. Still, I'd recommend that you accept the bank job.

You've shown that you're sensible enough to mind yourself as far as the drink is concerned."

My admiration for the man grew, not only because of his concise analysis and decisive conclusions, but also because he knew that I didn't drink alcohol. I was reminded of his detective work which led to him returning the school fees five years earlier. At that time, he had carried out his enquiries and consultations and then unobtrusively handed the money back to me. On this latest occasion, if I had made an appointment to see him, I would have concluded that he made some discreet enquiries in preparation for my visit. But I had arrived unannounced so that he had no opportunity to prepare. Yet, he knew that I didn't drink alcohol. I wondered how much more he knew about his students. A formidable man.

There was a flurry of activity in preparation for my departure from home to take up a job with the bank. My mother bought some essentials and, almost half a century later, I still have in my possession the polish brushes and a clothes brush which she purchased for me. My father presented me with a new, sturdy, cardboard suitcase which was much too large for my needs. At least, he was being consistent. He had already accompanied me to the drapers and the shoe-shop in order to kit me out for my departure. On each occasion, the items purchased were a couple of sizes too large.

"You'll grow into then very quickly. Look at how fast you're growing out of your clothes."

I had experienced a spurt of growth and was now a skinny, gangly, six feet tall teenager. An argument could be made that I would put on some weight, although my mother fretted that a landlady was unlikely to feed me as well as I had been fed at home. It seemed less plausible that my feet would get any bigger. Nevertheless, as I tried on shoes in the shoe shop, my father prodded at the toes in order to ensure that there was plenty of room for expansion. His ally, the shoe salesman, nodded and murmured in approval as I was made to walk around the shop in order, presumably, to ensure that the new shoes did not misbehave in some strange and unpredictable way. When I tentatively suggested that the shoes might perhaps be a size too big, the salesman knew where his duty lay; to please the person paying the bill, not the wearer of the merchandise.

"Your father is right. You're a growing boy. But let me show you some nice fashionable thick socks which will make the shoes feel more snug. You'll need two pairs, of course."

The ordeal was repeated in the drapery shop as I tried on various sports jackets. There was much tugging of sleeves, extending of arms and elbows, and rubbing of lapels between thumb and forefinger. Size, cut, and quality of cloth were not the only criteria, as my father explained when the salesman had departed into the dim recesses of the shop in order to collect a few suitable jackets.

"You can't be too careful when you're buying clothes. The lights and mirrors they have in these shops can make anything look good. That's why you see fellows walking down the street wearing jackets in all the colours of the rainbow."

He had a solution, of course. When I tried on each new jacket, I was obliged to step out of the shop onto the street and to "do a twirl" so that my father could ensure that the colour of the fabric was acceptable in ordinary day-light. It was true that the shade of the fabric could change significantly when relocated from the enhanced lighting of the shop into the more demanding light outside. While self consciously walking out of the store and pirouetting on the sidewalk, I had to run the risk of encountering smirking former schoolmates or, worse still, local girls who were quick to articulate their amusement at my obvious embarrassment. Shopping at mid-morning on a busy Saturday served to guarantee that there would be lots of people on the street so that I would have to bear the brunt of a few jibes.

"Nice jacket, Colman. But you need to do some more work on the cat-walking!"

"Colman. Ask for a refund from the modelling school."

"Make a run for it, Rushe! They'll be so glad to get rid of that jacket, they won't even bother to chase you."

In my quieter moments, as I packed my clothes and my few possessions into the suitcase and pondered my uncertain future, I knew that I was ready to leave home. Just as I would "grow into" my jacket, shoes, and suitcase, I was also ready to grow into my own life. I needed to forge an identity for myself away from the daily protection and comfort of my parents and family. I now understood what my father meant when he insisted that it was best for Mike to leave home rather than drift into the carpentry venture with my grandfather. Mike and I needed to find our place in the world. If we later drifted back towards the home-place, that was fine. We would have seen the world outside, gained experience, and earned our wings. We would either grow into the clothes with which we departed or we would acquire new ones which fitted us better and equipped us for our new lives.

As I prepared to leave, there was one issue which was on my mind but which I kept to myself. By now, the guitar was very much part of my life. I was in the habit of playing it most evenings. It had started as a routine to practise the instrument, on my father's advice.

"It's far better to practise for ten minutes each day than for two or three hours once a week."

In truth, although my playing had improved greatly, I spent at least as much time mindlessly doodling as practising. I found this helped me to relax and pass the time.

My father was also playing the guitar regularly. On rainy evenings after he came home from work, I heard him playing quietly as I did my homework. I knew that I would greatly miss the guitar when I left home and I was quietly determined to save some money in order to buy one as soon as possible.

"What is Dad doing with the guitar case?"

The old soft, canvas, guitar case had nestled unused and furred with dust on top of the wardrobe since he ceased to play in bands a few years earlier. Now the dust was brushed off and the guitar case was on the bed beside my suitcase. My mother, who was handing me some carefully folded and ironed shirts, paused and answered quietly.

"Daddy wants you to take the guitar with you until you can get one of your own."

Suddenly, I was fighting to hold back tears. Outwardly, at least, I had maintained a quite casual attitude about my imminent departure from home. This was partly due to a stereotypical teenage attempt to "be cool" and also because I was conscious that my mother was sad at my departure and would be even more upset if she saw any display of excessive emotion from me.

"But he'll be lost without it."

"Well, he thinks you'll be more lost without it and, anyway, he doesn't play it as much as he used to. Sure, he has the fiddle. He'll be alright."

Perhaps only a musician who plays habitually will really understand the sacrifice involved in being deprived of the opportunity to play for a prolonged period. My appreciation of the generosity of his gesture has grown as time went on. Two years later, I temporarily moved to England to find work during a bank strike. The stoppage was expected to be short-lived so I left my guitar behind in Dublin. The five months which I spent without a guitar made me determined never to allow the deprivation to be repeated and deepened my appreciation of the sacrifice involved in my farther's gesture.

As I look back now, I'm less certain that all the credit should go to my father. While writing about my parents, I've increasingly recognised my mother's study and subvert strategy. Did she plant the idea in my father's mind or did he decide on his own to pass on the guitar to me? I realise that it doesn't matter. Yet the generosity and thoughtfulness of the gesture has all my mother's hallmarks. My father, of course, had to endure the deprivation. Perhaps the credit should be shared.

The family support kicked in when I finally moved to Dublin. Patricia met me at the train station and brought me to "digs" which she had already vetted and approved. That same evening, Mike arrived from across the city and, as he had promised some months earlier, handed me a glistening, new, wrist-watch so that I would report on time for work in the morning. Mike had kept his word and Patricia had done her duty as elder sister. My parents would have nodded in quiet satisfaction. This was how our family was supposed to function.

Four months later, I had scraped together the money to buy an acoustic guitar and case at a second-hand shop in Dublin. I proudly returned the Hofner Club 50 to my father. He kept it and played it intermittently for the rest of his life. It is now one of my most prized possessions.

CHAPTER FORTY-THREE

Two Girls

Donogh O'Malley, the Minister for Education, introduced free secondary education in Ireland in September 1966. He also inaugurated a free transport system whereby children who lived over three miles from school would be provided with free daily school bus rides. The new arrangement helped to ease the financial burden on families and made secondary education more accessible.

For the students, the school buses had an added attraction; they provided an opportunity to mix with the opposite sex. Boys and girls could enrol in the Tech but the Convent and College were still single sex institutions. I was fifteen and unaccustomed to dealing with girls. Sisters didn't count. They were not real girls; the type who regularly reduced one to a stammering, red-faced, gawky, embarrassment in their presence. The school bus changed everything. Suddenly, we were thrown into close contact with these strange and exotic creatures. A chattering mass of teenage girls piled noisily onto the school bus each day, ignoring, entrancing, and annoying us boys in equal measure.

We had been warned. One of our teacher priests had strong views on the subject of girls. A variation on his cautionary speech was regularly delivered to his awed students.

"Girls are ok until they reach the age of twelve or thirteen. Suddenly, they think that they're grown women. They try to dress and act like grown-ups and they convince themselves that they succeed. But, in reality, they're just a bunch of hysterical, shrieking, teenagers totally devoid of reason or logic. Yet, they can run rings around teenage boys and make their lives a misery. I strongly advise you to keep well away from them during their teenage years. Wait until they're in their early twenties by which time many of them will have evolved into reasonably pleasant human beings".

Yeah! Right!

His warnings fell on deaf ears. My attention had already been grabbed by one girl who stepped on the bus each morning. For a time, our interaction was confined to nods and hesitant smiles. One morning, I mustered the courage and slipped into the vacant seat beside her. She didn't seem to mind and we chatted. Each morning after that, we sat together and we became more comfortable and relaxed in one another's company. During mid-term breaks or school holidays, we arranged to meet for dances or "hops". We were smitten in that unique way that teenagers reserve for their first big crush. We didn't think or talk about it. It just was what it was.

And then, suddenly, many months later, it wasn't.

She sent me a short note telling me that it was over. I was devastated.

I thought that I was successfully hiding my feelings when I went home that evening from Tommy Keane's farm. The others had finished their dinners earlier so that only my mother and Sean were in the kitchen. My mother was on my case.

"What's wrong? You're not eating."

I had planned to say that Mrs Keane had given us a massive dinner that afternoon. But I didn't want to lie...or to tell the truth.

"Ah, nothing. I'm just not hungry."

She was looking carefully at me. Then she sat down beside me, carefully smoothing her apron over her lap.

"Sean. Take that bucket and go to the pump for water."

"Ah, now. That's not fair. It's Colman's job to go to the pump in the evening."

"Off out with you to the pump and do what you're told, like a good boy."

Sean left, muttering with the righteous anger of the oppressed. My mother looked at me carefully and spoke quietly.

"Are you having trouble with that girleen."

At least it was out.

"She broke it off with me. I don't know what's behind it."

She nodded sympathetically.

"How? A note?"

"Yeah."

"And what are you going to do now?"

"Nothing, I suppose... I don't know."

I had thought about writing a note in reply but was undecided because of a combination of pride and the absence of a clear idea of what I wanted to say.

"Take your time and think long and hard before you decide what to do. God knows why she did it but it might be for the best. That girleen is just starting on her most important year in school. You'll probably be away in Dublin or somewhere else and the last thing she needs is the distraction of a long distance boyfriend when she should be studying for her Leaving. Maybe the best thing you can do for her is to leave her alone until she finishes school. I'm sure her father and mother would feel the same way."

I grudgingly conceded that my mother was probably right. Although I had composed endless notes in my mind, none of them sounded right and they were unwritten. Slowly, I came to realise that I should wait. If it was meant to happen, it would happen…

It was late 1970, about two years later. In Dublin, I had been going out with a girl for over a year when she invited me to spend the weekend with her family in the southwest of Ireland. I was pleased to be invited and we travelled south by train. Her family were welcoming and I warmed immediately to her parents, brothers and sisters. She and I went dancing and I was introduced to her friends. It was a most enjoyable time.

When next I went home to Murneen to see my family, my mother engineered a quiet moment alone with me. She got straight to the point.

"Are you serious about that girl?"

"Serious? Well… we get on very well… but, don't worry, I'll give you plenty of notice if I'm thinking of bringing her here for a weekend."

She looked at me sternly.

"That's not what I'm saying. It seems that she's serious about you if she brought you down to meet her family?"

"Well…maybe she is… But it's not as if we're engaged or anything. It's far from that. She just invited me for a weekend and it would have been bad-mannered to refuse to go."

I was on the defensive. My mother had hit a raw nerve. I was conscious that, in the relationship, I was in favour of "taking it slow" while my girlfriend was more committed. I tried to convince myself that this was because she was two years older than me.

"It's not a big deal. There's no hurry. She knows where we stand.

We'll see how things work out."

"You need to make sure that you're not leading that girl up the garden path."

"She knows that we..."

"And another thing. You should be thinking about what her mother and father and her friends will be saying. When a girl from the country brings a boy home for the weekend, she is showing her friends and family that she is serious about him and has expectations. If he agrees to go, everybody will think that he feels the same way about her. If you're not serious about her, you shouldn't go. You have a responsibility to think about the impression it gives to others and to protect the girl, even if she doesn't see things that way."

"I understand what you're saying. But it's not really like that..."

She knew that she had made her point, despite my inadequate and evasive response. She continued in a more kindly tone.

"Mike tells me that she's a lovely girl from a nice family. I'd hate to think that she was caused any upset or embarrassment. It's not fair to let things drag on and to get her hopes up if she's going to be disappointed. You should give it a bit more thought. Now. How about a nice cup of tea...?"

Not long afterwards, after much soul-searching I ended the relationship.

CHAPTER FORTY-FOUR

The Letter

We were sifting through my father's possessions after his death when an envelope was handed to me.

"It's a letter from you to Dad."

I couldn't remember writing to him but, when I read the letter, the memory came flooding back. Unsurprisingly, my mother's influence was a key factor in the correspondence which took place about two years after I left home.

Following the settlement of the bank strike which resulted in a significant increase in salary, staff were obliged to work many months of overtime in order to clear a back-log of work. As a result, I had some spare cash which I wanted to give to my parents. I thought that they might use it to go on holiday to England to visit my aunts and uncles.

When I mentioned my proposal to my mother, she had other ideas. She confided her concern that my father was still thumbing to work and, as people were becoming increasingly wary of hitch-hikers, he was not getting lifts as easily as before. Sometimes, he arrived home soaking wet as a consequence of standing on the roadside as cars and lorries whizzed by. My mother was trying to persuade him to buy a car but, unsurprisingly, he had other priorities. He preferred that they should continue to grow their savings in order to build an extension to the house. Adding a new bedroom would enable him to relocate the kitchen and create a larger and more comfortable living area. I understood my father's thinking. He considered that buying a car was a selfish move; he would be the main beneficiary from the car purchase whereas the whole family would benefit from the proposed house extension.

My mother's strategy of study and subversion had not yet resulted in a change of opinion on my father's part. Now she saw another opportunity.

"If you just hand him the money, he'll put it towards the house extension. He definitely won't spend it on a holiday or anything like that."

"I could talk to him and try to persuade him."

"No. Here's what you'll do. Write him a letter when you're sending the cheque. Tell him that you'd prefer that he spent it on a car. Don't tell him what to do; you know how stubborn he can be. But let him know that you hope that he'll buy a car. I think that might do the trick. He listens to you. I'll do the rest."

Her idea about the letter was a master stroke. Like Patricia and Mike, I was regularly writing home because my parents did not yet possess a telephone. But all letters were sent to my mother who also wrote all replies. This one would be different. It would be addressed directly to my father and the cheque would be made out in his name. My mother knew instinctively that a letter would be far more impactful than merely handing over the cheque while making a suggestion about its usage. He would find it much more difficult to go against my written wishes and the letter would, in a sense, absolve him of any guilt he might feel about not prioritising the house conversion.

My mother's subversion strategy worked. A few weeks later, he was the proud owner of a used car and was taking driving lessons. Soon he was driving to work and ferrying my mother to Mass and to town for her weekly shopping.

My father could have borrowed sufficient funds to buy the car without any help or urging from me but he had a complex relationship with the concept of borrowing.

"If you want a car, wait until you have saved enough to pay for it. Most of the cars cluttering up the roads are owned by the hire purchase companies. If you want something badly enough, you'll save for it."

I poked fun at his oft quoted advice.

"Thank God people don't follow your advice. Otherwise, I'd be out of a job."

"It's different with banks. It's ok for people to borrow for their business or to buy a house. But I draw the line at loans for cars…"

Despite his antipathy to borrowing, he utilised a unique strategy which enabled him to fund the replacement of his car. He visited the local credit union and obtained a personal loan of a few thousand pounds to be repaid over two years. He immediately walked from the credit union to the post office and used all the money which he had just borrowed in order to buy a savings bond. Each week, he visited the credit union in order to make his payments until the loan was fully repaid. Then he got another loan and bought an additional savings bond. Eventually, when he needed funds to change the car or to pay for some house improvements, he encashed sufficient savings bonds to finance the outlay.

I explained to him that his strategy made no financial sense. The amount of interest he was earning on his savings bonds was less than the loan interest which he was being charged by the credit union. It made more sense to make weekly payments into a savings account and thereby avoid paying any interest on borrowings. He disagreed and explained.

"That's not the point. It's all about human nature. I know that, in theory, I could just save my money every week so that I'd have enough to pay for whatever I wanted. But life doesn't work like that. There would always be some pressing use for the money and there's no way that I would save regularly every week. But when I owe the money, I know that I'll make my repayments without fail. I couldn't face the people in the credit union if I missed a payment."

Just over a year later, work began on the house extension. The catalyst for the beginning of the project was the belated arrival of a water supply in Murneen so that the house renovations could now incorporate a bathroom as well as the planned extra bedroom. Until the early seventies, the people of Murneen had drawn water from the well or the pump. A few locals, including my father, organised a Group Water Scheme. This system was designed to bring running water to rural areas which were not served by a public water supply. Grant aid was provided by the local authority but such schemes were privately owned, operated, and maintained. All prospective participants had to make an initial contribution and regular ongoing payments. Some households opted out but most joined the scheme.

Planning permission was obtained and a bricklayer and plasterer were contracted to erect the extension to the house. My brother Mike offered his expertise with plumbing and electricity while the woodwork was delegated to my grandfather who manufactured and installed windows, shelving, and doors. An added bonus was that our house was finally going to have a back door.

Trouble arose while my grandfather, assisted by Mike, was doing the carpentry work. My father, who had been working in the garden, came in and pointed out that a door frame was not straight. My grandfather was furious.

"Are you telling me how to do carpentry after I've been at it for fifty years?"

He angrily packed up his tools, grabbed his bicycle, and headed for home. My father, who always had a great relationship with my grandfather, immediately regretted the incident. He brought Mike out to the garden so that he could look in through the back door at the frame of the internal door. Mike agreed that there was a problem. The brickwork over the internal door was not level. My father got on his bike, followed, and overtook my grandfather. He apologised for his remark and tactfully explained that Mike was in agreement with him that there was a problem with the brickwork. My grandfather had huge respect for Mike and valued his judgement.

"If Michael says that the top of the doorframe isn't straight, he must be right. Get the bricklayer back to fix it. Then I'll finish the carpentry work."

The bond between my grandfather and Mike was a strong one. Apart from their shared enthusiasm for carpentry, they regularly went fishing together. Mike sometimes received unusual titbits of advice.

"You don't smoke, Michael. Do you?"

"No. I don't. Why do you ask?"

"A good carpenter should be a smoker."

"Why? I thought that smoking would be dangerous with so much timber around."

"A carpenter who smokes will stop work now and again for a cigarette. He'll take the opportunity to stand back and look at the work that he's after doing and, if he made a mistake, he'll spot it and rectify it. The non smoker won't spot his mistakes until it's too late and then it's a major job to put things right."

As I mentioned earlier, Granda Rushe's childhood and his presence for a time in the children's section of the Workhouse was an issue "not talked about". There were vague murmurings about a house fire as a possible reason for the breakup of his family. In the late 1970s, however, in response to questions about our family history by my brother Sean, our grandfather broke his silence and revealed much more detail about his childhood. My father had already been aware of some, but not all, of his father's traumatic childhood. I was later able to corroborate much of the detail from public records and from an interview which I carried out with John Rush, my grandfather's younger brother, who shared the same experiences.

The Rushes were a sea-fishing family who lived in Claddagh, an ancient fishing village on the outskirts of Galway City. The parents developed drinking problems with the result that, in about 1904, the four younger Rushe children were taken into care. They were installed in the children's wing of the workhouse in Galway, under the control of the Poor Law Union. By this time, the older Rushe children had already left home to find work or had married. One married sister lived nearby and she took Margaret, the youngest sister, from the Workhouse and brought her up with her own family.

The young brothers did not fare so well. In accordance with the normal practise of the Poor Law Union, Michael, John, and Patrick were told that they were to be removed from the Workhouse and placed with a farm family who would look after them. My grandfather described how he and his two brothers were sent on the train from Galway to Tuam where they would meet their new foster family. When they alighted from the train, however, they discovered that three separate families were waiting to meet them. They had presumed that they would live together with one family.

My eighty year old grandfather tearfully described the scene at Tuam railway station which took place when he was aged five or six. In their desperation not to be parted, the three brothers clung to one another so that they had to be forcibly prised apart in order that they could be claimed by their host families. Patrick, the eldest, was lucky to be placed with an elderly childless couple who treated him well. John, the youngest, was allocated to a family in which there already were three children. He was treated badly, was not allowed to eat or sleep near the family, and ran away twice before being recaptured. My grandfather, the middle child, was unwilling to be specific about the treatment which he received from his host family, apart from revealing that he was very unhappy and was glad when he was eventually separated from them and installed in nearby Glenamaddy Workhouse. While he was an inmate of the workhouse, he had to attend a local school and he recalled being bullied by some local children who assumed that he was illegitimate.

During this period, he received one visit from his mother; his father had died in 1909. On a summer afternoon, mother and son sat and talked on the grassy bank adjacent to the workhouse in Glenamaddy. He never heard from her again. She died at Galway Workhouse, where she had been working as an attendant, in 1915.

Finally, my grandfather's luck and his life changed irrevocably when he was placed with Maurice and Sarah Mitchell, a childless couple who cared for him, arranged an apprenticeship as a carpenter, and later erected a workshop for him beside their home. For some unexplained reason, Sarah Mitchell gave his name as "Tom" Rushe when he attended the local school at Leitra and he was to be known by that name for the rest of his life. He was living with the Mitchells when he met Mary Reynolds, my grandmother.

CHAPTER FORTY-FIVE

Moonlight In Mayo

"I was thinking that we might go home for the weekend."

"Home? Is this not your home?"

"You know what I mean. Down home to Mayo. We'll go down home for the weekend..."

My wife teasingly points out to me that, when I mention home, I am invariably referring to Murneen and not to where we were living as a family. Weekends spent in Murneen were eagerly anticipated by my wife and, later, by our two children. By the time Kay, my youngest sister, left home to embark on a nursing career, there were already a steady stream of grandchildren heading regularly towards Murneen to visit their grandparents. Before arranging such a visit, it was necessary to check whether anybody else had booked in. In the earlier years, it was sufficient to write a note and to await a reply. As time went on, we prevailed upon my parents to have a telephone installed and this greatly simplified the process.

The first port of call on the visit home was Granny and Granda Rushe's house in Claremorris. Since early childhood, we had been conditioned to unfailingly pay a visit to Granny's on our way to and from Murneen. In truth, it was always a welcome diversion. When we were younger, there was the certainty of tea and biscuits, cakes or bread and jam. In our teenage years, Granny commenced a practice of handing out a small but most welcome amount of pocket money. She was quite conspiratorial in the manner in which she carried out this activity.

"This is just between us. There's no need to mention it to your grandfather."

"Grand. Thanks, Granny."

"If I'm away from the house, it'll be left for you on the mantelpiece behind the statue of the Blessed Virgin. You can take it when your grandfather isn't looking."

I felt slightly guilty about keeping a secret from my grandfather but this didn't deter me from taking the money. One one occasion, I called on my way home from school. Granny was out. While Granda was in the back kitchen making the obligatory pot of tea, I retrieved the booty from behind the statue and slipped it into my pocket.

After we finished our tea and I was about to leave, my grandfather hesitated.

"Ah. Tell me this and tell me no more. Did your grandmother... look after you this week?".

He rubbed his thumb and forefinger together.

"Oh. She did. Thanks."

"Good man. Say no more. I never mentioned it. Alright?"

"That's grand. Not a word."

Now, a decade later, we instinctively made Granny's our first and last port of call on our weekends down home. While we sat in my grandparents' kitchen, having our customary cup of tea, their delight at holding and cherishing their great grandchildren was a joy to watch.

On one such visit, my grandmother warmly greeted my wife.

"Oh Bridget. You look great! You got fat!"

My mother later laughingly reassured Bridget, who had not put on any weight, that she had been the recipient of a compliment. My grandmother was from a generation which regarded weight loss as a possible sign of some wasting disease. Putting on weight was an indicator of rude good health. One of the greatest compliments which my grandmother could give was to suggest that you had added a few pounds.

After we arrived in Murneen, there was another welcoming cup of tea before commencing the task of unpacking bags and assembling a cot which had been carried on the roof-rack of our family car. In the meantime, children were being fussed over by doting grandparents. The groundwork was laid for an attachment which would eventually result in a most warm, intimate, and affectionate bond between the generations.

"Did you bring the music?"

My father watched anxiously as bags and toys emerged from the car boot. My wife reassured him, shaking her head in mock exasperation, as the guitar case was finally retrieved.

"Don't you worry. He'd forget the child's cot if I wasn't keeping an eye of him but the guitar will always be the first thing in the car."

Soon, my father and I were in the back bedroom playing music. He had gradually reverted to playing the fiddle again after years as a guitarist. It took a while for him to, in the parlance of musicians, "get his chops back" but soon he was playing with the freedom and abandon of his youth. In order to loosen up, he ripped through an Irish air, usually one of Sean Maguire's tunes, before swinging into "Battle of New Orleans", "Jambalaya" and "Darktown Strutters Ball". Then on to the more measured, melodic, tunes such as "Autumn Leaves", "Carolina Moon" or "Somewhere Over The Rainbow".

He might pull a slip of paper out of his pocket, from his fiddle case, or from the mantelpiece. This could contain the name of a recently discovered singer or musician or it might list the title of a tune which he thought would sound well when played on fiddle and guitar. After playing and talking for a while, we returned to the living room for another cup of tea. An additional music session was sure to take place over the course of the weekend.

Another ritual was a walk around the garden with my father in order to view his latest improvements. In our earlier years, my mother had taken charge of the front garden, planting flowers and ensuring that the grass was cut. As my parents got older, my mother had less energy for this work and my father had much more time on his hands, especially after his retirement. He devoted his spare hours to the garden, extending the lawn area, planting shrubs and flowers, and shaping and trimming hedges. He achieved wonderful results and eventually had the type of garden which passersby paused to admire.

When I delve into my cerebral filing cabinet to retrieve memories of these visits to Murneen, I am assailed by vignettes of bright, summer days. Playing football or cricket with our two children in the garden while my mother and Bridget sit in the sunshine, watching, chatting, and usually knitting. My father reading his Sunday newspaper or, more likely, wandering around the garden, dead-heading the roses, and removing some weeds from the base of a recently planted shrub.

Thoughts of Sunday dinner brings other memories. My mother casually demonstrating her full array of cooking skills. Delicious soup which she described semi-apologetically as "just something to keep you going until the dinner is ready". Then the main event. A plate laden with food for the body and soul. Seasonal vegetables from the back garden. Flowery boiled potatoes and a few roast potatoes for good measure. Perhaps two varieties of meat. Roast chicken. Roast beef.

And then, dessert.

"Colman? Would you like custard or cream with your hot apple tart? Or will you have both as always?"

"Both, please."

"You have no shame."

Of course, many of the trips west were on wet, miserable days or in winter when my mother's fear of frost on the road resulted in her urging us to start our return journey early on Sunday afternoon. As we loaded the car, she might hand me a package contained one of her apple tarts or perhaps a cooked ham shank. She and my father hugged the children and, when goodbyes were said, she stood alone on the roadside, waving her hand until she slid from our view as the car crested Day's hill. A reassuring phone call confirming our safe arrival about three hours later set her mind at ease.

After our marriage, most of our Christmas holidays were spent with my wife's family in England. But sometimes, in our earlier years, we spent Christmas in Murneen. On one such occasion, after nightfall on Christmas Day, my father proposed that he and I go for a walk. My mother wasn't impressed.

"It's freezing cold and it's dark. You're mad to be going out at this time."

"Ah sure we just want some fresh air and to stretch our legs after that dinner. Colman wants to go, don't you, Colman?"

Overcoated and gloved, we stepped out onto the road and turned right. The initial shock of the biting cold soon dissipated as we picked up pace and strode west along the road. It was a gloriously bright clear moonlit night. Under a sparkling canopy of frost-polished stars, we could just about make out the distant streetlights of Ballinrobe and the glow in the sky over Claremorris. Twinkling lights from farmhouses dotted the Mayo plain. There were no car headlights to be seen. The only sound was the occasional, sudden, dog-bark nearby which was gradually followed by delayed, plaintive and ever fainter responses from other dogs many miles away. One could imagine the sound of the dogs spreading ripple-like across the county until it broke weakly on the shores of the Atlantic Ocean, forty miles away.

We walked in silence until, gradually, my father began to talk. He asked me about my job and the conversation widened to the work and lives of my brothers and sisters. He slowed and stopped.

"I think this is far enough. Maybe we should head back."

We stood and took in the star-bright scene. Just as we turned to retrace our steps, he paused.

"There's something I wanted to say. Mammy and I are delighted with the way ye have all turned out. We're very proud of the lot of ye."

It was a remarkable statement from a man who rarely if ever touched on the personal in his talks with his children. I had often talked at length with him about music, politics, and current affairs. He regularly spoke to me with obvious admiration and pride about the achievements and activities of my brothers and sisters. But occasional enquiries about whether I enjoyed my work were as close as he got to an intimate, personal talk with me. I was unsure how to respond to him.

"We know that but it's nice to hear it. But you and Mam deserve the credit for the way we turned out."

He shrugged his shoulders. He was unconvinced.

"We just did what we thought was the right thing at any time. We can't take too much credit for that."

"Well. If any of us was in jail, people would say that the parents were at least partly to blame. So you may as well take the credit while you can."

He laughed.

"I suppose that's one way of looking at it," he said as we turned towards home.

CHAPTER FORTY-SIX

Old Friends

My mother's parents were the first of my grandparents to die. Cappamore Granny died in 1958 when I was seven. My only memories of her death were my mother's grief when hearing the news and the unexpected, hastily arranged, night drive south to Cappamore. Mrs Gavin, a neighbour, had received a telegram informing her about the sudden death and asking her to break the news as gently as possible to my mother.

After his wife's death, my grandfather lived on in the Cappamore house with his unmarried son, Mike Joe, and his youngest daughter Philomena. While I was sitting my Leaving Certificate examinations during two hot and humid weeks in 1968, my mother received a letter from him. He had thoughtfully enclosed a ten shilling note to enable me to buy bottles of orange or lemonade which I could carry into the examination hall to quench my thirst. The news of his sudden death reached us a few weeks later, before my examination results were published.

The circumstances of the deaths of my Rushe grandparents are more clear in my mind. This is because they resided nearby so that we had regular contact with them, and they lived on until the 1980s.

Granny Rushe was the first to go. She had been deteriorating slowly for a few years. There were no significant illnesses or medical problems but she seemed to be getting physically smaller and her movements were more laboured. She retained her mental faculties but, to her vast amusement, she could suddenly remember and recite poems in English and Irish which she had learned as a child at school and from her mother.

"I don't know if I'll see another year. I think this winter will take me."

Half seriously, half joking, she confided her fears to me. She was of the view that people of her age usually died during the winter months. In the spring, her mood would brighten.

"You're going to have to put up with me for another while."

As 1982 drew to a close, she seemed to be less pessimistic than in a few previous years.

"Please God, I'll see another Christmas," she said confidently.

Before dawn on January 4, she got out of the bed she shared with Granda, stood at the window, moved the curtains aside, and looked out at the night sky. Having closed the curtains, she climbed back into bed and, without fuss or any apparent discomfort, her breathing stopped.

My grandfather knew immediately that she was dead. He thought about going next door to raise the alarm; the Warner family had often reassured him that he should not hesitate to call on them, day or night, if there was a problem. But he saw no point in disturbing the Warners during the night. He quietly lay beside Granny, his companion for close to sixty years, and waited until dawn. When he heard movement which confirmed that the Warners were up and about, he went next door and soon was on the phone to my father.

"I knew that she was gone. There was no point in disturbing everyone until morning", he later explained.

Following my grandmother's death, my parents intensified their efforts to care for my grandfather while enabling him to preserve his independence. My father dropped by each morning on his way to work in order to light the fire for my grandfather and to deliver the daily newspaper. As always, he also dropped in on Granda on his way home from work to have a chat and a cup of tea. My grandfather continued to shop and cook for himself but my mother insisted that he come to Murneen each Sunday for dinner. My father collected him by car after Sunday Mass and, later in the evening, dropped him back home.

My sisters, Kay and Patricia, volunteered to clean his house thoroughly on a regular basis. His house in Claremorris continued to be the first port of call for his grandchildren and great grandchildren when they visited Murneen. My father and mother also brought him to visit his grandchildren in their homes. During one such visit to our house on the east coast, my wife took a photograph of me, our son Stephen, my father, and my grandfather. This photograph of four generations of our family is a treasured heirloom.

In October 1986, my grandfather decided to travel to England to visit his youngest daughter, Chris, who had been widowed a year previously. While staying with Chris in Coventry, he became ill and was admitted to hospital. My father decided to visit him and I offered to accompany him on the journey to England.

We stayed with Chris in Coventry and visited my grandfather in the hospital. My first impression was that he looked more frail than when last I'd seen him. He was delighted to see us and remained in good spirits during our visit. Chris revealed that she was planning to travel back to Ireland with him when he had recuperated and would remain with him indefinitely. To my grandfather's mock horror, she pointed out that she would have to take her boisterous dog with her.

"Dad. Would you like me to come back to Claremorris with you?"

"That would be grand, Chris... but I might have to shoot the bloody dog!"

As we left the hospital ward having said our goodbyes, I turned to wave. He slowly waved back and I was again struck by his frail appearance. Despite the optimism about his recovery and eventual return home to Ireland, I had a feeling of certainty that I would not see him alive again. Two weeks later, on November 9, 1986, he passed away.

He was brought home and laid to rest beside my grandmother, his daughter Patsy, and my sister Mary, at Crossboyne cemetery near Claremorris. Following the burial, as I stood at the graveside beside my father, a friend stepped forward to offer his condolences. He shook my father's hand.

"Coleman. You can take great comfort from the fact that you did everything possible to look after your mother and father while they were alive. You can't have any regrets."

My father nodded in gratitude.

"Thanks. But I always look at it this way. If your children see you looking after your parents in their old age, there's a fair chance that they might look after you when your own turn comes."

CHAPTER FORTY-SEVEN

Two Of Us

When I eventually brought a young woman down home for the weekend to meet my family, she and I had already decided that we were going to marry. My main concern was whether Bridget and my mother would "hit it off". I was confident that my mother would welcome the visitor and try to make her as comfortable as possible. Similarly, Bridget's tact, generosity, and good nature would ensure that she would be an accommodating, friendly, and flexible guest.

But it wasn't as simple as that.

Bridget, a fully qualified teacher, was an Englishwoman from a professional family who was raised in a leafy city suburb. I was bringing her to a home which still had an outside toilet and lacked running water. While I was confident that Bridget could cope, I knew that my mother would be on edge.

Unlike my father, my mother found it easier to relate to "down to earth" people. She was less comfortable with those whom she referred to as big shots. In the company of such people, my father usually took the lead and chatted away on any subject. My mother's response would be: "I couldn't wait to get away. I didn't know where to put myself." I worried that my mother would be intimidated by Bridget and might not relax in her company. Bridget was understandably apprehensive, knowing how closely knit we Rushes were as a family.

Whatever tension was in the air was dissipated by Mike who was home for the weekend and who teased Bridget unmercifully. She was immediately defended from Mike's playful jibes by everybody else...except me, as she later pointed out. Her ability to take a ribbing and to dish it out endeared her to all as did her willingness to adapt to the lifestyle of the family.

What pleased me most was the rapport which was instantly established between Bridget and my mother. They developed a mutual admiration, affection, and respect which was unwavering in the years which followed. Who knows or understands why some people form such a close bond? The two women shared many characteristics. Both were kind, considerate, and empathetic but disliked displays of pomposity, elitism, or ostentation. Under pressure, each possessed a strength of character and a quiet determination to do the right thing even if this was unpopular.

When we started our own family, my mother loved the way that Bridget managed our children.

"Bridget is a real mother".

When I overheard her saying this to Mrs Glynn, I knew that there was no greater compliment.

Bridget greatly admired my mother's cooking and, during one visit, asked whether she could watch and write down some recipes as my mother prepared dinner. My mother agreed and, armed with pen and notebook, Bridget joined her in the kitchen. The project was a failure, to the disappointment but amusement of both women. The main problem was that my mother never measured her ingredients. She relied upon a combination of instinct and experience when cooking. A perplexed Bridget was encouraged to add "a pinch", a "biteen", or even a "small biteen" of some ingredient. My mother's gravy and soups, which Bridget particularly admired and which I loved, seemed to be conjured up in a most haphazard manner. She revealed that, when making soup, she used whatever suitable flavouring she could find in the cupboard. She might be making vegetable soup but could randomly add part of the contents of a packet of chicken soup.

"How much?"

"Not too much. Just a biteen. Sure you can always taste it and add some more if it needs it, can't you?".

"How hot does the roasting tin need to be when you're making the gravy?"

"Hot enough… but not too hot. You don't want to burn it."

Their attempt at collaboration was not a complete write-off. Bridget could make a great apple tart. Not as good as my mother's, as she would ruefully point out, but still delicious.

My mother was careful to avoid interfering in the bringing up of her grandchildren. She willingly offer an opinion or advice if it was sought but otherwise kept her counsel. She generally did not become involved in the relationship between Bridget and me but sometimes, deliberately or otherwise, she made an impact.

In one of our earlier visits, we were watching some late-night television show with my father when my mother announced that she was going to bed. She paused at the door as she was leaving.

"I'm off to bed but Colman, if you feel like a cup of tea before you go to bed, Bridget will make it for you."

"I will not! He's big and ugly enough to get off his backside and make it for himself."

My mother joined in my father's loud burst of laughter as she retreated.

Another of her interventions was more effective. We were down home in Murneen in early December. Bridget mentioned that she preferred to put up the Christmas tree and decorations a few days before Christmas. I advocated that I would wait until Christmas night after the children had gone to bed so they could experience the magical feeling of my youth when we rose on Christmas morning to see the tree and decorations for the first time.

Later, out of earshot of the others, my mother took me to one side and spoke quietly.

"When you get home, decorate the house for Christmas the way Bridget wants it and don't be waiting for the last minute. I know that we had our own way of doing it when you were small but Bridget's family did it differently. That girl is a long way from home and I'm sure she feels the distance between herself and her family at Christmas. She deserves to have the kind of Christmas that reminds her of home."

Need I say that I put up the tree and decorations as soon as we got home?

My mother and father sometimes travelled across the country to visit us during the 80s. We lived a few miles from the border with Northern Ireland and on one occasion, my mother proposed that she and Bridget would travel across the border to Newry to do some shopping. Depending on the euro/sterling exchange rate, prices could sometimes be more favourable in Northern Ireland. Another factor was the opportunity to buy some items which might not be readily available south of the border.

While some people in our area travelled regularly to Northern Ireland, others avoided crossing the border because of concerns about bomb threats, car hijackings, and shootings which were occasional symptoms of the political unrest.

Bridget, a relatively unexperienced driver at that time, drove both of them north. Just south of the border crossing, before they entered Northern Ireland, they were stopped by the Gardai and by Irish Army personnel. It was explained to them that the road ahead was closed and would remain so for some time because of a bomb threat. As Bridget was turning the car to head home, they were approached by the driver of another car.

"If you're going to Newry, I know how to get there by using the back roads. You're welcome to follow me if you like."

Apart from the official border crossings on the main roads, there is a complex network of narrow secondary roads which cross the border. During the "troubles", these unapproved roads, as they were officially designated, were sometimes used by local people but travellers ran the risk of encountering IRA roadblocks and of having vehicles hijacked.

The two women looked at one another.

"I'm happy to go if you are, Bridget."

"Oh. What the heck!"

They took off behind the lead driver and, with Thelma and Louise-like abandon, were soon hurtling through a confusing succession of grassy laneways and narrow roads, trying desperately not to lose sight of the car in front. They were relieved when they eventually recognised the outskirts of Newry and they were soon patrolling the shop aisles. Their hopes that the main road would be reopened for their return journey were dashed. Undeterred, they drove out of Newry on the same road which they had used earlier. They soon spotted and followed a number of cars with Republic of Ireland registration plates. Their trust was rewarded when the cars led them safely back across the border. They arrived home flushed with excitement, like two teenagers who had escaped from parental control for a few hours.

The two women shared a passion for knitting and this provided the opportunity for a most revealing photograph. They are sitting side-by-side on collapsible chairs in front of the Murneen house on a bright summer day. Both are knitting; balls of wool on their laps. Bridget has a mischievous smile, as if she has just made some conspiratorial comment, possibly about the photographer. My mother's face is creased with laughter. It is a joyful image. Despite the age difference, they seem more like sisters than mother and daughter-in-law.

CHAPTER FORTY-EIGHT

Into The Mystic

"When I was last back in Ireland, I was surprised at how much our tastes in music have changed. Your dad had much more modern tastes. He liked the new stuff far better than I did."

New York based Paddy Clarke, my father's childhood friend and band-mate, was expressing his admiration and envy at my father's capacity to keep abreast of and appreciate new trends in music. Paddy admitted that his own appetite for new music was stunted by the rise of the bebop movement in jazz in the 1940s and killed off in the 1950s by the advent of rock and roll. Paddy still loved music but listened mainly to the early jazz performers and to the big swing bands. My father retained an enthusiasm for new music and, even in his 80s, could get excited about some new artist or performance.

He had a passion for good singers. His early love of Louis Armstrong, Bing Crosby, and Frank Sinatra evolved in the 1960s into an appreciation of Ray Charles, Tom Jones, and Irish singers such as Dickie Rock and Pat McGeegan.

He was initially wary of the Beatles. He admired the songs but suspected that the musicianship on their records was attributable to session players. His breakthrough came in 1967 when he saw the "Our World" TV broadcast which demonstrated the extent of the Beatles involvement in arranging and recording as well as playing their music.

He saw an early performance by Colm Wilkinson on TV and earmarked him as a great singer long before Wilkinson went on to achieve worldwide fame when he originated the on-stage role of Jean Valjean in Les Miserables. Other favourites included such song stylists as Anne Murray, Eddi Reader, George Jones, Willie Nelson and Tommy Fleming.

My father scanned a slip of paper which he had pulled from his fiddle case.

"Did you hear this new fellow, Al Green?"

It was in the 1990s and he had just seen Al Green on a television show. I explained that the singer had been hugely popular in the early 1970s, had taken a sabbatical from music for about a decade, and was now recording again.

"How did I not know about him?"

His voice betrayed a sense of wonder and possibly a hint of annoyance that I had not previously brought such a great singer to his notice. As a result of the encounter, I trawled through my record collection in order to see if I could find any other gems which he might have missed and I put some likely candidates on cassette tapes for him. One such discovery was Merle Haggard, who became a firm favourite of my father. I also included some instrumental music in my selection albeit with mixed results. He did not share my passion for Miles Davis but he loved Clifford Brown. A compilation of tracks featuring fiddler Johnny Gimble also became very popular with him. Other fiddle players whom he admired included such disparate stylists as Stéphane Grappelli, Sean Maguire, Frankie Gavin, and Yehudi Menuhin.

The bebop jazz guitar virtuosity of Irishman Louis Stewart appealed to him but he was equally passionate about the more populist guitar playing of Bert Weedon, Duane Eddy, and the Shadows. He admired rather than loved the playing of Jimi Hendrix but I had no trouble convincing him of of the merits of Peter Green.

"I knew you would", he said when I told him that I had already heard and admired Norah Jones. He urged me to check out Stacey Kent's sublime version of the old Fred Astaire song "Let Yourself Go".

He was mesmerised and charmed by the sweet soulful voice of Aaron Neville when he heard his duet with Linda Ronstadt, whom he also admired. As a result, I had to compile a tape of Neville's work as a solo performer and as a member of the Neville Brothers. He played it constantly. When I explained that the Nevilles came from New Orleans, he nodded. That explained it, as far as he was concerned.

He had admiration for the technical prowess of singers and instrumentalists but was equally enthused by performers. When I asked him who his favourite singer was, his answer was considered and thoughtful.

"I would have to say that Sinatra is the best singer I've heard although it's a close run thing between himself and Bing Crosby. I know that it's fashionable nowadays to like Sinatra but I think that Crosby doesn't get the credit he deserves. But it's not just about singing. It should be about entertaining, too. Not all great singers are good performers. The best man I ever saw to work a room was Josef Locke."

In the light of his high musical standards, it was particularly gratifying that he rated my own musical ability.

"Colman is a far better guitar player than I ever was."

He said this at his retirement party when somebody suggested that he accompany his own singing on guitar. In fact, he preferred to have me provide musical backing for him if he was singing in public. Before he sang with the band at the wedding of one of his grandsons, he politely asked the guitarist to relinquish his place and his instrument so that I could play as he sang. He tore through a medley of "Your Cheating Heart", "Take These Chains", "Singing The Blues", and "Bill Bailey", bringing listeners to their feet and on to the dance floor, applauding, and calling for an encore.

He tentatively suggested on a few occasions that I should consider embarking upon a career as a professional musician. I reassured him that I had a career which I was enjoying and did not relish the uncertainty which a musical career would entail. I had some experience as a full-time musician which reinforced my view. I was off work during the summer of 1976 because of a bank strike but I was playing music six nights a week and comfortably supporting our family. However, I quickly became bored as a result of playing the same things every night. I knew that my father would have preferred if I had followed a musical route but I assumed that he would accept my explanation. I was wrong, and his preoccupation with the matter was to result in some tension between my father and my wife.

It was the late 70s. Bridget and I had been married for a few years and had a son, Stephen. Perhaps my father entertained the hope that I might opt to follow a musical route. When he broached the subject with Bridget, he articulated his suspicion that I would prefer to embark on a musical career but that I was constrained by the financial responsibilities associated with an early marriage and a young son. Bridget was hurt by his suggestion that I was pining for a musical career without her knowledge and resented the implication that she or our marriage were thwarting my ambitions. She firmly told him that she was fully supportive of any action which I might decide to take in order to pursue a music career. She added that, as a qualified teacher, she could easily get a job in order to help support our family and she was quite willing to sell our house and to relocate if this would be of benefit to me.

I was appalled when Bridget told me the details of my father's intervention. She repeated her willingness to support me if I wanted to pursue a different path and reassured me that we could manage financially in such circumstances. We agreed hat there was little to be gained by reopening the issue with my father. However, I would continue to regularly reiterate to him my satisfaction with my business career and my lack of ambition to become a professional musician. I suspect that, over time, he reluctantly accepted my decision while privately regretting it. My brother Sean told me about a conversation about me which he had with my father: "He once told me you were good enough as a musician to play with anyone in the world. High praise coming from him."

My father's openness to new music and musicians was matched by his willingness to explore other areas, for example his love of expressionist art. But there soon arose an even more surprising example of a willingness to experiment and innovate. I don't know what motivated him to experiment with Transcendental Meditation. Perhaps his doctor suggested it or maybe it was his own desire to find a way of coping with pressure. As the 1970s progressed, he had developed a tendency to become quite impatient and intolerant if things did not progress to his satisfaction. For example, he became agitated if he was left sitting for too long in the car while my mother did the shopping. She usually met a friend or acquaintance, resulting in a prolonged chat before she hurried back to the car where he sat in a foul mood. If he dropped her off to visit a friend, he expected her to be ready to leave when he returned to pick her up at the appointed time. Otherwise, he might impatiently blow the car horn, to her acute embarrassment.

He read in the newspaper that a TM introductory course was being held in Dublin and he enrolled for the weekend sessions, travelled to Dublin, and stayed over with Patricia. He arrived home, armed with the knowledge and techniques necessary to embark on his new regimen. This seemed to consist of spending some time meditating each evening after he came home from work. He may also have had a similar session each morning. His only concern was that, if the neighbours knew that he was meditating, they would think that he was away with the fairies. My mother overcame the problem by explaining apologetically to any callers:

"Coleman is saying his prayers in the bedroom. He'll be back out for his dinner shortly."

It's possible that some neighbours knew the truth, and they may indeed have been told secretively by my mother. But, as far as he was concerned, his secret was intact.

The results of the meditation routine were remarkable and long lasting. I immediately noticed a calm and a patience about him which had been markedly absent previously. Things which had stressed him in the past were now tolerated with equanimity. In his mid 50s, my father had found within himself a meditative calm and peace.

CHAPTER FORTY-NINE

Celebration

It was my mother's idea. She decided that she should arrange a party for her grandchildren. They were all regular visitors to Murneen and they loved to see their grandparents. But my mother wanted more. Wouldn't it be lovely if grandparents, children, and grandchildren were all in Murneen at the same time and could get together to eat, have some fun, and spend the day together? Also, the cousins would get to know one another.

There were obstacles to be overcome. The party would have to be arranged on a date which would suit as many people as possible.

No problem. Pick a date and we'll be there.

Where would we all stay? There would be almost thirty people if everybody showed up.

Easily managed. We could book into B&Bs or hotels for one night. Or some could travel on the day.

What about food?

We can have a buffet. Each of us can provide something. Patricia and Kay will decide and tell everybody what to bring.

What if it rained? Nearly thirty of us would be packed into the house. The children will be driven mad.

Please God it will be fine. The night before, Mam will leave the headless statue of the Child of Prague outside to keep the rain away.

Does that ever work?

Who knows? Anyway, have faith. We'll manage.

On August 8, 1992, a gloriously sunny Saturday, my parents were joined by their six children with their six spouses, and their 14 grandchildren. Technically, one was not a grandchild. Paul, who was Kay's young stepson, was embraced by my mother and became an honorary Rushe grandchild. Cryptic notes under the heading "Big Day" in my mother's journal convey her feelings about the occasion.

"Great day. Very fine... All here and big meal and fun outside. Loads of photos... Great, great day"

Mike placed his camera on a tripod to take a group photo of all twenty-eight of us. There are also photos of the group of fourteen grandchildren and various images of children playing football, eating, and generally enjoying themselves in the sunlit garden. The party became one of the family's most treasured memories and is still spoken about with warmth whenever we meet.

Another treasured occasion had taken place five years earlier when our parents celebrated their 40th wedding anniversary. Patricia and her husband John had gone to Murneen with the stated intention of bringing my mother and father to Breaffy House Hotel near Castlebar for a celebratory meal. When they entered the dining room to claim their table, it was already occupied by their remaining five children and spouses, as Patricia had arranged. The surprise and delight on my parents' faces are captured in various photographs. My mother's journal is again revealing.

"P. Came. Went to Breaffy. What a night. Big surprise and best night out ever."

My father's 80th birthday was in April 2004, almost seven years after my mother's death. We had a party in Claremorris to celebrate. His grandchildren were in attendance as were many of his friends and neighbours. As a present, I gave him a copy of a book which I had just completed about our family history and which sported a cover which was created and bound by my daughter Kathryn, now a professional bookbinder. I accompanied him on my guitar when he sang "Tennessee Waltz" and he brought the house down.

Now that my father and mother are no longer with us, we have a family celebration each year to honour their memory. Each August, we return to Claremorris, and stay overnight in a local hotel. We have an informal celebratory meal on Saturday night and attend an anniversary Mass for my parents in Barnacarroll church on Sunday morning. The event affords us an opportunity to spend time with one another, to visit family graves, and to reconnect with neighbours and friends. Apart from my siblings and their spouses, attendees can sometimes include nieces, nephews or aunts. There is no pressure to attend; it is accepted and acknowledged that work, family, or social obligations will sometimes result in the non-attendance of some of our siblings and we continue to meet and visit one another regularly on other occasions during the year. But the August event has evolved into a most enjoyable, informal and relaxing family occasion. Exactly as my parents would have wished.

CHAPTER FIFTY

Father And Son

'Did you bring the music?"

The heat of the open fire and the familiar, comforting, clicking of my mother's knitting needles were making me feel drowsy after my three hour car journey.

'You know well that he never comes without it,' she said.

'I'd be afraid to show up otherwise".

My mother smiled.

'Will we go to the room?' said my father. 'Or maybe you're tired after the journey. Sure we can leave it until tomorrow, if you like.'

'No. I'm just getting lazy here. We'll give it a go.'

'I'll have the kettle on when ye're finished,' said my mother.

As we left the warmth of the kitchen, we chatted.

'Did you see that TV programme with Grappelli and Yehudi Menuhin?'

'I watched it. Two great musicians with different styles. They have great respect for one another.'

'They do. Menuhin is technically the better musician but when he tried to play with Grappelli, there was something missing. It's difficult to put your finger on the reason why.'

'He doesn't swing,' I said.

He nodded thoughtfully.

'You hit the nail on the head. Yehudi doesn't swing.'

In truth, I had mixed feelings about 'going to the room'. I loved playing music with my father and we had been doing so on each visit since I left home thirty years earlier. But now he was in his late seventies and he was not playing as cleanly and smoothly as in the past. I didn't say anything and wondered whether he noticed. On one occasion, when he was having trouble adjusting the tension on the bow, I offered to buy a new one and we drove to a shop in Westport to get a replacement. But his playing was still inconsistent. On my previous visit home, I guessed that he hadn't practised for a while because the fiddle was out of tune when he removed it from its case. He became frustrated as he struggled to adjust the tuning pegs which squeaked in protest. After a few uncomfortable tunes, he put aside the fiddle and sang a few songs to my accompaniment.

So it was with some misgivings that I removed my guitar from its case in my parent's bedroom. He was vigorously applying some rosin to the bow as I seated myself on the edge of the bed. Then, tucking the fiddle under his chin, he drew the bow across the strings to check the tuning. This time, there was no need to use the tuning pegs. A minor adjustment to the fine tuners was all that was needed.

At least, he has been practising, I thought to myself.

'Give me a G,' I said.

He looked on impatiently as I checked the tuning on my guitar.

'Play that intro to "Bill Bailey"'.

I chorded the eight bars at a fast tempo and he joined in. Immediately, I recognised that he had been practising. His tone was clear and his fingering was smooth. He played the melody and then paused to allow me to solo. I played my usual combination of chords and single note runs for the thirty-two bars. Then, he cut in and, like a bird taking flight, he began to improvise. His phrases usually lasted for four bars and started in the upper register before gradually working their way down along the finger board. Then the process was repeated as he discovered ever more complex and melodic ways of playing his way down through the scales. His facial expression together with the set of his chin reminded me of the similar look on the face of my grandfather as I used to watch him in his carpentry workshop.

'A carpenter has to hold his face right when he hammers a nail,' my grandfather would say with a twinkle in his eye in response to my childish enquiry.

I added my best percussive vamping accompaniment and he responded to my musical prompting by carrying on for an further thirty-two bars before repeating the melody and finishing with a flourish.

'We'll try "Snowbird"', he said.

Slightly slower tempo now. He played the melody for sixteen bars and then repeated it but this time he bowed two strings at the same time so that a harmony line sounded simultaneously with the melody. It was a long time since I had heard him attempting this double-stopping technique. After allowing me to solo, he came back in and continued with a combination of double-stopping and single string playing.

'"Spanish Eyes". That calypso rhythm,' he said.

No time for small talk now.

As we traded solos and covered our normal repertoire including "Oh, Lady Be Good", "Jambalaya", "Darktown Strutters' Ball" and "The Glory Of Love", it was clear that he had been practising regularly. He stood with his back to the empty fireplace and, with his right foot tapping to the beat, he swayed to the rhythm as his dancing bow seemed to draw ever more inventive melody from the fiddle and release it around the room. As each tune ended and another began, I didn't consider it necessary to say anything. He knew that he was playing well and he knew that I knew. That was enough.

'Do you have anything new?' he asked.

I had been working on "Last Date", an old Floyd Cramer tune. He had overheard me idly experimenting with it when last I was home and had remarked that it had potential. I played the tune and, as I attempted to replicate the style of Cramer's honky-tonk piano, he watched and listened carefully.

'That's a good one,' he said. 'People would stand in the snow to listen to that.'

I smiled to myself. I'm in my 50s, I thought, and my father's praise is still capable of making my day.

He sang and played 'Tennessee Waltz' before we finished. Whatever about the occasional lapses in his fiddle playing in the past, his singing had never deteriorated. Indeed, it had acquired a different timbre as he got older which made the voice even more expressive.

We chatted easily as we replaced our instruments in their cases. I returned to the kitchen.

'I'm ready for that cup of tea. I'll scald the pot,' I said to my mother. My father was in the bathroom.

'How did you get on?'

She often spoke with affection and amusement to others about the music sessions "in the room" but it was unusual for her to ask about our playing. She must have noticed my surprised response to her enquiry because she explained.

'He has been in there practising away for two hours every evening since you rang to say that you were coming.'

She was at the end of a row in her knitting and was closely examining what she had done.

'I can well believe it,' I said. 'He was in great form. I haven't heard him play as well for a long time.'

'Did you tell him?'

She was looking directly at me now.

I shrugged.

'Ah, he knows. Musicians know when they are playing well.'

She wasn't about to be diverted.

'He often encouraged you when you were learning to play. Even if you knew you were doing well, I know it used to put a spring in your step.'

I felt uncomfortable. I knew that she was correct but I found it hard to envisage myself praising my father.

'Fathers are expected to praise and encourage their children,' I said. 'It doesn't seem right the other way round. Anyway, that man would take offence if he thought he was being *plámásed*.'

She wound some wool around a finger and was poised to start knitting another row but she waited.

'He was down on himself after the last time you were here because he thought you were disappointed with the way he played. Daddy is getting old, you know. He didn't find the practising easy and he listens to what you say ... especially when you talk about music. You should tell him if you think he is playing well. He needs encouragement. People change when they get older.'

The following evening, as my mother prepared dinner, my father and I played again. As before, the repertoire consisted of swing tunes together with one or traditional Irish airs which showed traces of the influence of Sean Maguire and a few slower tunes when he sang and played soulful solos. His playing was even better and more carefree than the previous evening. Finally, he put the fiddle down.

'That was grand. It's always better to leave something in the well,' he said. 'We'll leave it at that.'

'You must have been practising a lot. I haven't heard you playing so well in a long time.'

He had his back to me as he put the fiddle in its case.

'It doesn't get any easier as you get older,' he said. 'But practise always helps, I suppose.'

'I was just thinking. The next time I come down, I'll bring my tape recorder. We can record a few tunes while we're on top of our game. I'll give you a bit of notice when I'm coming so that you can be loosened up.'

He was facing me now.

'That's a good idea. It'll keep me practising in the meantime.'

I rose to leave the room but stopped at the door.

'One other thing, while we're talking. Don't be putting yourself under pressure. If you don't have the time or inclination to practise, there's no problem. You have the voice to fall back on and it's getting better with age. I'll still bring the guitar anyway.'

'Do that. But don't forget to bring the tape recorder the next time.'

He followed me into the other bedroom as I put my guitar in its case.

'I enjoy our sessions,' he said. 'But I know that sometimes when you call, I'm struggling a bit and it can't be much fun for you. But I look forward to playing.'

'So do I but you're too hard on yourself. Whether you've practised or not, your playing always swings."

His face brightened.

'Do you think so? Sometimes it's hard to judge. Some evenings I think I'm playing well and at other times, I wonder if I'm fooling myself.'

'There's some fight left in you yet. Grappelli is older than you and he's still recording.'

He laughed.

'As the song goes, "it don't mean a thing if it ain't got that swing".'

'The dinner will be on the table,' I said. 'We'll be in the wars if we let it get cold.'

'That woman doesn't understand the attraction of music,' he said with a smile.

'I suspect that she understands a lot more than we realise,' I said.

CHAPTER FIFTY-ONE

Let It Be

Each year, the bank in which I worked issued to customers a lavish wall calendar, featuring photographs or reproductions of art works. My mother pestered me for a copy which she would hang on the kitchen wall. In addition to the large version, the bank distributed a smaller calendar or planner, suitable for recording appointments and events. My mother would be on my case each Christmas, seeking the smaller version. It was only after her death that I discovered the reason. She was using the planners to keep a journal or diary.

My mothers main writing outlet consisted of letters to family and friends and they were a joy to read. The letters were unplanned and spontaneous. Her style might be described as stream of consciousness; she wrote down whatever came into her mind and she changed topics on a whim, sometimes in mid sentence. The reader might discern a link between one subject and the next, but not usually. The best way to read the letters was to go with the flow, glean as much information as possible, and then read the letter again in the confidence that more would be revealed the second time around.

Another eccentricity was the formatting of her letters. If she was reaching the end of the letter and knew that she was running out of news, she avoided starting on a new page. Instead, she wrote on the margins of the letter, her handwriting becoming smaller as she ran out of space. When reading, it became necessary to turn the letter sideways and follow a sentence up one side of the page, across the top, and down the other side before reaching her conclusion and sign-off. My wife loved these letters. She claimed that she could almost hear my mother's voice as she read the words.

The eccentric writing style is replicated in the journal. As a result of the size and unsuitability of the appointment calendars, my mother is obliged to be terse in her comments and inventive with her use of space. Margins are liberally used when the events of the day cannot be condensed to fit into the allocated area. The written notes consist of brief comments and reflect the patterns and phrases which she utilised in everyday speech but which look unusual when written down. When she writes "wicked bad", "lovely day entirely", or "horrid day", you know that she could be describing either the weather or her mood. "Killed out" signifies that she is tired after a challenging day. "Mayo beaten horrid" indicated that the county football team had suffered yet another humiliating defeat. Abbreviations were liberally used to conserve writing space. "C, B and all" indicated that I had arrived for the weekend with my wife, Bridget, and our two children. "C gone 2.30 rang 6" shows that we left Murneen after dinner on Sunday afternoon and telephoned at 6pm to reassure her that we had arrived home safely.

She commenced her journal in 1985 and continued until 1995; about two years before her death. The entries are a mixture of the banal and the deeply personal and private. It is discomforting to trace from the writings her deteriorating health and her occasional bouts of melancholia. But it is uplifting to read of her joy at the births and achievements of grandchildren and her pleasure at the keenly awaited and regular visits and even phone-calls from her children.

There are occasional unexplained gaps where no entries are recorded for a few days and at times an unease is sensed by the astute reader. For example, one instinctively detects the understandable parental apprehension when Kay announced her relationship with Danny, a widower who was quite a few years her senior and who has four children, the youngest of whom was not yet a teenager. Kay, the youngest of our family and the last to leave home, was now a qualified nurse but was still, in my mother's eyes, the baby of the family. She was working in Donegal, in the far north of Ireland, but I suspect that my parents harboured the unspoken hope that she would eventually move back home, get a nursing job locally, and be available to care for them as they got older. Now, their "baby" was going to settle far away in Donegal and would assume the role as wife to an older man and step-mother to his children.

In March 1987, Kay was coming home to help my mother prepare for the Stations, a local tradition which involved the celebration of Mass in the homes of parishioners. Kay brought Danny with her to meet my parents. The visit was a resounding success. The entries in the journal reflect the change from apprehension to delight. Danny was described as a "very, very nice fellow". The additional "very" was a rarely awarded and precious accolade. When Danny departed three days later, leaving Kay to remain for a further week, my mother wrote a brief note. "D went. All missed him a lot". All apprehensions had evaporated. The relationship with Danny was further enhanced when he and Kay brought Paul, his youngest son, to Murneen. My mother immediately took him "under her wing" and, as far as she was concerned, acquired another grandchild.

A year later, after Kay and Danny's wedding, my parents visited their home in Donegal for the first time. They had a house in Carndonagh and a mobile home parked beside the sea at the Isle of Doagh a few miles away. My mothers notes reveal her impressions. "Lovely home"..."had lovely evening"..."went long walk"..."had lovely day entirely"..."big walk in evening". Kay and Danny were delighted that both my parents, but especially my mother, loved the area. She treasured the long empty beach and walked for miles along the sandy shoreline. She was also instantly at ease among Danny's family and was charmed by the friendly and relaxed attitude of the local people.

Over time, an implicit understanding grew that, when my father died, my mother would move to Donegal to live with Kay and Danny. Later, when they were planning to build a new house beside the sea on the site of their mobile home, they incorporated a ground floor bedroom which would be ideal for my mother when she eventually relocated.

In hindsight, the widely shared presumption that my father would predecease my mother seems naive. As he grew older, my father was constantly worrying about his health, almost to the point of hypochondria. The smallest ache or pain seemed to impact on his confidence and he regularly imagined that he had a serious, possibly terminal, illness. My mother had genuine health problems but yet she seemed indestructible. One felt that when my father contracted some serious health setback, he would succumb to it quite quickly.

There were visits to Donegal at least twice yearly, all of which were written about in glowing terms by my mother. She and my father also made visits to the homes of their other children during this period and my mother's journal shows how much she enjoyed these breaks but her writing seems to come to life when she details her latest trip to Donegal.

Cryptic notes in the journal also reveal the health problems which my mother was experiencing. She had suffered from rheumatism and arthritis in the past but now here seemed to be constant pain in her leg and hip. She was in hospital in Galway for one week in January 1990 but her problems continued. She notes that she was diagnosed with arthritis and a slipped disc in July. During her stay with Kay in Donegal in September, she was unwell. A month later, she was admitted to Merlin Park Hospital in Galway in order to have a hip replacement operation.

The operation took place on October 28. Almost immediately there were complications. She was unwell and in much pain. She was not healing as quickly as expected and there were problems with swelling and skin rashes. The medical staff were perplexed by her post-operative condition and it was decided to revisit her medical details.

"Mrs Rushe. You told us that you had no allergies - no allergic reaction to penicillin or any other medicines?"

"I did indeed, nurse. I never had any problems like that. I'm only allergic to cheap jewellery."

"Pardon?"

"It's just a little family joke. If I wear any nickel plated jewellery, I break out in a rash. I always say that I'm allergic to cheap jewellery."

Her casual attempt to strike a lighter note with the nurse uncovered the underlying reason for her post operative problems. Nickel was one of the components in her artificial hip and was the reason for the negative reaction of her body after the operation.

A nickel-free artificial hip had to be sourced and, in the meantime, my mother was obliged to remain in hospital to recover her strength. Her 65th birthday was celebrated in hospital and her stay was punctuated by regular visits from family, friends, and neighbours. My father, who had retired from CIE a few months earlier, was her most constant visitor and supporter. She had surgery on December 14 and again on December 21. She was finally discharged on January 15, having been in hospital for three months. She was delighted to be home in time to immerse herself in crafting her 1991 supply of Saint Brigid's crosses.

Over the remaining years until her death in 1997, there were a number of visits to hospital including a replacement for her other hip. She did not allow the discomfort and occasional pain to rule her life. She hosted the gathering of children and grandchildren in 1992 and holidayed in England where she and my father attended a family wedding, after which they travelled around that country to visit their siblings and families. There were also regular visits to the homes of sons and daughters around Ireland. Perhaps the reducing frequency of entries in her journal was a sign of her lessening vitality. Her final entry was made on 16 May1995. It read: "At doctor".

On June 24th 1997, my parents celebrated their 50th wedding anniversary and there was another family celebration to mark the occasion. My mother was joyful but, in photographs, looks tired and weak. We had just returned from a trip to England to attend the ordination as a priest of my cousin Michael Ryan, the eldest son on my father's sister Mary Rushe and my mother's brother Johnny Ryan. My mother insisted on making the journey even though travelling was becoming increasingly difficult for her. It is tempting to speculate that she would have lived longer if she had not undertaken the arduous journey. A viewing of a video recording of the event, however, gives pause to such conjecture. Although she uses two walking sticks to support herself and to aid her movements, she looks happy and proud. There is video footage of the extended family celebrating, eating, and drinking in the garden of Johnny and Mary's house. My mother looks relaxed and radiant. Her three sisters and her brother are present as are my father with his two sisters. They are surrounded by nieces and nephews and their children. As I watch the video, it is almost impossible to believe that my mother would be dead within three months.

In September, my wife and I were in Manchester when we received a call that my mother, who was in hospital in Castlebar, was gravely ill. It was a momentous time for me and my wife. Our youngest, Kathryn, was leaving home, having achieved her ambition of being accepted to study art at Manchester University. We had taken the ferry to England in order to transport her things and were getting her settled in her student accommodation when the call came. I immediately drove to Holyhead to catch the next ferry back to Ireland and drove across the country to Castlebar.

I had been warned by my sisters that my mother had lost consciousness and was unresponsive. When I walked into the hospital ward, she was surrounded by my father, brothers, and sisters. Patricia was holding my mother's hand and she leant forward to speak in her ear.

"Now, Mammy. We're all here now. Here's Colman. He just arrived."

My mother suddenly moved her head and made an unintelligible murmuring sound before lapsing into deep sleep again. We took it as a sign that she was now contented that all her family were around her. I was left alone to hold her hand and to talk to her for a while before my sisters inveigled me to accompany them to the hospital cafe for a coffee and sandwich. As we sat chatting quietly at a table, I was suddenly and unexpectedly overcome by a wave of grief. For the first time, it fully dawned on me that I was losing my mother. Patricia turned towards me and saw the tears streaming uncontrollably down my cheeks. I apologetically tried to hide my face but she took my hand.

"Ah! I was wondering when it would hit you. Don't worry. Now it's your turn. We've all been there."

My mother slipped away that night. Fittingly, Patricia and Kay were with her as she died and my father and my brothers were nearby.

As I left the hospital later with my father, I spoke to him about how much she was loved and how much I admired what she had achieved in difficult times. He nodded in agreement.

"She could make a home out of two sticks".

Her death was caused by antibiotic resistant septicaemia. It seems likely that she acquired an infection during one of her many hospital visits.

The church was thronged for her funeral. Her sisters, the nuns, in consultation with the family, selected the items which were placed on the altar to symbolise her life.

Flowers from her garden.

The framed photo taken at the family party which she had organised for her grandchildren.

Her rosary beads and prayer book.

Her apron.

A Saint Brigid's Cross.

During the service, I played some music and my brother Kieran recited the poem "Resurrection" by Vladimir Holan:

Is it true that after this life of ours we shall one day be awakened
By a terrifying clamour of trumpets?
Forgive me God, but I console myself
That the beginning and resurrection of all of us dead
Will simply be announced by the crowing of the cock.

After that we'll remain lying down a while...
The first to get up

Will be Mother…We'll hear her
quietly laying the fire,
Quietly putting the kettle on the stove
And cosily taking the teapot out of the cupboard.
We'll be home once more.

CHAPTER FIFTY-TWO

Don't Get Around Much Anymore

A few years previously, any suggestion that my father could cope while living alone following my mother's death would have been regarded as completely unrealistic. Here was a man who was approaching his seventieth year and whose cooking skills were minimal. He could boil an egg and, at a push, could probably produce a cooked breakfast provided somebody had done the shopping for him and also showed him how to switch on the cooker. For decades, my mother had taken responsibility for all their cooking and housework. My father had no experience or interest in the operation of utilities such as the washing machine and the microwave.

His inexperience in household skills was not his only problem; my father also lacked the social skills which might make sole living more viable. He was polite and courteous towards anybody who visited the house. Nevertheless, he had little meaningful contact with neighbours. He left the social networking to my mother and, unlike her, he never dropped into a neighbour's house for a chat and a cup of tea. He drove my mother to the shops each week but sat in the car reading the newspaper while she shopped and chatted.

He would have been completely ill-equipped for lone living but fate was to change all.

My mother's reduced mobility, which was caused by her hip problems in her later years, resulted in a change in the management of the household and my father entered willingly into the new routine. My mother sat in the living-room by the fire and gave my father instructions and encouragement while she monitored the sounds emanating from the kitchen.

"Turn the heat down now and let it simmer".

"It's time to put in the carrots and the onion".

"And put the pan of potatoes on the other ring now. They'll take about twenty minutes."

As well as learning how to cook, he also became experienced in cleaning the cooker, kitchen, and bathroom. The mysteries of the washing machine and microwave were also unravelled for him.

My mother compiled the shopping list and sent my father to test himself against the previously unexplored mysteries of the supermarket. Because of her knowledge of the locations of items on the shelves, she would compile the shopping list so that, if he followed her instructions, he could work his way down through the list as he pushed his trolley along the aisles. Despite his early apprehension, he was soon an experienced grocery shopper.

His shopping expeditions also had an unexpected but welcome outcome. He had never been comfortable with small talk which he describing as "gossiping" and which he regarded as the preserve of women. He used to joke that, because of her chatting, my mother would take an hour to do the shopping which should be completed in about ten minutes. Now, as he shopped, he was constantly being greeted and questioned, sometimes by women whom he barely recognised...

How is Kitty? Will you tell her that I asked about her? Is she still waiting for a hospital appointment? How are you coping? Are you expecting any of the family for the weekend? Is Patricia still in Dublin? She went to school with my eldest...

Common courtesy dictated that he paused, responded, and chatted. Soon, he was completely at ease as he trawled through the supermarket aisles. On one of my visits home, I accompanied him as he did the shopping and was amazed at the manner in which he interacted with fellow shoppers, made a careful selection at the meat counter, and bantered easily with the women who checked out his groceries. My mother had trained and prepared him for sole living.

As the family sat and talked in the house in the evening following my mother's burial, my father made it clear that he was going to live alone in the house for as long as he possibly could. But there was something on his mind.

"While we're all here together, there's something I want to say. I know the reason you all came here so often was to see Mammy. But now that she's no longer here, I hope that you'll all still continue to visit now and again..."

There was a chorus of reassurances that we didn't just come to see Mammy but to see him as well. We stressed that we would continue to visit as before. He seemed gratified but the look of apprehension remained. He approached the issue from a slightly different angle.

"It'll be a lot harder than you think. Everything here will remind you of Mammy. You'll look up and find yourself expecting her to suddenly appear from around the corner or to walk out of the kitchen. It won't be easy and, without thinking, you might find yourselves wanting to avoid it..."

We reiterated our reassurances but later, as we spoke among ourselves, we wondered whether he might have a point. Murneen would be irrevocably changed for us in the absence of our mother. Despite our intention to make regular visits, it would be easy to defer a trip or to trust that a brother or sister would travel instead.

Patricia and Kay, ever the organisers of their willing brothers, decided that matters should be formalised. We would set up a rota for visits to Murneen so that one of us would visit my father each weekend. Patricia would visit next weekend, Michael the following weekend and the rest of us, in order of seniority, after that. As a result of this arrangement, each of us would see our father once every six weeks while he would have a visitor every weekend. If, for family or other reasons, we were unable to visit on our specified weekend, we would make a phone call and swap weekends with another person on the list.

We also agreed a rota of phone calls. Each of us was allocated a day when we would make our weekly telephone call to chat to my father. I selected Friday as I had developed a habit of phoning my mother before I left work at the end of each week.

A few days later, Patricia posted to each of us a list of our visiting dates. The rota of visits and phone calls worked well and had unexpected benefits. By spending regular weekends with our father, often alone but sometimes accompanied by our spouses or children, we each developed an even stronger bond with him.

His lifestyle changed but he soon adjusted and developed a new routine. As a pensioner living alone, he was entitled to some home help which was provided by the local Health Service. Funding was provided to enable a local person to call to the house on weekdays in order to cook an evening meal and to perform some cleaning duties. As an alternative to cooking for himself, my father sometimes went to a pub in Claremorris for lunch. Each morning, he drove to town to collect daily newspapers for himself and for Mrs Glynn. While dropping off the newspaper next door, he remained for a chat and cup of tea with Mrs Glynn and Brenda, her daughter.

My father was to remain in Murneen for another seven years. This was not just due to the regular contact with his children and the support of the Health Service. Friends and neighbours also provided a supportive environment which challenges the general perception that older people living in the countryside are no longer cared for by their community. The local caregiving was often so unobtrusive that it only became apparent to his children over time and was usually unnoticed by him. Neighbours kept watch for signals. Were curtains opened or closed at unusual times? Why was the outside light not switched off? Was there smoke from the chimney? Who owned the car which was parked outside? When neighbours were concerned about something, they made discreet enquiries or, if necessary, invented an excuse to ring on his doorbell.

If he failed to answer his phone when one of his children called, we had the option of phoning Brenda from next door who might explain that he was outside mowing the lawn and obviously couldn't hear the phone ringing. Or Brenda might get a call from one of the staff in the pub in Claremorris when my father didn't turn up for his usual Tuesday lunch. Brenda might point out that he had a hospital appointment or that he was away for a few days visiting one of his children. He could not have continued to live alone for so long had it not been for the support of the community.

I brought him to Belfast to attend the graduation of our son Stephen. He was proud that the first of the new generation of the family had graduated from university and his pleasure was enhanced when he saw that Queens University had employed a jazz band to entertain the guests as we partook of strawberries and cream in the quadrangle.

In 2002, my wife and I invited him to travel with us to London to attend the university graduation of our daughter, Kathryn. After the ceremony in Westminster Central Hall, the students and their families streamed out into the sunlight to celebrate and take photographs on the green area in front of the building. Suddenly there was a commotion as a motorcade of vehicles swung in towards a building across the street.

"It's Nelson Mandela!".

"Where?"

My father, who was painstakingly organising us to pose for his camera, suddenly lost all interest in our family group and joined the stampede of students, parents and grandparents who were dashing across to get a better view of the great man. Mr Mandela alighted from the main vehicle, turned in response to the spontaneous burst of applause from across the road and waved warmly and smilingly as cameras flashed before entering the building. My father, who had been an admirer of Mandela for many years, was thrilled at the coincidence of events and marvelled at the affection shown to Mandela from people of all ages who were gathered for the graduation ceremony.

In the afternoon following the ceremony, my father had arranged to meet and have lunch with his old friend and bandmate, Bill Gleeson. When I asked him how he wanted to spend the following morning, he immediately suggested that we visit St. Paul's Cathedral which he revealed was his favourite building in London and which he had often frequented while working in the city. During our visit, he struck up a conversation with a guide about the changes, renewals, and renovations which had taken place over the half century since his last visit. Their enthusiasm was a joy to behold as they exchanged information and shared their passion for the magnificent building.

Another welcome development in my father's later years was the growth in his relationships with his grandchildren, most of whom were now teenagers or young adults. My mother had been a great favourite with them and, now that she was gone, my father seemed to assume the role of confidant. They visited him, on their own or with their parents. Soon, grandfather and grandchild were seated together in a quiet corner or in the garden, deeply involved in intense conversations. These encounters, knowingly referred to by amused parents as "the interview", were not confined to the grandchildren. A boyfriend or girlfriend or even a casual caller might be introduced to him and would soon be engrossed in conversation.

"Oh God. I see that poor girl is having the interview!"

I do not know the nature or content of such personal conversations. As we have seen, he did not have deep discussions with his own children when we were growing up. What is indisputable is that these chats made a great impression on many people. The girlfriend of a nephew, who had "the interview" before embarking on a lengthy, international, back-packing expedition, later sent him a postcard from each new location which she visited. A poet whom he met and talked to later wrote a poem dedicated to my father and published it in his next collection.

My father was unaware that one of his grandchildren was gay. The misguided decision not to tell him was influenced by well-intentioned parents who thought it best that he should not be burdened with the information shortly after my mother's death. As time passed, it seemed as if the withholding of the truth was a betrayal of their close and trusting relationship, so the grandchild decided that he should be told. Anxious parents, aunts, and uncles looked out through the kitchen window in Murneen as grandfather and grandchild stood together and talked under the trees at the end of the garden. My father immediately held out his arms, they embraced warmly, and then walked away slowly, arm in arm. The misty eyed watchers in the window were equally proud of both of them. My father offered his love, support, and reassurance. He made it clear that the grandchild, and any partner, were welcome to come and stay with him at any time.

The many photographs taken at my fathers 80th birthday party include quite a few which show that he had lost some of his former sparkle. He seemed frail. He complained regularly about pains and aches and it was not always clear whether his ailments were real or imagined. What was certain was that he had lost some of his mobility. It took him longer to stand or sit and, if he was seated for a prolonged period, he became quite stiff and sore until he had an opportunity to slowly loosen up.

I made a phone call to my father each Friday in accordance with the rota which Patricia had instigated. My brothers and sisters also phoned him so that he received a call almost every day. While my mother was alive, my father sometimes answered the phone but, after a few awkward words, he passed the receiver to her. By necessity, he became much more comfortable on the telephone after her death. He was happy to answer the phone and to chat but seldom if ever made any outgoing calls.

One evening in late August 2005, our phone rang. When Bridget, who answered the call, told me that my father was on the line, I picked up the receiver with some foreboding. He answered my immediate enquiry by assuring me that he was well. He revealed that he had been following the TV coverage of the devastation caused to New Orleans in the wake of Hurricane Katrina and he explained that he had watched in disbelief at what he perceived to be an inexcusably inadequate response by the authorities.

"It's the richest country in the world and there are bodies floating down the street! It wouldn't happen in a third world country. I can't understand it."

He had a great affection for the USA and its people. He admired its films and music as well at its status as a land of opportunity for its own citizens and for immigrants. He had visited the USA to spend time with Paddy Clarke, his school friend and bandmate, and loved the country. He was not uncritical of its failings, particularly in areas such as race relations, but he had a conviction that the American people, despite their differing political viewpoints, had an innate sense of justice and would always eventually do the right thing. Now, his confidence was being undermined. The city which he regarded as a musical beacon for the world was, quite literally, drowning. To compound his sense of loss, he had just heard that Fats Domino was missing and it was feared that he had been lost in the flooding. Who knew that other musicians might be missing or dead?

We talked for a while and I tried to offer reassurance by suggesting that the rescue plans might merely be delayed. He wasn't convinced.

"I know that you have an ambition to visit New Orleans. I hope that there is something there for you to see."

A few evenings later, the news broke that Fats Domino had been rescued and was now safe. I immediately phoned my father to pass on the welcome information. He was delighted but also disheartened at the pace of the response and the negative news coverage.

"Looting? If I was there myself, I'd be breaking into supermarkets to get fresh water and food. Just because you can show a photo of some idiots stealing a TV set doesn't mean you can call everybody else looters."

Almost exactly four years later, I was seated in Café Du Monde in New Orleans, having a coffee and beignets. Earlier, accompanied by my daughter, Kathryn, I had taken a sobering and depressing tour of the areas of the city which were still scarred in the aftermath of the storm. A street-performing trumpeter sat outside the cafe playing jazz standards. Unexpectedly, he played a beautifully haunting version of "Danny Boy". As the plaintive Irish melody mingled with the city sounds of Jackson Square and with the steam horn of a riverboat on the nearby Mississippi, I regretted that my father did not get a chance to see and experience the city which had such an influence on him.

CHAPTER FIFTY-THREE

You Better Move On

My father's relationships with his grandchildren also smoothed the transition to the final stage of his life. My daughter, Kathryn, was coming home from London for a few days and particularly wanted to visit her grandfather. I picked her up at Dublin airport and we drove west into the Mayo night. My father was delighted to see his grandaughter and to hear about her life and work in London. As they chatted, I thought that he had become physically frail but he was in great spirits and, it seemed to me, bubbling with confidence.

The three of us were relaxing after dinner when, seemingly casually, he asked me a question.

"Colman. Do you think that I'm still fit to look after myself while I'm living here on my own?"

I was taken aback by the question. I knew that my sister Kay had told him on many occasions that he would be welcome to stay with her and her family in Donegal whenever he felt that he no longer wanted to live alone. It seemed to me that he was coping well on his own although I realised that eventually, he might have to move. I answered truthfully but in a manner which was intended to boost his self-confidence.

"I think you're doing fine on your own and that you should carry on alone for as long as you can."

"That's what I thought myself."

Even as he nodded in satisfaction, I had an vague feeling that there was some subtext to his query. Later, when I was alone with Kathryn, it became clear that, unlike me, she had recognised immediately that the question was loaded.

"There's something going on, Dad, and I think you might not have helped. You should talk to Patricia or Kay."

I immediately phoned Kay to discover that both of my sisters were becoming quite concerned about our father. Brenda from next door had promised to let them know if there was any change in his condition. Recently, Brenda had observed that he was regularly quite tired and she had notified Kay. After he delivered Mrs Glynn's newspaper in the morning and accepted the offer of a cup of tea, he would often fall asleep on his chair. Brenda had also seen him sleeping in his car after he returned from town and parked inside his front gate. Kay regretted not letting me know of her concerns about him and understood my response to his question.

"He's ok on his own for the time being, as you told him. But Patricia and I are worried that, unless he moves soon, he'll refuse to move at all. You know how stubborn he can be."

When I dropped in next-door to visit her and her mother, Brenda reiterated her concerns.

"You know that I'll keep a close eye on him for as long as he's in Murneen. And, in a way, we'd hate to see him going away. Mam will miss him an awful lot. But he'd be far better off with Kay. And she would no longer be constantly worried about him."

The following evening, as Kathryn and I prepared to leave Murneen, the three of us were having a cup of tea. Kathryn suddenly reintroduced the subject.

"Grandad. You remember when you asked Dad yesterday about living on your own...?"

He turned and looked at her quizzically.

"Why? Do you not think I'm ok to stay here on my own."

"It's not that. Dad is probably right when he says that you're fine for the time being. But there's another way of looking at it. Unless you make the decision for yourself, sooner or later, somebody is going to have to tell you that it's time for you to move... and Grandad, you won't like that."

I knew that the comment had an impact on him. If I, my brothers or sisters had ventured to speak in those terms, he would probably have taken offence. He was silent and didn't mention the subject again. He was in good form as we left and, as my mother used to do, he remained on the road to wave at our departing car until we crested Day's hill.

A few nights later, I received a phone call from Kay with the startling news that Dad had made a decision to move to Donegal to live with her and her family. He had a number of conditions which Kay itemised carefully:

1. If, after a period, he didn't settle in Donegal, he would return to Murneen.

2. He did not want the house in Murneen standing empty and deteriorating. As soon as he was content to settle in Donegal, he would sell the Murneen house. Each of us would eventually get an equal sixth share of the proceeds and this was also reflected in his will. Michael and Colman would organise the selling of the house.

3. If one or more of us wanted to retain the Murneen house, for example as a holiday home, each of the remaining siblings would first have to be paid one sixth of the professional valuation of the property.

4. He would make a weekly payment from his pension to Kay and Danny in order to cover his food and other living expenses.

5. As a pre-condition of his leaving Murneen, he stipulated that all six of us must be in agreement with his decision to live with Kay and with the proposed financial arrangements.

The setting of conditions and the nature of the conditions themselves, reveal much about my father's mindset and obsessions. He abhorred family disputes and was of the opinion that the vast majority of such arguments tended to revolve around financial matters and inheritance. His solution was that each of us should benefit equally from his assets, irrespective of our individual family or financial circumstances. Kay should not gain or be at a loss financially as a result of his location with her and her family. If any of the remaining five of us had a problem with the proposed arrangement, he wanted it sorted out now and not after his death.

His pre-conditions also took account of the reality that an old, unheated, empty houses in a rural location can deteriorate quite rapidly.

We all quickly confirmed our agreement to the conditions and Kay hastily set about arranging the move in case he had second thoughts. None of the family proposed to keep the house so Mike and I decided to wait until spring before placing it on the market for sale. Although we were confident that Dad would not exercise his option to return to live in Murneen, we didn't want to appear too hasty in arranging the sale of the property. We reassured Dad that, in the interim, we would take turns to travel to Murneen to check on the house, to mow the lawn, and maintain the gardens.

On my birthday, 17 November 2004, Kay and I boxed the items

which Dad would need or like to have with him in Donegal. My car was filled and Dad's car had barely enough room for Kay and himself. He hadn't displayed much emotion about his departure but his stoicism crumbled when he bade a tearful goodbye to Mrs Glynn, my mother's closest friend and their neighbour for fifty years. Following an emotional visit to my mother's grave, we set off for Donegal. Kay drove my father's car and I followed.

A few hours later, we were warmly welcomed by Kay's husband. Danny sat us down to recover from the journey with tea and sandwiches before excusing himself. While the three of us chatted, I could hear noises and activity in the background. I assumed that Danny was unloading the cars but this was only part of the truth.

Danny reappeared and, when we had finished out tea, invited my father to inspect his bedroom. I already knew that the room was comfortable and spacious with a beautifully scenic view across the Donegal sea inlet to Lagg Chapel, with sheep-filled fields, and green hills in the background. But the real delight was inside the room. My father's favourite framed photographs, which that morning had been removed from his living room and bedroom in Murneen, and which had earlier been boxed by Kay, were now hanging on the walls or adorning the surfaces of his new room. The noise which I'd heard had been Danny hanging the pictures.

"It feels just like home", I said, as I thanked Danny for the most thoughtful and meaningful gesture.

"It is his home now", he replied.

As Kay and Danny's teenage children, Mark and Sinead, arrived from school and joyfully greeted their grandfather, I knew that he was in the right place.

Children and grandchildren continued to travel to Donegal to see him. He loved the local area and the friendliness of the people. His health continued to slowly deteriorate and there were a few visits to hospital for tests and treatment. On one such occasion, I visited him in Letterkenny Hospital. He was glad to see me and we chatted until a hospital worker arrived to make his bed while he sat alongside on a chair. She began to chat distractedly to my father as she went about her work.

"How are we today?"

"No use complaining. I'm like everybody else. Sometimes happy. Sometimes sad."

"Sad? Why would you be sad?"

He winked at me.

"In sooth. I know not why I am so sad: It wearies me.."

"What?"

"...you say it wearies you..."

" Wearies me? I didn't say anything at all. Sure, I'm grand, thank God."

She patted down the bedspread.

"...but how I caught it, found it, or came by it,

What stuff 'tis made of, whereof it is born,

I am to learn..."

She paused in her work, looked at me enquiringly and then at him as he went on.

"...and such a want-wit sadness makes of me,

That I have much ado to know myself."

She sidled over until she stood by me, all the while watching him.

"Is that man alright? What in the name of God is he on about? Is he rambling?"

"No. He's just reciting Shakespeare. The Merchant of Venice. Act 1-Scene 1."

She nodded, leaned closer to me in a conspiratorial manner, and spoke quietly.

"Sure, it's not the same way they all go."

My father grinned widely when I told him what she said.

CHAPTER FIFTY-FOUR

Take These Chains

Terezín
"No room has ever been as silent as the room
Where hundreds of violins are hung in unison."
-Michael Longley.

As his health deteriorated, my father was sometimes difficult to manage and, at times, placed Kay and Danny under pressure. He was not sleeping well and regularly called loudly for Kay during the night. She had to balance her work shifts as a full-time nurse, her obligations in the home with two teenage children, and her workload in caring for my father. Danny took a lot of the strain, helping my father who was increasingly in need of assistance in the shower and bathroom. Kay's two children who lived at home and her step-children on their visits were extraordinary supportive.

Occasionally, Kay telephoned me and asked for my help. Unlike the rest of my siblings, I had now retired from work and was available to travel to Donegal at very short notice. Within a few hours of her call, I arrived at their house in order to provide some assistance or moral support.

In response to one such call, my wife handed me an overnight bag almost as soon as I put the phone down, and I was on the road to the north west. When I arrived, my father was sleeping but was not expected to have a peaceful night. I went to bed, having left instructions that I was to be called if needed, and fell into my usual deep sleep.

I woke in the morning to find that, as expected, Dad had a bad night but Kay and Danny had taken turns to attend to him. Kay hadn't called me, having adjudged that I needed sleep after my journey, but she tried to assuage my guilt by telling me that my presence and support were a comfort to her.

When I came downstairs, I found Kay and Danny with my father in his room. While Kay was changing the bedsheets, Dad was seated beside the bed. He made a wretched figure as he was hunched in the chair with a blanket draped shawl-like over his head and shoulders. The top of the blanket was pulled forward so that his face was in deep shadow and only the tip of his nose was clearly visible. I was put in mind of an old, frail woman. His bare feet were steeped in a basin of water which Danny had just provided in order to give him some relief; one of his symptoms was swollen ankles which resulted from water retention. I was shocked at his appearance. I suddenly knew without doubt that he had only a very short time to live.

"Dad. How are you this morning?"

"Ah!"

He shook his head slowly and resignedly.

Kay spoke softly to him.

"I'll be ready to let you back into bed in a minute, if you like. But it might be better for you to bathe your feet for a short while."

He made no reply. It was clear that he wasn't in the humour for talking and I looked around the room. My eyes fell on his guitar which was on a stand nearby. I picked up the old familiar Hofner guitar and, as I checked the tuning, I could feel him watching me from the dark recesses of his shawl. I began to fingerpick the melody of "Take These Chains", the old Ray Charles hit which was a particular favourite of my father. As I started the second chorus, adding a few extra flourishes in an effort to keep him interested or at least distracted, I was startled by what seemed like a moaning sound emanating from the hunched figure. Kay anxiously stopped what she was doing and stared at him.

"What's wrong?", I asked. I had stopped playing.

"Keep playing", she murmured. "I think he's trying to sing."

Sure enough, the initial moaning sound had now given way to a more musical one. He was not yet singing the words but was half-humming the tune and, to my amazement, was hitting the right notes. I immediately recognised that there was a problem. He was trying to sing about half an octave higher than was usual for him. I was playing in the key of D but he normally sang the song in A. This wasn't a problem on the earlier part of the verse which was in a low register. Nevertheless, I knew that when he got to the "take these chains" in the

329

final line, he would need to hit a D above high C, which would cause him to struggle, even on a good day.

As he straightened his back to fill his lungs, the shawl has slipped back and I could see his face clearly as he looked at me. Now he was mouthing the words. His voice was much weaker and thinner than usual but his pitch was perfect.

"We're in the wrong key. Will I change it down?"

He shook his head.

"Keep going", he said, in a pause between the lines of the song.

"Oh, my faith in you is gone,
And the heartaches linger on.
Take these chains..."

He hit the high note perfectly, looked at me with a knowing half smile..

"...from my heart and set me free."

He sang the second verse. His confidence was such that he was now tapping his foot in time to the music. Unnoticed by him, this was causing the water to lap over the rim of the basin onto the carpet. Danny, whom I have often ribbed for his tendency to be overly house-proud, walked back into the room with a large jug of warm water, replenished and reheated the water which was lapping around my father's ankles, and pretended not to even notice that his prized carpet was being saturated. Kay and Danny left me and Dad alone.

"Play one yourself."

I can't remember what I played but, when I finished, I played the intro to "Tennessee Waltz". The key was more favourable to him this time and he sang along.

"Do you know that song 'Rambling Rose'? I think it was Dean Martin."

"I do. And it was Nat King Cole."

I began to pick the melody.

"Nat King Cole? Are you sure. It seems more like a Dean Martin song".

I sang and played it as he listened carefully. When I finished, he mused distractedly.

"You know, there's one thing I could never figure out about that song."

"What's that?"

"It's a good song. It's easy to sing. And everyone likes it. But still, you never hear anybody singing it anymore. I wonder why that is…?"

He was tired now. Kay re-entered the room.

"I think you should have a lie down now for a while. Then maybe you can get up later and ye can sit in the kitchen and have another tune."

He did get up later. He didn't sing but he listened to me play for a while before nodding off to sleep in his easy chair.

Two weeks later, he was in the Hospice in Letterkenny. When I arrived Kay and Danny were with him and after talking to us for a while, he drifted off to sleep. I persuaded Kay and Danny to go home and said that I would sit with him for a few hours more. Some of the nursing staff looked in now and again and quietly spoke to me about his condition. They felt that he probably had only a few days left and thought it likely that he would sleep for at least a few hours more. I was about to leave at 6pm when I realised that he was wide awake and looking at me.

"Are you still here?"

"Kay and Danny are gone home. I though I'd wait awhile."

"Good. I'm glad they went. They're run off their feet."

A nurse put her head around the door.

"I thought I heard voices. Do you need anything?"

"I'd love a cup of tea and maybe a bit of toast."

"Certainly. I'll organise that."

When she left, my father chatted away. He seemed brighter and more care-free than I had seen for weeks. A nurse or helper brought in tea and toast. Immediately, he began to chat to her. Another nurse walked in,

"I was wondering what the racket was," she said kindly.

"We're just making arrangements to go dancing," said my father. "Do you have a car?"

"I do but I'm hardly dressed for dancing."

A younger nurse entered, attracted by the laughter. My father greeted her.

"Isn't that just typical? You just walked in and already I have a problem."

"What did I do wrong? I just heard the noise and stepped in to find out what what was going on."

"That's the problem. You see, it had taken me at least ten minutes to finally figure out which of these nurses was the best looking. Now you walked in and I have to start all over again."

I decided to leave them to their banter and fun. I told him that I'd see him tomorrow and walked down the corridor as the sound of laughter receded behind me. I realised that the nurse who seemed to me to be in charge, was following me. I waited. She looked back as a fresh peal of laughter escaped from my father's room. She turned to me.

"I hope you don't mind. But the staff rarely get a response from a patient here. They don't often get an opportunity to have a bit of fun with one."

"Not at all," I reassured her. "It's great to see him in such good form."

She looked at me carefully.

"I hope you don't think this changes anything about your Dad's condition. We often see sudden variations like this but they're very short lived. But it's lovely while it lasts."

The following morning, it was immediately evident that his condition had deteriorated overnight. A nurse spoke quietly to me.

"If any family members want to see him before the end, they should get here as soon as possible."

My remaining brothers and sisters arrived during the afternoon. We waited as he slept. A cassette of his favourite Ray Charles songs played quietly in the background. When a priest arrived, we feared that Dad would wake up and become annoyed or frightened when he realised that the Last Rites were being administered. Our apprehensions were unfounded. He awoke, looked at the priest, and mouthed the responses before drifting off to sleep again. In the early hours of the following morning, with his two daughters watching him, and his sons sleeping in the next room, he slipped quietly away.

The following day was 17 November 2006. My birthday. Exactly two years after we had driven him from Mayo to Donegal, we followed our father's hearse back down to Mayo. Members of Danny's family, friends and neighbours from Donegal accompanied my father on his last, long, journey home to Mayo. We were welcomed by multitudes of friends and neighbours who helped us to lay him to rest beside my mother in the hillside cemetery at Barnacarroll.

Chasing November Blues (in memory of Coleman Rushe).
By John O'Rourke.

I feel I can try
And reach out
Towards the blue Christ

In the red fishing boat
Beyond the turn-over
Of these dark-water
November waves.
Na tonnta.
So lourd!
And majestic.
I envisage him
As blinding light
For all intents and purposes
All elements earthly gone.
His shape is alternatively
Angelic,
Trans-atomic
Trans-human,
As he hovers now
Towards snow-covered Nephin;-
Bleached turfstack.
For some moments
On the morning of his sailing
The skyline towards
Balbriggan and Malahide reflected
A sultry orange exotic place dawning.
Sea-music filled ether
Reverberated with the words
Of Michael Longley's Terezín.

CHAPTER FIFTY-FIVE

Love Child

"The voice of parents is the voice of gods, for to their children they are heaven's lieutenants".
- Shakespeare.

Truth and revelation arrive in mysterious and unexpected ways. Previously overlooked or misinterpreted information can provide a new insight into events and can radically change perceptions.

Both of my parents were enthusiastic and supportive when I began to research our family history. They hoped that I might be able to cast some light on unanswered questions regarding both the Ryans and the Rushes. They were also pleased that some information about their ancestors would be recorded and would be available for their grandchildren and future generations.

At an early stage in my genealogical research, I was visiting my parents in Mayo and was asking questions and taking notes. I balanced a notepad on my knee as my father sat opposite me in the living room. My mother was listening as she prepared Sunday dinner in the kitchen and she joined in the conversation as I asked questions about my grandparents and great grand-parents. I was also sharing with my mother and father some insights which I had gleaned from Census returns and other sources.

My mother was fascinated by information which I had unearthed about her grandfather in Limerick. Owing to her father's reticence in discussing his childhood, she knew nothing about her paternal grandparents. I told my mother that her grandfather had died in 1899 at the age of 35, leaving a widow and six young children. Nine years later, the mother also died so that my grandfather, Mick Ryan, was an orphan at the age of thirteen. Some of his older siblings had already emigrated to the USA and the others soon followed. Mick was brought up by his grandmother and he later worked as a servant boy and lodged with neighbours on their farm. It seems that contact was not maintained between Mick Ryan and his siblings in the USA. My mother was previously unaware that her father had brothers and a sister.

Some information about my father's family had also come to light. I had obtained marriage details for some of the Reynolds, Granny Rushe's family which was of special interest to my father. He was anxious that all the information should be recorded as soon as I had finished my research. We were in agreement that it should be a readable family history; people would be much more likely to read a narrative than to peruse a succession of birth, death and marriage records or Census reports.

"There's one thing I meant to say to you", said my father.

"What's that", I asked distractedly, looking at the note-pad on my knee. I had listed other questions which I wanted to ask and didn't welcome the digression.

He paused.

"When you're writing everything down, you might find that some things don't add up. Don't leave anything out. Don't be worried about causing embarrassment to anyone."

He had my full attention now. My first thought was that he was speaking about the experience of his own father in the workhouses. In many Irish families, this was the kind of family history which was "not talked about". But we had often discussed this in the past and he already knew that I would write about it when I had completed my research.

But the tone of his voice indicated to me that this was something different. Something new. Something sensitive.

"What kind of things won't add up?"

The normal kitchen sounds associated with preparation of dinner had ceased. I knew that my mother was listening.

He paused again.

"Well, when you compare Granny and Granda's marriage certificate with my date of birth, you might see that they don't quite add up. But you should put the correct information down on paper. Things are what they are. There's nothing that needs to be hidden. Nothing for anybody to be ashamed of."

I sensed that he was choosing his words carefully. I decided not to ask anything else. I could check the facts. He seemed relieved.

My mother's voice came from the kitchen.

"Set the table, Colman. There's a good boy! The soup will be ready in a minute."

I laughed.

"I'm a bit long in the tooth to be called a boy!"

"Shake yourself or your father will fall down with the hunger!"

I was reasonably certain that she had been listening and waiting for us to finish.

As soon as I arrived back to our home on the east coast that evening, I examined my genealogical files. I had thought about my father's comments on my long drive east and wondered whether his mother might have been pregnant before his parents married. Perhaps they married when they discovered that she was expecting a baby. Maybe my father was born only a few months after the wedding.

I knew my father's date of birth was April 4, 1924. I rustled through my disorganised bundles of documents and notes until I eventually located my father's birth certificate. His mother's name was listed as Mary Rushe. I figured that she would have been listed as Mary Reynolds if she was unmarried when my father was born. Somewhat relieved, I continued the search and found my grand-parents' marriage certificate. It confirmed that they were married in January 1923. What was my father talking about? Did he erroneously think that he was illegitimate? But, why? Did somebody mislead him when he was younger? Was it a prank played on a young boy or young man? And what would I do now with the information?

He had said that I "might" see that the dates didn't add up. Might. Not definite. Was he uncertain? Strange.

During my next visit, we spoke more about my research and findings. He didn't mention our previous conversation and I decided to let the subject rest until I wrote the family history. This took much longer than I expected but I finally presented him with a copy of the book, "Not From The Wind" on his eightieth birthday in 2004. After he had a chance to read it, he thanked me and told me that his only regret was that my mother didn't live to see the finished work. He was delighted with the book, showing it to everybody who visited him. He didn't mention our earlier talk. I didn't want to cause him any discomfort and decided to let things lie.

While working on this book, I revisited my old research material. I wanted to identify the local church in which my grandparents were married. My original untidy collection of documents and notes had since been reorganised. I now had separate files for each branch of the family and a rudimentary index system. Despite repeated searches, I could not locate the marriage certificate for Granny and Granda Rushe. In my Ryan file, however, I came upon the marriage certificate for my mother's parents and noticed that it was dated January 1923. Oops! 1923? Had I made a mistake when following up on my father's comments and looked at the marriage information for the wrong grandparents?

I applied for a marriage certificate for Granny and Granda Rushe. By now, I was sure that I had erred. I had checked the marriage cert for my Ryan grandparents instead of my Rushe grandparents when examining the circumstances of my father's birth. The certificate arrived. It revealed that Michael Rushe and Mary Reynolds married on April 28, 1924; three weeks and three days after the birth of my father. I scrutinised the records of the marriage and birth more closely.

My father was born on April 4.

"Tom" Rushe and Mary Reynolds married on April 28.

The marriage was recorded on the register a month later on May 28. The marriage date is quoted correctly on the register as April 28.

My father's birth was registered on June 2. Again, the date of birth is recorded correctly as April 4.

I knew from my genealogy work that there was normally a delay of a few days after a birth or marriage before the event was registered. But, in this case, there an extraordinary delay of two months before the child's birth was registered. It seems likely that registration of the birth was deliberately deferred until after the registration of the marriage of his parents. As a result of the delay, his mother's name appears as Mary Rushe on the birth certificate. Otherwise, it would appear as Mary Reynolds, her name when the child was born.

What are the implications of this birth outside wedlock? This kind of thing should not happen in Catholic Ireland in the 1920s. Of course, there were unplanned pregnancies and babies born before marriage, even in the pervasive, rigidly Catholic, atmosphere of rural Ireland. There was a clearly defined strategy to be adopted in such unfortunate cases, however. This was designed to minimise any shame or embarrassment to the family and to avoid causing scandal in the parish.

The first and preferred option was to arrange for the "fallen woman" to marry the father as soon as possible after the pregnancy was discovered. If the father was available, acceptable to the woman's family, and willing to marry, the nuptials were hastily arranged. The "early" arrival of the baby, some months later, could be obfuscated or explained as a premature birth.

The other option was to send the pregnant woman away to relatives or to the Magdalen Laundries, a church-run enterprise which was set up to give employment to the unfortunate woman and to hide her from public view. When the child was born, it was placed for adoption and details of its location and future life were denied to the mother. Some few women were accepted back into their homes by their parents following their spell in the Magdalen Laundries but most were abandoned, being regarded as "a disgrace to the family". The luckier ones managed to emigrate but others had no option but to remain in the Magdalen Laundries, sometimes for years, before accumulating some savings with which to escape.

The fate of the children was precarious. In 1924, a general Registrar's report stated that "one in every three illegitimate children born alive in 1924 died within one year of its birth and the mortality rate amongst these children was about five times as great as in other cases."

The horrors of the treatment of Irish unmarried mothers and their babies have only been fully revealed and understood in Ireland quite recently as a result of a detailed government sponsored report into the involvement of church and state in the Magdalen Laundries. The scandal later came to international attention following the release of the Oscar nominated film "Philomena".

Following the publication of the government report, many of the elderly survivors of the laundries were invited to the Dail, the Irish parliament, to receive a public apology from the Irish Government. Enda Kenny, the prime minister, apologised for the state role in the scandal which he characterised as "a national shame". He acknowledged that, while Ireland "had created a particular portrait of itself as a good-living God-fearing nation", the reality which these women experienced was much different. They encountered a "cruel, pitiless Ireland distinctly lacking in a quality of mercy" and a people who were "judgemental; intolerant; petty; and prim". He identified the unhealthy subservience of the state to the Catholic church and pointed out that the people "lived with the damaging idea that what was desirable and acceptable in the eyes of the church and the state was the same and interchangeable".

But in facing and taking responsibility for our dark and shameful history, we should also acknowledge the occasional shafts of light which broke through the dark clouds. There were a few noble people for whom the accepted mores were unconscionable. Furthermore, they had the courage and perseverance to rebel, to forge their own path, and to take the consequences.

We will never know fully the circumstances surrounding the decision of my grandparents to flout convention and to keep their child. There are unanswerable questions. Did Mary Reynolds remain at home to give birth or did she leave, perhaps to stay with relatives, and return after her baby was born? Why did she and "Tom" Rushe not get married as soon as she became aware that she was pregnant? Did Mary conceal the pregnancy until the last possible moment? Did my grandfather's own experiences while in care and in the workhouse make him determined not to allow his son to be removed from his mother and taken into "the system"?

But these questions are unimportant. What is remarkable is that a decision was made to break with convention. Mary Reynolds would not be disowned or temporarily banished to the Magdalen Laundries. The couple decided to keep the baby and to marry a few weeks later. In doing this, Mary and "Tom" showed themselves to be people of exceptional courage and determination.

It also seems inescapable that they were supported in their decision by Mary's widowed mother. After all, it was almost invariably the parents of the pregnant woman who banished her from the home in order to preserve the outward appearance of family respectability. Clearly, Mrs Reynolds supported the decision of the young parents. As a young woman, Mary had emigrated and spent some years in Newfoundland before she returned to Ireland and married William Reynolds. Perhaps her broader worldview and experience was a factor in her tolerant approach towards her daughter's dilemma. It would have been virtually impossible for the couple to keep the child without her help. Her continued support is demonstrated by the fact that, after their marriage, Mary and "Tom" and the baby lived with Mrs Reynolds in Meelickroe or in nearby Ballinlough, for four years.

What of the local community? How did the friends and neighbours of the Reynolds family respond to the event? It was usually the disapproval of local people, buoyed by the clergy, which drove families to ostracise the unmarried mother. Subsequent events provide no evidence of such opprobrium. In later years, my grandmother was happy to bring her young children on holiday from Claremorris back to her home place in Meelickroe or to nearby Leitra to visit Sarah Mitchell, who had fostered my grandfather. This would not have happened if my grandmother had any fears about the reaction of locals. Sarah Mitchell sometimes travelled to Claremorris to visit the Rushes and she attended the wedding of Mary Rushe and Johnny Ryan. I have been in touch with another woman from Leitra who, as a child, accompanied her aunt on visits to the Rushes in Claremorris. Such displays of friendship and support speak most eloquently of the exemplary reaction of the local community. Perhaps this can be partly attributed to the local respect for the Reynolds family. This was articulated to my brother Sean by a neighbour who said that William Reynolds was remembered as a "man to whom people turned when they were in trouble".

How did Mary's two older brothers react to her dilemma? Is there a clue in the lifelong and unexplained hostility which my grandmother displayed toward her eldest brother, Martin? When he died, she refused to attend his funeral or to have him buried in the Rushe family grave at Crossboyne. I and my brothers and sisters had attributed her uncharacteristically hostile attitude to a disapproval of Martin's lifestyle and particularly his drinking. Nevertheless, her other brother, Jack, was quite partial to a drink or two and she was very fond of him.

Following the death of their father, Martin, as the eldest son, would have seen himself as head of the household when his sister's crisis pregnancy came to light. Was he less than supportive of his sister in her time of need? Did he want to follow the normal practise and banish her from the home and have the baby given up for adoption? If so, this seems like a plausible explanation for the lifelong rift between them.

Another question arises. When did my father become aware that he was born before his parents married? Did he make the discovery himself or did they tell him? If so, did he discuss it with his parents? I am satisfied that his sisters, who were a few years younger than him, were not aware of his situation. As I look back, I am fairly certain that my mother knew. At least that was the clear impression I got at the time my father spoke to me to warn me that the dates "didn't quite add up".

But again, the answer is not important. What is inescapable is that there were three people who emerged from this episode with enormous credit. I am immensely proud of my grandparents, "Tom" Rushe and Mary Reynolds and of my great-grandmother Mary Reynolds née Egan. Here truly were "heaven's lieutenants" who were willing to do what is best for their children and to flout convention no matter what the consequences.

And what of the impact on my father and my mother? Were they inspired by the display of dedication and perseverance in the face of adversity which was repeated when my grandparents had to deal with the early deaths of their children Mickey Rushe and his sister Patsy? Does this help to explain the courage and persistence demonstrated by my own parents as they safeguarded their children while dealing with the recurring problems which assailed them in later years?

Another strange and shocking insight coincided with my discovery. A few days after I shared the new information about Dad's birth with my brothers and sisters, news broke about the discovery of the remains of 796 dead babies. They had been buried in waste land beside a church-run home for unmarried mothers in Tuam, which is seventeen miles south of Claremorris. This is the town where my grandfather was torn from his two little brothers after they were discharged from the workhouse. The babies in the home died at an average of one death every fortnight between 1925 and 1961.

Unmarried mothers who were rejected by their families were sent to such institutions where the babies were born. The babies were sometimes adopted but, it now transpires, many died from infection, disease, or malnutrition. The order of nuns who were in charge of the home were paid a capitation fee by the government in order to feed and clothe the children. Early statistics imply that the child mortality rate within such homes was over 50% compared to the national average for "marital" children of 15%. As I write, there are demands for a full public enquiry about this home in Tuam and many others scattered around the country where, it is suspected, there were similar outrages.

796 babies is a statistic. An appalling, shameful statistic, yes. But still a statistic. But the shock was more profound to me when I realised that, but for the grace and courage of my Rushe grandparents and my Reynolds great-grandmother, my father could have been such a statistic. He could have suffered neglect or death in a home like the one in Tuam or he could have been adopted - effectively sold to adoptive parents - with every effort made to thwart any future attempt to trace his whereabouts.

In recent times, the appalling treatment in the past of Ireland's unmarried mothers and their children was brought to public attention. The initial reaction was to blame the nuns and other religious who operated the institutions such as the Magdalen laundries and care homes. They facilitated the adoption of babies, and later refused to provide information to searching and grieving mothers. Successive governments, which colluded in this cruelty and exploitation, also justifiably bore the brunt of much criticism. But as a nation, we have been more reluctant to face the reality that the problem originated in the Christian family homes of Ireland. Daughters who became pregnant were often thrown out and disowned. Otherwise, steps were taken to hide the "embarrassment" and "disgrace to the family" by sending the expectant mother to one of the church run institutions. She was only allowed to return home after the adoption or abandonment of the baby.

The institutions and practises, distasteful as they were, came into existence because of the failure of families and individuals to deal with the pregnancies in a charitable and, dare I say it, Christian manner. The clergy reinforced the view that pregnancy outside marriage must be punished vigorously and the state was unforgivably subservient to the Catholic church. Nevertheless, the blame should first be laid at the feet of the heartless or cowed parents and the shiftless, faint-hearted, and cowardly fathers who abdicated their responsibility when the woman became pregnant. The appalling institutions became a necessary evil because many families and fathers failed to support the pregnant women.

CHAPTER FIFTY-SIX

Everyday People

"Saint Patrick was a gentleman. He came from decent people"
- Irish folksong.

I embarked upon a quest to better understand my parents by writing about them. To belie Tolstoy's claim that happy families are all alike. To demonstrate that a happy childhood is worth your while, despite what Frank Mc Court may feel. To show that your mum and dad do not necessarily fuck you up.

On my journey, I rediscovered not just my parents but also inspirational grandparents and great grandparents. My father's parents overcame extraordinary obstacles with the courageous support of Mary Reynolds, my great grandmother. My mother's father, Mick Ryan, was orphaned at an early age and had lost touch with his siblings. Yet he emerged unscathed to marry happily and raise a family while choosing not to burden his children with details of his painful, parentless youth.

My parents decided to continue this practise of refraining from passing on their problems, anxieties, or worries to their children. The writing process has given me a new appreciation of the sequence of setbacks which our family endured and my parents' extraordinary performance in dealing with them and shielding us children.

I marvel at their energy and perseverance. By today's standards, my mother's workload in Streamstown with small children and meagre utilities while my father was in London seems unmanageable. Listing her daily routine gave me a new appreciation of how much she did and makes me wonder how she coped.

But necessity can propel people to new heights of achievement. One sometimes has little choice but to rise to the challenge. Who knows what each of us can achieve when faced with seemingly unsurmountable obstacles?

Many parental activities are driven by necessity; others are optional. Parents have obligations such as feeding, educating, and clothing their children. But there are also things which parents do not have to do. Some parents are motivated to persevere with these optional activities because they enjoy doing them or because they know that their children will benefit.

Dad enjoyed helping me with music and encouraging the various extra-curricular interests and talents of my siblings. My mother derived satisfaction from observing the results of her encouragement and support with homework and job applications. I'm also sure that she was at her happiest when engaging with and chatting to a plethora of tiny children scattered around the kitchen floor.

But there were other activities that must have been unwelcome chores for my parents. Mam had no interest in boxing but set her alarm clock and got me and Mike out of bed in the small hours to listen to the radio commentary. Dad shepherded three of us around Dublin, or brought me to Salthill, in order to keep a promise. He allowed me to take his treasured guitar when I left home.

As I look back, these are the moments when I see my parents at their best.

What else did I learn about my parents from the writing process? I already knew that, broadly, my mother's contribution to the Rushe family dynamic consisted of child-rearing, home-making, setting and insisting upon behavioural boundaries, and constant engagement with her children. My father worked at his day job and also around the home to provide the family income and gave moral support and guidance.

But I've come to realise the major impact on me and my siblings was not the constant flow of advice, guidance, and encouragement from my parents. Parents teach, not by words, but by actions. We watched them and, later in life, we replicated their actions. I and my brothers and sisters cared for and maintained a close relationship with our parents in their declining years. We did not do this because we were regularly told as children that this was the right thing to do. We merely followed the example of our parents in caring for their own parents, our grandparents. Our continuing close bond as siblings replicates the relationships which my parents had with their own brothers and sisters.

There is much to be learned from my parents' method of raising their family. Yet, I wonder whether their actions are applicable to parenting nowadays. Demands on parents were different in the 50s and 60s. TV didn't provide a distraction, at least for the older Rushe children. Any danger of inappropriate information flowing towards their children was nullified by selectivity in the newspapers and magazines entering the home. Nowadays, the ubiquity of internet access and social media present a much more difficult problem for parents.

Unlike many family units nowadays, ours was a two-parent household with my mother working in the home on a full-time basis. Her decision to remain at home was not an optional one; it was dictated by the marriage bar then in existence. Nowadays, two generations after my parents era, it is unusual for young couples to decide that one of them should work in the home in order to care for their young children. There are many reasons for this phenomenon but financial considerations are usually paramount. Two salaries are needed in order to pay the mortgage and to finance the lifestyle to which the partners aspire.

People of my generation, who reached marriageable age when the ban on women in the work-place was revoked, were more open to exploring the possibilities of stay-at-home parenting. They were content to rent a home or to buy a small two-bedroom semi-detached property and to maintain a low-key inexpensive lifestyle while their children were in their formative years. When the children went to secondary school, the stay-at-home parent had the option of returning to part-time and later to full-time employment.

We live in different times. There are many aspects of the parenting practices of my mother and father which could be beneficially replicated by young parents today. Yet, I am reluctant to be proscriptive in recommending specific methods of child-rearing. Instead, I venture to put forward a word of caution. We should be aware that, while our children may not take our advice and do as we say, they are much more likely to do as we do. If we behave ethically, with kindness and consideration, in our dealings with others, and if we display tolerance of different lifestyles and acceptance of diversity, our children will do likewise. If we have a dysfunctional relationship with our own parents, we should make whatever sacrifices and compromises are necessary in order to repair it. Just imagine the impact that this will have on our children! Even if we are ultimately unsuccessful, our children will be motivated by our effort. Either way, we win. Our actions will have inspired them, not our words.

Although it sounds trite, my parents would be happy and contented to be described as decent people. Bill Melia gave me my first job on his farm because my mother was "a decent woman". I read somewhere that Hollywood actress, Grace Kelly, who regularly visited Mayo and who later purchased her ancestral farm in the county, described her Irish ancestors as "decent people". At the time, it struck me that this was the kind of accolade to which my own parents aspired.

The word "decent" is most often heard nowadays when describing dress or behaviour. In the Mayo of my youth, it had a more refined meaning when used to describe people. Decent individuals or families had earned a reputation for respectability, morality, and integrity. They could be relied upon to do the right thing. The decent thing.

My parents were decent people.

They came from decent people.

So did I.

Printed in Great Britain
by Amazon